Books are to be returned on or before
the last date below.

0 9 DEC 2010

LIBREX-

Olympic Tourism

Olympic Tourism

Mike Weed

ELSEVIER

AMSTERDAM • BOSTON • HEIDELBERG • LONDON • NEW YORK • OXFORD
PARIS • SAN DIEGO • SAN FRANCISCO • SINGAPORE • SYDNEY • TOKYO
Butterworth-Heinemann is an imprint of Elsevier

Butterworth-Heinemann is an imprint of Elsevier
Linacre House, Jordan Hill, Oxford OX2 8DP, UK
30 Corporate Drive, Suite 400, Burlington, MA 01803, USA

First edition 2008

British Library Cataloguing in Publication Data
A catalogue record for this book is available from the British Library

Library of Congress Cataloging-in-Publication Data
A catalog record for this book is available from the Library of Congress

ISBN: 978-0-7506-8161-2

For information on all Butterworth-Heinemann publications visit our
web site at books.elsevier.com

Printed and bound in Hungary

08 09 10   10 9 8 7 6 5 4 3 2 1

Contents

List of Tables

List of Figures

Preface

As a subject for academic analysis, tourism has reached a stage of relative maturity (Downward and Mearman, 2004). A cursory review of journals serving the subject area reveals a number that have been in existence for over 25 years (e.g., *Tourism Management*, *Annals of Tourism Research*), with the *Journal of Travel Research* publishing its 45th annual volume in 2007. Similarly, the range of journals reveals the diversity of issues considered (e.g., *Tourism Geographies*, *Tourism Economics*, *Journal of Sustainable Tourism*, *Journal of Travel and Tourism Marketing*). Downward (2005:308) describes the study of tourism as characterized by 'an emphasis on management and resource allocation' but 'within an eclectic approach to disciplinary context'.

Similarly, research on the Olympics and the Olympic Movement has burgeoned in the last 20 years. Academic research has focussed on Olympic politics (e.g., Espy, 1979; Hill, 1996) the impacts of the Olympic Games (Lenskyj, 2002; Preuss, 2004), and the history and ideology of the Olympics and the Olympic Movement (Girginov and Parry, 2004; Toohey and Veal, 1999). In addition, there has been a keen journalistic and popular culture interest in the machinations of the Olympic Movement (e.g., Jennings, 2000; Simson and Jennings, 1992) and Olympic impacts (Lee, 2006; Payne, 2005), with the latter sustaining, almost single-handedly, an industry in the prediction of economic impacts (see, e.g., IVC, 2002; PricewaterhouseCoopers, 2005). However, despite the significant growth in both consultancy reports and academic research on the economic impacts of the Olympic Games, there is little published research that explores the extent and nature of Olympic tourism.

With a general lack of research on Olympic tourism, it would seem sensible to turn to research in the areas of events management (e.g., Berridge, 2006; Masterman, 2004) and sports tourism (e.g., Hinch and Higham, 2004; Weed and Bull, 2004), which are supported by the journals *Event Management* and *Journal of Sport and Tourism*, respectively. While much research in the former has tended to focus on the minutiae of events operations and management (Wilson, 2006), research in the latter tends to be more wide-ranging and multi-disciplinary and, of course, has a clear tourism focus. Weed (2006a) conducted a systematic review and meta-evaluation of peer reviewed sports tourism research published between 2000 and 2004 inclusive in which 80 articles from 24 journals were reviewed. Of these articles, eight were explicitly about Olympic-related tourism, whilst many more investigated tourism to mega- or major-events. Overall, 40 per cent of these sports tourism publications had an events focus. As such, it would seem that the academic sub-field of sports tourism provides a useful starting point for an analysis of Olympic tourism, and much of the contextual content in the first two chapters of this book is drawn from research on the relationship between sport and tourism.

This leads to a general comment on the approach taken throughout this book. It is perhaps possible to identify a continuum of types of academic books. At one end of the scale is the text book, in which there is no attempt to generate new knowledge. Existing knowledge is simply presented in a way that is easily digestible for student learning. Examples of this type of book might be *An Introduction to Leisure Studies* (Bull, Hoose and Weed, 2003) and *Understanding Sport: An Introduction to the Sociological and Cultural Analysis of Sport* (Horne, Tomlinson and Whannel, 1999). At the other end of the scale are texts that have been written to both present and inform research, and that largely comprise new ideas developed from original research and approaches. Examples of such texts might be *Sports Tourism: Participants, Policy and Providers* (Weed and Bull, 2004) and *Sport and Tourism: Globalization, Mobility and Authenticity* (Higham and Hinch, forthcoming). In between are a range of other approaches, including those that might be seen as *advocacy* texts, arguing for the acceptance of a particular field of study or approach (e.g., *Sport Tourism*, Standeven and De Knop, 1999; *Adventure Tourism: The New Frontier*, Swarbrooke et al., 2003), and edited collections that present the views and perspectives of a range of different authors on a particular topic. Such edited collections might range from those that, like some text books, are fairly introductory in nature (e.g., *Sport and Adventure Tourism*, Hudson, 2003) to those that present a more advanced collection of readings (e.g., *Sport Tourism Destinations*, Higham, 2005; *Sport Tourism: Concepts and Theories*, Gibson, 2006). This book takes a different approach again, and one that might be characterized as lying midway between the text book and the research text. Given that there is little research on Olympic tourism *per se*, but that there is a great deal of research that might be seen as *foundational* to the study of Olympic tourism in the areas of tourism, Olympic studies and sports tourism, this book seeks to apply both cutting-edge and long-standing research from these three areas to develop an understanding of Olympic tourism. As such, many of the models and frameworks presented throughout this research have been *adapted from* previous research and applied to the Olympic tourism context. In this respect, while this book does not present new research, it does attempt to develop knowledge through the application of existing frameworks to a new context. Nothing more than this is intended for this book, and it is hoped that it will encourage others to develop programmes of Olympic tourism research to reinforce, refute, or refine the approaches discussed and suggested within.

This book is presented in two parts, with Part 1 discussing the concepts and approaches that might inform an analysis of Olympic tourism, and Part 2 illustrating these through an examination of previous and forthcoming Olympic Games in the 21st century. Whilst the chapters in Part 2 are designed to illustrate different issues from the first part of the book, unlike other books that use case study chapters, the subjects of these chapters have not been the result of strategic choices to illustrate specific issues as, obviously, they have been dictated by the Games that have and will take place. As such, the coverage of issues developed in Part 1 of the book will inevitably be partial in the applied chapters in Part 2.

The five chapters in Part 1 represent an attempt to build an understanding of Olympic tourism from providing a context of product and behavioural types (Chapters 1 and 2) through a consideration of the detail of Olympic tourism flows (Chapter 3) which informs an examination of strategies to develop Olympic tourism (Chapter 4) and the way in which such strategies can be affected by the actions of policy-makers and planners (Chapter 5).

Chapter 1 examines the relationship between sport, tourism, and the Olympic Games. As an introduction to the book, it sets out to briefly establish the significant relationship between sport and tourism, and to discuss how sports tourism might be conceptualized and understood. It then utilizes an adapted version of Weed and Bull's (2004) *Model of Sports Tourism Types*,[1] which

---

[1] Both Chapter 1 and Chapter 2 provide contextual material from the sports tourism literature to underpin the more detailed and specific discussions in the remainder of the book. In particular, these two chapters draw heavily on material previously published in Weed and Bull (2004).

has been updated to include a consideration of 'vicarious' activities as discussed by Weed (2005a), to discuss how activities related to the Olympic Games might be the basis for each of the five types of sports tourism (Tourism with Sports Content, Sports Participation Tourism, Sports Training, Sports Events, and Luxury Sports Tourism) featured in the model. In addition, the potential for the Olympic Games to stimulate generic tourism is identified. This chapter is intended to demonstrate the wide range of sports-related and generic tourism provision that comprises *Olympic tourism products* in the pre-, during and post-Games periods. The chapter concludes by proposing the following definition of Olympic tourism: 'Tourism behaviour motivated or generated by Olympic-related activities'.

Following on from the discussion of the supply-side of Olympic tourism in Chapter 1, Chapter 2 examines the demand-side, the Olympic tourists themselves. Whilst Chapter 1 discusses the potential for an Olympic Games to stimulate generic tourism, the interest of this text is on how such tourism is stimulated rather than on the behaviours of such tourists. As such, Chapter 2 focuses on the Olympic-related sports tourist, with the detail and stimulation of generic tourism being discussed in Chapter 3, and covered in depth in Chapter 4. Chapter 2 commences with a consideration of the concepts that can inform an understanding of the motivations and behaviours of Olympic-related sports tourists. The role of Olympic-related activities in the broad sports tourist profiles identified by Weed and Bull (2004) is then considered, thus establishing three sport-related *Olympic tourist profiles* (Primary Sports Tourists, Associated Experience Sports Tourists, and Tourists Interested in Sport). The final part of the chapter outlines Weed and Bull's (2004) *Sports Tourism Participation Model*, which is then used to identify a range of *types of Olympic tourist* (e.g., 'Incidental', 'Occasional', 'Driven') and their associated behaviours and consumption of different *Olympic tourism products*.

Taken together, Chapters 1 and 2 establish a range of sports-related *Olympic tourism products* (plus the potential for the Olympic Games to stimulate generic tourism) which are consumed by various *types of Olympic Tourist* that will exhibit one of three broader *Olympic tourist profiles*. This provides the context for Chapter 3, which examines the detail of Olympic tourism. Chapter 3 utilizes Preuss's (2005) *Model of Event-Affected People*, which has previously been used to inform economic analyses rather than to understand behaviours, to identify a range of categories of *Olympic tourism flows* in the pre-, during, and post-Games periods. These flows are discussed in relation to the *Olympic tourism products* identified in Chapter 1, and the

Olympic tourist profiles and the *types of Olympic tourism* discussed in Chapter 2. A key factor in understanding such flows is their potential to be positive (e.g., a trip to watch the Olympics that would not have been taken without the Games), negative (e.g., a trip out of the host city/region to escape the Games) and neutral (e.g., a trip to a host city/region that would have been taken at another time that has been switched to co-incide with the Games). The second part of Chapter 3 utilizes Leiper's (1979) long-standing model of the tourist system to discuss the potential travel propensities of populations in Olympic tourism generating regions, and the effect that factors in the Olympic tourism desti-nation region, such as unfamiliarity and cultural distance, might have on such travel propensities. This model leads to a discus-sion of the *stratified geography* of tourism flows in which the level of analysis can change the effect of the flows. Specifically, that a trip from the host city/region to another region in the same country to escape the Games will be a negative flow for the host city/region, a positive flow for the other region, and a neutral flow for the country as a whole.

Having established the context for Olympic tourism in Chapters 1 and 2, and discussed the detail of *Olympic tourism flows* in Chapter 3, the analysis moves, in Chapter 4, to examine ways in which this knowledge might be applied to the devel-opment of strategy. Chapter 4 focuses on *leveraging Olympic tourism* – the development of strategies and tactics to maximize positive outcomes in relation to Olympic tourism. The chapter adapts Chalip's (2004) *General Model for Sport Event Leverage* to the Olympic context, and uses the understandings of Olympic tourism products and flows and Olympic tourist profiles and types to examine Olympic tourism development strategies. The chapter extends Chalip's (2004) model both temporally (i.e., to the pre-, during, and post-Games periods) and geographically (i.e., to the host city/region, to other regions in the country, and to the country as a whole), examining the way in which the Olympic Games can be harnessed as a leveragable resource in each of these cases. Two 'opportunities' are identified within the model: Olympic tourism and Olympic media. In the former case the focus is on strategies to directly generate Olympic tourism in the pre-, during, and post-Games period, whereas in the latter case the focus is on using Olympic media to enhance destination image and thus lead to a longer-term boost in both sports-related and generic tourism business.

The final chapter in the first part of the book, Chapter 5, exam-ines policy and planning for Olympic tourism, and the ways in which this might facilitate the strategies for the development of Olympic tourism described in the previous chapter. The chapter commences with the adaptation of Weed and Bull's (1997a) *Policy Area Matrix for Sport and Tourism* to the Olympic context to illustrate the range of areas that Olympic tourism policy might address in a set of *Olympic Tourism Policy Rings*. The chapter then discusses the emergence of transient Olympic Policy Communities in Olympic host countries before utilizing Weed's (2001b) *Model of Cross-Sectoral Policy Development* to discuss the ways in which policy-makers in a range of sectors might most effectively collaborate in developing policy to facilitate the effective leveraging of Olympic tourism discussed in Chapter 4.

The second part of the book commences with a consideration of tourism and the Winter Olympic Games (Chapter 6), which tend to be overlooked in Olympic-related research. This chapter illustrates the potential for Winter Olympic Games to stimulate a wider range of *Olympic tourism products* (as discussed in Chapter 1) than the Summer Games because much of the infrastructure developed for a Winter Games can support the development of extensive Sports Participation Tourism products in addition to the range of Sports Events, Sports Training and Tourism with Sports Content products that are common to both the Winter and Summer events. However, while the range of *Olympic tourism products* related to a Winter Games may be wider than that for the Summer event, the overall size of the Olympic tourism market for the Summer event has the potential to be much larger.

Chapter 7, written by Professor Graham Brown, of the University of South Australia, a key figure in the analysis of the Sydney Games of 2000 (see, for example, Brown, 2000, 2001; Faulkner et al., 2001), discusses the tourism strategies developed for the first Olympic Games of the 21st century held in Sydney. As many authors have noted (e.g., Chalip, 2004; Faulkner et al., 2001; Payne, 2005), much of the stimulus for a move towards a leveraging approach to the development of Olympic tourism (as discussed in Chapter 4) emerged as result of the approach taken for the Sydney Olympics. Brown discusses in Chapter 7 some of the strategies employed by the Australian Tourist Commission, and the partnerships which were developed for Olympic tourism delivery (see discussions in Chapter 5), such as the Sydney Tourism Olympic Forum (which was established six years prior to the Games in 1994). Brown's chapter suggests that there were early indications that Sydney's leveraging and policy partnership approaches were set to simulate a long-term post-Games tourism benefit. However, the outbreak of severe acute respiratory syndrome (SARS) in Asia and the terrorist attacks on New York on September 11, 2001, rendered useless any further attempts at evaluating a post-Sydney tourism effect.

The IOC has placed considerable emphasis in recent years on the transfer of Olympic knowledge from one host to another, and following the Sydney Games in 2000, the (later to be successful) Vancouver bid for the 2010 Winter Games commissioned a study from Inter Vistas Consulting (2003) which drew heavily on the leveraging lessons from Sydney (see Chapter 6). However, the discussions of the Athens Games of 2004 in Chapter 8 show that, despite the country's place at the centre of Olympic ideology and culture, the city generally failed to capitalize on the opportunities that Olympic tourism can present (as discussed in Chapters 1 and 2). The Athens Games are a clear illustration of Ritchie's (1999) comment that 'a successful event and successfully marketing the host city are distinctly different concepts'. Athens, unfortunately, was characterized by a lack of planning for Olympic tourism, and as such serves as a negative example that highlights the importance of developing the types of leveraging strategies and policy partnerships discussed in Chapters 4 and 5.

The discussions of the 2008 Games in Beijing in Chapter 9 are the first of a prospective Olympic Games. Despite a chequered history within the Olympic movement, China has shown considerable enthusiasm for the Olympic Games, with Beijing having bid unsuccessfully for the 2000 Games before being awarded the 2008 Olympics. Similarly, despite still adhering to many of the norms of a central planned economy, China in general, and Beijing in particular, has shown signs of wishing to develop a more 'market-oriented' economy, and the 2008 Olympics have been harnessed as a central part of a policy that is attempting to promote Beijing as a global city for both business and tourism. However, a key perception for the 2008 Beijing Games is the issue of cultural distance between China and many of the traditional Olympic tourism generating regions (see discussion of Leiper's model in Chapter 3). The strategies that can be employed to overcome this cultural distance are a key part of the discussions of the Beijing Games in this chapter.

The final substantive chapter of this book, Chapter 10, discusses the most distant Olympic Games at the time of writing (June 2007), those to be held in London in 2012. The discussions in this chapter show that long-term planning and leveraging strategies for an Olympic Games are now accepted as being a necessity if the potential positive impacts of Olympic tourism are to be realized. The focus of Chapter 10 is on the way in which planning for Olympic tourism is taking place, both at a UK level, and throughout the constituent nations and regions. As such, the chapter examines the extent to which the *stratified geography* of *Olympic tourism flows* discussed in Chapter 3 has been understood by those responsible for delivering the benefits of London

2012, particularly as this is the Games that has had the most opportunity to learn from previous Olympic hosts.

In concluding this text, an *Afterword* comments on the approaches to understanding Olympic tourism taken throughout the book. In particular, the potential variability of the Olympic tourism context for different Olympic hosts is examined, and the need for future empirical Olympic tourism research is highlighted.

Acknowledgements

I would like to express my appreciation to the various staff at Elsevier-Butterworth Heinemann, particularly Fran Ford, who has been supportive throughout a number of missed deadlines, for their continued support for this project and the help they have provided.

I am also grateful to my colleagues at Canterbury Christ Church University, particularly my Head of Department, Dr Chris Bull, for their support in allowing me the space to work on this and a range of other research projects.

Finally, infinite thanks to my wife, Sonja, for her patience and understanding, and for her selfless loving support throughout this project, particularly in the 'final push' to the finishing line.

Sport, tourism and the Olympic Games

Although now overshadowed by the bombings on July 7th, Wednesday July 6, 2005, was a joyous day for London and the UK as the city celebrated beating the favourite Paris to win the race to become the host for the Games of the XXXth Olympiad in 2012. Trafalgar Square was overrun with both overseas and UK tourists who came to watch and celebrate the IOC announcement. Stratford in East London, one of the world's most multicultural places, a fact not lost on IOC members, held a party to celebrate the area's regeneration over the next seven years. The Olympic Games would be coming to London, and according to a range of commentators, this would provide a range of benefits for the tourism sector in the UK. The nature and extent of these benefits, and how they might be planned for and maximized, not only in London's case, but in the case of all Olympic hosts, is the subject of the analysis in this book.

As an introduction to the book, this chapter sets out to briefly establish the significant relationship between sport and tourism, and to discuss how sports tourism might be conceptualized and understood. It then utilizes a slightly updated version of Weed and Bull's (2004) *Model of Sports Tourism Types* to discuss how activities related to the Olympic Games might be the basis for each of the five types of sports tourism featured in the model. In addition, the potential for the Olympic Games to stimulate generic tourism is identified. As such, the chapter demonstrates the whole range of sports-related and generic provision that comprises Olympic tourism products in the pre-, during, and post-Games periods. The chapter concludes by proposing a definition of Olympic tourism.

Sport and tourism

Research in the field of sports tourism has burgeoned over the last 15 years. Work by Glyptis (1991) and the subsequent report commissioned by the Great Britain Sports Council (Jackson and Glyptis, 1992) were some of the early substantive works in the field, while other reviews were carried out by De Knop (1990) and Standeven and Tomlinson (1994). The focus of these early works was on advocacy, attempting to establish sports tourism as a legitimate field of study, and one with a potentially significant range of impacts. The first full text relating to sport and tourism was the 1999 work by Standeven and De Knop which, while largely descriptive, outlined the range of economic, socio-cultural, environmental, and health impacts of sports tourism.

In the late 1990s and early 2000s, a range of authors have carried out more detailed examinations of the sports tourism field in relation to *inter alia*: policy (Weed, 1999; 2003a), destination development (Vrondou, 1999), seasonality (Higham and Hinch, 2002), participation patterns (Jackson and Reeves, 1998; Reeves, 2000), economic impacts (Collins and Jackson, 1999), and spectators (Weed, 2002a). Furthermore, in the last few years a number of student texts (e.g., Hudson, 2003; Ritchie and Adair, 2004; Turco, Riley and Swart, 2002) and more research-oriented books (e.g., Higham, 2005; Hinch and Higham, 2004; Weed and Bull, 2004) have been published, as well as special editions of *European Sport Management Quarterly* (2005, Vol.5, No.3), *Sport in Society* (2005, Vol.8, No.2), *Journal of Sport Management* (2003, Vol.17, No.3), *Current Issues in Tourism* (2002, Vol.5, No.1), *Journal of Vacation Marketing* (1998, Vol.4, No.1), and *Tourism Recreation Research* (1997, Vol.22, No.2). The existence of these works demonstrates academic interest in the area, while their content clearly establishes sports tourism as a real and significant phenomenon in contemporary society.

In a recent five-year (2000–2004) 'systematic review of sports tourism knowledge', Weed (2006a) searched 38 hard copy peer-reviewed journals in the broad sport, tourism and leisure subject areas and found 80 articles that fell within the sports tourism field. There was a clear growth in the field, with only eight articles published in 2000, compared to the publication of 24 articles in 2004. Unsurprisingly, the most studied activity was event sports tourism (40% of articles), with outdoor and adventure sports tourism (29%) and skiing and winter sports (15%) being the only other two significant areas. In terms of the phenomena investigated, the largest area of investigation was behaviours (38%) with other work taking place on impacts (25%), provision, management and marketing (24%), policy (8%), and definitions, classification and conceptualization (6%). Combining phenomena and activity, the single largest area of investigation was the impacts of event sports tourism (23% of articles), something that is clearly of relevance in a text on Olympic tourism. However, as the rest of this chapter, and indeed this book, will show, Olympic tourism is about much more than the tourism impacts of the event itself.

Implicit in these publications is a recognition that sports tourism is a significant cultural, social, and economic phenomenon (Weed and Bull, 2004). While statistics about the sporting elements of tourist trips are notoriously difficult to extrapolate, Collins and Jackson (1999) conservatively estimated that, at the turn of the millennium, sports tourism was worth £2.5 billion annually to the UK, whilst Jackson and Reeves (1996) had earlier provided a 'guesstimate' that figures of 10–15 per cent of holidays in Northern Europe having a sports orientation are not unreasonable.

There have been a number of attempts to define sports tourism, but few attempts at conceptualizing the area. Typical of many such definitions is that offered by Standeven and De Knop (1999:12) that 'sport tourism' comprises:

> All forms of active and passive involvement in sporting activity, participated in casually or in an organised way for non-commercial or business/commercial reasons, that necessitate travel away from home and work locality.

Such a definition, while allowing an inclusive approach to the study of sports tourism, does little more than combine widely accepted definitions of sport (cf. Council of Europe, 1992) and tourism (cf. British Tourist Authority, 1981). As such, it is really no definition at all as it does not add anything to an understanding of the area that could not be established from definitions of sport and of tourism as it simply identifies tourism activity involving sport. In fact, such a definition would seem to cast doubt on whether sports tourism is a serious subject for study, or whether it is merely a convenient descriptive term with little explanatory value. Other authors (e.g., Gammon and Robinson, 1997/2003; Robinson and Gammon, 2004; Sofield, 2003) have attempted to separate out 'sports tourists' (for whom sport is the primary purpose of the trip) and 'tourism sportists' [sic] (for whom tourism is the primary purpose), and to further classify these categories into 'hard' and 'soft' participants. However, the flaw in such work is that it is dependent on defining tourism activity in terms of sport, or sport activity in terms of tourism, and as such inevitably establishes a subordinate role for either tourism or sport in an understanding of the area.

I and others have argued elsewhere (Downward, 2005; Weed, 2005a; Weed and Bull, 2004) that sports tourism is a synergistic phenomenon that is more than the simple combination of sport and tourism. As such, it requires an understanding of both sport and tourism (cf. Standeven and De Knop's definition above), but it needs to be conceptualized in a way that is not dependent on definitions of sport and of tourism, and which allows its synergistic elements to be understood. One way in which this can be done is to examine the features of both sport and tourism and establish an understanding of sports tourism derived from those features.

Sport can be seen as involving some form of activity (e.g., kayaking, cycling, etc.), be it formal or informal, competitive or recreational, or actively, passively or vicariously participated in. Furthermore, sport also involves other people, as competitors and/or co-participants. For vicarious and passive participants, the people element is likely to be both other vicarious or passive participants (e.g., other spectators) and the active participants (e.g., competitors). Similarly, active competitors and co-participants may experience other people as active and/or vicarious or passive participants. Even activities that are sometimes participated in alone (e.g., mountaineering, running) are likely to involve other people because participants may reference their participation in terms of the subculture of the activity and thus experience a feeling of 'communitas' (Turner, 1974). Similarly, tourism involves other people, either as co-travellers and/or as hosts. Even solitary tourism entails passing through areas that have been constructed by other people or other communities, and it is rare for a tourist to complete a trip without encountering other travellers. Tourism also involves visiting places outside of the tourist's usual environment. There is, of course, a travel element, but this is either an instrumental factor in arriving at an 'unusual' place, or the travel takes place in or through 'unusual' places. Considering the interaction of these features of sport and tourism, it is possible to arrive at Weed and Bull's (2004:37) conceptualization of sports tourism as 'arising from the unique interaction of activity, people and place'. Notice here that the focus is on the 'interaction' of activity, people and place, thus emphasizing the synergistic nature of the phenomenon and moving it away from a dependence on either sport or tourism as the primary defining factor. Thinking about sports tourism in this way establishes the phenomenon as *related to but more than the sum of* sport and tourism, and thus establishes sports tourism as something that cannot be understood as a tourism market niche or a subset of sports management. Consequently, the understanding used in this text is that:

> Sports tourism is a social, economic and cultural phenomenon arising from the unique interaction of activity, people and place.

What, though, does this conceptualization tell us about the tourism potential of the Olympic Games? There are, perhaps three important things to consider. First, we know that sport is an important tourism phenomenon (cf. Collins and Jackson, 1999; Jackson and Reeves, 1996) that provides *people* with exciting and stimulating tourist experiences (Hinch and Higham, 2005). Second, we know that Olympic cities are, in the vast majority of cases (e.g., Sydney, Athens, and London), some of the world's foremost city tourism destinations, providing vibrant and often multicultural *places* for domestic and international visitors. Finally, we know that the Olympics is the world's premier sporting event, providing travellers with varied active, passive, and vicariously experienced *activities*. Consequently, Olympic hosts experience the interaction of sport as a tourism draw with world city tourism destinations and the Olympic Games as the world's premier sports event, thus providing the potential for a wide range of highly significant tourism benefits.

The next question, therefore, is what is the scope and nature of Olympic tourism? The simple view would be that Olympic tourism comprises the visits of spectators, athletes, officials, and dignitaries during the Games themselves. However, this is far from the full picture. The IOC announcement that a city is to host the Olympic Games should be the 'B of the Bang' for that country's tourism industry, the start of a tourism phenomenon potentially lasting 10–15 years and leaving a lasting legacy for the future organization and co-ordination of tourism in that country. In addition to tourism generated during the games themselves, potential pre- and post-games tourism may arise from a range of sports tourism types, and it useful to take a look in detail at these types before establishing a definition of 'Olympic Tourism' that can inform the rest of the text.

A Model of Sports Tourism Types

In one of the pioneering works in the field, Glyptis (1982) investigated the links between sport and tourism in five European countries and made some comparisons with Britain. She identified five 'demand types' – namely: general holidays with sports opportunities, activity holidays, sports training, spectator events, and 'up-market' sports holidays – which, although proposed as relating to demand, essentially amount to a supply side categorization of sports holidays. Weed and Bull (2004) modified these categories to reflect the nature of contemporary sports tourism and used them to examine the range of sports tourism provision. In modifying the categories, Weed and Bull (2004:123) noted that the 'activity holidays' category, whilst perhaps not initially intended to do so, has come to imply outdoor adventure or countryside pursuits such as rock climbing, potholing, or hiking or trekking. Consequently this category was renamed as 'sports participation holidays' to encompass the full range of sports activities that might take place as a prime purpose of a tourist trip. The 'spectator events' category was seen as useful because it allowed for the 'passive' aspect of sports tourism. However, Weed and Bull (2004:37) noted that other categories, such as general holidays with sports opportunities, may also include passive sports tourism. In addition, it was seen to be important to allow for active involvement in sports events, particularly mass participation events such as the big city marathons. Consequently, Weed and Bull (2004:37) proposed that this category could be more usefully labelled as 'sports events'. The final category, 'up-market sports holidays' has been identified (Weed, 2001a) as being characterized not by the nature of the sports opportunities offered, but by the luxurious nature of the accommodation and attendant facilities provided. As such, Weed and Bull (2004:37) proposed that it would be useful to label this category as 'luxury sports holidays' to more accurately reflect this. In addition to the updating of the individual categories, one final modification was required to allow for the inclusion of day-visits, which the vast majority of tourism definitions now include. This was achieved by simply replacing the word 'holidays' with 'tourism' where necessary in the categories. As a result, the updated sports tourism types proposed by Weed and Bull (2004) were:

- Tourism with sports content

- Sports participation tourism

- Sports training

- Sports events

- Luxury sports tourism.

These types were illustrated by Weed and Bull (2004) in their Model of Sports Tourism Types which also showed the key features of such types. In this text, Weed and Bull's model has been updated slightly to include the consideration of an additional feature, that of 'vicarious' participation in sports tourism (see discussions below). This updated model is shown as Figure 1.1.

In considering the features of the sports tourism types shown in Figure 1.1, perhaps the most obvious feature is that sports tourism may involve multi-sport or single sport participation. This is one of the dimensions identified by Standeven and De Knop (1999) in their categorization of sports tourism, and all of the five types of sports tourism may involve either single sport or multi-sport participation. A further feature of sports tourism, identified by Glyptis in her 1982 categorization and

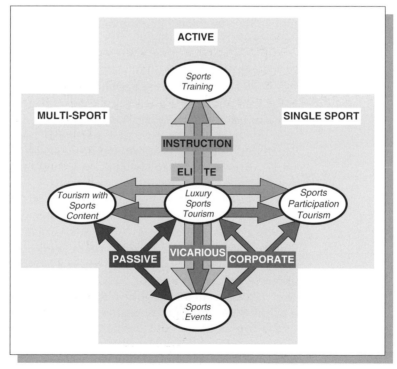

Figure 1.1
Model of Sports Tourism Types.
Source: adapted from Weed and Bull, 2004.

utilized in much of the subsequent literature (Hall 1992a; Jackson and Glyptis, 1992; Standeven and De Knop, 1999), is its potential to be either active or passive. While each of the sports tourism types discussed here may be active, passive participation can only take place in the tourism with sports content (e.g., incidental spectating), sports events (as a spectator) and luxury sports tourism (e.g., as a corporate hospitality guest) types. More recently, it has been argued (Weed, 2005a) that there is also a 'vicarious' element to sports tourism participation, and this element, as noted above, represents an updating and development of Weed and Bull's (2004) model and is shown in Figure 1.1. Many sports spectators consider themselves to be much more than passive participants, although they are not actively taking part in the sport itself. Such spectators feel that they are interacting with the active participants and, as such, might be described as experiencing the sport 'vicariously' through such participants. This might be true of spectators in the case of sports events, luxury sports tourism and tourism with sports content as noted above. However, as visits to sports attractions and museums become more widespread, such 'vicarious' involvement may also be a part of sports participation tourism, where the participation is the 'imagined' (Gammon, 2002) journey and 'vicarious' experience that takes place.

The five features identified so far exist on dimensions where the features are mutually exclusive: Multi/Single sport and Active/Passive/Vicarious activities. Consequently, features are associated with sports tourism types insofar as each type of sports tourism *may* potentially display that feature, rather than the feature being a defining part of a particular sports tourism type. The remaining features identified do not exist to the exclusion of other features, but they are still associated with sports tourism types as potential features.

As the following discussions will detail, sports training is not only about elite training, but might also incorporate elements of 'advanced instruction'. However, instruction is also a potential feature of tourism with sports content (e.g., water skiing instruction on beach holidays), sports participation tourism (e.g., advice about technique on a skiing holiday), and luxury sports tourism (e.g., advice from a resident professional on golfing holidays). In each of these three cases 'instruction' is not the prime purpose of the trip as that would define the activities as sports training. Consequently, instruction might feature as a part of four of the five sports tourism types. Sports training is also readily associated with elite sport although, as with instruction, this is not the only sports tourism type that might potentially involve elite sport. Elite sport may feature in both sports events (e.g., Olympic

Table 1.1
Potential Features of each Sports Tourism Type

	Multi-Sport	Single-Sport	Active	Passive	Vicarious	Instruction	Elite	Corporate
Tourism with sports content	•	•	•	•	•	•		
Sports participation tourism	•	•	•		•	•		•
Sports training	•	•	•			•	•	
Sports events	•	•	•	•	•		•	•
Luxury sports tourism	•	•	•	•	•	•	•	•

Games) and luxury sports tourism (e.g., National squad 'get togethers' at luxurious facilities). Finally, involvement in sports tourism as part of a corporate group can be a feature of sports participation tourism (e.g., outdoor activity management training), sports events (e.g., corporate hospitality), and luxury sports tourism (e.g., a weekend in a country house hotel as a reward for corporate performance). A summary of the potential features of each sports tourism type shown in Figure 1.1 is summarized in Table 1.1.

Each of the features described recur in relation to at least three of the sports tourism types, and three of them – multi-sport, single-sport, and active participation – may be a feature of every sports tourism type. It is perhaps useful to take one of the sports tourism types as an example to illustrate the potential features identified in the model. The model shows that sports events may be either multi-sport (e.g., Olympic Games) or single-sport (e.g., Football World Cup), may be active (e.g., as a participant in the Chicago Marathon), passive (e.g., as a neutral spectator at a New York Yankees Baseball Game), or vicarious (e.g., as an emotionally involved spectator at an Ashes cricket test match), may involve elite sport (e.g., international championships), and may involve participation as part of a corporate group (e.g., the corporate hospitality boxes at Royal Ascot Horse Racing Events).

Sports tourism types as a basis for Olympic tourism products

Developing a model such as this is useful in the context of studying sports tourism provision because an understanding of the nature and potential features of each sports tourism type can assist in examining and developing the most appropriate strategies to provide for such types. In the context of Olympic tourism, the model can help identify the range of tourism that might be generated by hosting an Olympic Games. The following discussion, therefore, examines each sports tourism type in more detail, and identifies those types that might be developed as Olympic tourism products.

Tourism with Sports Content

This category is the broadest of the sports tourism types. Its defining characteristic is that sport is not the prime purpose of the tourism trip. Given such a defining characteristic, this category may overlap with Sports Events and Luxury Sports Tourism, where it may also be possible that sport is not the prime trip purpose.

In exploring this category, it is perhaps useful to begin with the simplest form of sports tourism, that where sport is not an organized part of the holiday, where sports facilities or opportunities do not play any part in the choice of destination, and which would often take place spontaneously rather than being pre-planned. Examples of such activities may be a trip to the local swimming pool, perhaps due to other activities being limited due to bad weather, or a trip to watch an ice hockey match as an alternative evening activity. In each case, the participation has not been pre-planned, nor has it been part of the organized element of the holiday. Some research suggests (see Judd, 2002) that city breaks may often be most conducive to this element of sports tourism, as such breaks often involve a significant element of 'wandering around' the city and tourists may be attracted to events, activities or facilities that they had previously no knowledge of. The recent growth in 'sports museums' may be an example of this. Visits to such attractions, such as 'Halls of Fame' or 'Stadium Tours', as with many museums, can often be a spontaneous activity (Gammon, 2002; Snyder, 1991), and some aspects of Olympic-related tourism may be of this nature. However, such 'spontaneous' Olympic-related tourism, as it is not pre-planned, does not contribute to the generation of visits to a destination, although it can be harnessed as part of strategies to maximize tourist spending once at a destination.

Of course, the activities described above may, in other circumstances, be a planned, though not prime purpose, part of a tourism trip. Once sport becomes such a planned part of the trip, it is possible to examine the range of activities by reference to the importance of sport as a tourism decision factor. This is one of the categories used by Jackson and Weed (2003) in the Sports Tourism Demand Continuum, and subsequently used within the Sports Tourism Participation Model (see discussions in Chapter 2). In illustrating this element, it is perhaps useful to begin with examples where sport can be a major tourism decision factor, despite not being the prime purpose of the trip. In such cases sport can be the deciding factor between a number of different tourism destinations, in effect, it is a 'Unique Selling Proposition' for providers. As an example, a family may wish to take a city tourism break and, as described by Moutinho (1987), may have narrowed the choices down from a 'total opportunity set' of options, to a 'decision set' of three or four choices. However, this is but one element of the holiday decision making process, comprising eight stages, described by Cooper et al. (1998):

1. Tourism need arousal

2. Recognition of need for tourism

3. Involvement and search for information

4. Identification of alternatives

5. Evaluation of alternatives

6. Decision

7. Purchase

8. Post-purchase behaviour (anticipation and doubt).

The third, fourth, and fifth stages listed above are those that correspond to the opportunity set reduction process described by Moutinho (1987). In many cases, if sport is perceived as important to the family, then opportunities for sports spectating and participation may be the deciding factor between destinations in the fifth stage above. In the case of Olympic cities, the opportunities to visit Olympic sites to take a tour, to watch an event, or to participate in sport may be an important part of the decision making process for potential tourists, while not being the prime-purpose, or even a central purpose, of the trip.

Sport can also be a part of tourism planning once the destination choice has been made. In such cases there may be elements of sports participation or visits to events, facilities or attractions that are considered 'must see' or 'must do' activities when visiting a particular area. For example, for many non-American tourists visiting the USA, a trip to an American Football or Baseball game may often be regarded as such. As part of broader research on sports spectator motivations and behaviours in 2002 (see Weed, 2003b), a number of focus groups and interviews were conducted with sports spectators, the following is an excerpt from one such focus group:

> **INTERVIEWER:** *... so what about sports spectating outside Europe? Has anyone travelled across the world to watch sport?*
>
> **RESPONDANT:** *Well, not specifically to watch, but I went to New York this year – my girlfriend and I went to visit a friend of hers who lives out there now. As soon as I knew we were going I wanted to see the (New York) Yankees play, I've never seen a baseball match, and don't really follow it, but its something that you've got to do if you visit the States isn't it.*
>
> **INT:** *What about your girlfriend, did she want to go to the game too?*
>
> **RESP:** *Yeah, that's the strange thing. She doesn't really follow sport at all over here, but as soon as I suggested it she was dead keen – she said going to a baseball match in New York was the same as visiting Buckingham Palace for American tourists in London. She didn't seem to think it was sports spectating in the same way as watching football is here, she'd never come to football with me in England.*

There are three interesting things in this example. First, this example of sports tourism falls into the 'Visiting Friends and Relatives' sector which, similar to the city breaks described above, are often particularly conducive to incidental sports tourism (Jackson and Glyptis, 1992). Second, the visit to the baseball game became a part of the holiday plans from the first moment the destination choice was made as a 'must see/do' part of any visit to that city, but it was not a decision factor itself. Finally, the game was seen as more than a sports event, particularly by the respondent's girlfriend, who saw it as a representation of the country's culture. Whilst this is only isolated qualitative evidence, taken from a study that had other aims, it does give an indication of the types of factors that can be important in this type of sports tourism. It seems reasonable to assume that the VFR sector is important, that sports activities on general holidays can be an important part of pre-destination planning (Cooper et al., 1998; Moutinho, 1987), and that in some cases sport can be seen as a cultural representation of the destination (Hinch and Higham, 2005). In relation to Olympic tourism, the second and third elements, in particular, may be important. Certainly, in many cases Olympic-related activities on general trips are likely to be pre-planned. This may take the form of plans to watch a sport event at an Olympic site, or to visit Olympic related attractions. However, the global cultural importance of the Olympics should not be underestimated. The way Olympic hosts interpret the Olympics and the venues chosen can be a representation of host culture. For example, the archery competition in the London 2012 Games is set to be held at Lords, the home of cricket, and the customs and symbols of cricket and this venue are often seen as being derived from a particular view of Englishness. Conversely, Australia, which hosted the 2000 Games in Sydney, would interpret cricket in an entirely different way, seeing it as a way of demonstrating a particularly rugged Australian identity where sport is a key part of the national character. The Athens Games of 2004 used the event to emphasize the country's historic heritage, with images of the ancient Olympics and the Greek Gods being fore-fronted throughout the games. An example of this is the hosting of the shot-put competition at Ancient Olympia rather than, as is customary, at the athletics venue. As such, Olympic venues and attractions are as much a representation of host culture as they are a reminder of the forthcoming or past hosting of the Games.

Sports Participation Tourism

Whilst the previous category is the broadest in terms of both range of activity and types of provision, the Sports Participation Tourism category (where sport is the prime purpose of the trip) is perhaps the most obvious – essentially it refers to sports holidays, which is what most people would think of when they come across the term sports tourism. As with the previous category, there are some overlaps with other sports tourism types, particularly luxury sports tourism. Overlaps with other categories are best dealt with by exclusion. In this respect, active participation in sports events, except at the most basic level, is excluded from this category, as is any extended form of instruction or training. This category, therefore, encompasses the remainder of multi-sport or single-sport sports participation tourism.

A fairly obvious framework for examining this category is to consider multi-sport and single-sport trips. The most obvious single sport is perhaps skiing, and entire texts have been dedicated to this topic by other authors (e.g., Hudson, 2000).

Here, as with many aspects of the previous category, the major tour operators are the main providers, although they are obviously dependent on local destinations for much of their product. There is often demand for some form of instruction on ski-trips, although where instruction is the prime purpose of the trip such holidays would fall into the sports training category. Also, the non-sporting aspects of the trips can be important (see discussions of the Associated Experience profile in Chapter 2) and, whilst the sport provides the prime-purpose and stimulus for the trip, the 'apres ski' experience may often mean that some ski-trips fall into the luxury sports tourism category (Weed, 2001a) where the emphasis is as much on conspicuous consumption as it is on sports participation.

Of course, skiing and a range of other winter sports are part of the Winter Olympics. There is a key difference between much Winter Olympic tourism and that generated by the Summer Olympics. While in each case there will obviously be a significant number of tourists coming to watch the event itself, pre- and post-Winter Olympic tourism is often much more focussed on the recreational use of the Olympic facilities, such as ski-resorts and cross-country skiing trails. Following the 1988 Winter Olympics in Calgary, for example, the Canmore Nordic Ski Centre attracted 40,000 cross-country skiers in its first year of post-Olympic operation (Whitson and MacIntosh, 1996).

At this more recreational end of the sports tourism spectrum are sports where the sport itself may be the method of transport for the trip, such as hiking, cycling, and sailing. Taking the latter case as an example, sailing sports tourism can be divided into two distinct categories: that where the boat itself is the transport and accommodation for the trip; and that where the sailing takes place in the same place (e.g., at a lake or coastal venue) and the accommodation is provided nearby (Jennings, 2003). Sailing providers include commercial boat hire companies and marina developers, specialist commercial sailing holiday operators (that own a lake, equipment, and accommodation) or networks of sailing clubs from the 'not-for-profit' sector that organize exchange visits. In each of these cases, the prospect or the actuality of having been an Olympic venue will obviously be a fairly 'unique selling proposition' for most of these organizations and the wider destination in which they are located. Furthermore, such destinations may often be part of strategies to spread the Olympic tourism spend beyond the host city because their particular resources are often not found in such cities.

While there are a whole range of other examples of sports participation tourism, not least a range of adventurous and outdoor activities, the Olympic aspects of this sports tourism type are largely limited to those sports where sports tourists can experience the Olympic courses, venues, or facilities. In many cases, such experiences are much more likely to be part of tourism with sports content (e.g., taking the opportunity to swim in the Olympic pool whilst on a more general trip) or sports events (e.g., taking part in a Marathon run over the Olympic course). However, sports tourists may also 'vicariously' experience Olympic courses, venues, or facilities, through the Olympic related visitor attractions or halls of fame that have previously been mentioned in the tourism with sports content category. Such visits have been compared to 'pilgrimage' (Gammon, 2002) and may involve a certain amount of wish-fulfilment or 'place collecting' (Urry, 2001). Although little is known about this particular aspect of sports tourism participation (Gibson, 2002), it is obviously a significant group to consider within Olympic tourism.

Sports Training

Generally, the Sports Training category is much narrower than the previous two sports tourism types discussed above. However, in examining Olympic tourism it is a very important type. It comprises, quite simply, sports tourism trips where the prime purpose is sports instruction or training. This might range from a weekend instruction course for beginners on how to sail a dingy, to an elite training camp at an altitude for a national athletics squad (Weed, 2001a).

It is possible to identify three areas within this category: 'learn to' courses, advanced instruction, and elite training. In the first area, the purpose of the trip is to learn to play a sport. Sailing has already been mentioned, and within the UK the Royal Yatching Association (RYA) accredits residential courses at facilities throughout the country. Southwater Watersports, for example, offers residential instructional holidays in a range of watersports for individuals, couples, families and groups of adults or children. In addition to learning to play sports, coach education and training can also be included. Many courses to train coaches are residential, and as such should be considered as part of this 'learn to' category (Pigeassou, 2002). The similarity between coach education and learn to play is that in both cases some National Governing Body standard or certificate is often the end product of the course. In the Olympic context, such tourism is likely, like that in the sports participation tourism category, to be made more attractive by taking place at an Olympic venue.

In relation to athletes and participants, the same providers often cater for both advanced instruction and elite training. Club La Santa in Lanzarote is a good example of such a facility, with a range of sports on offer at top class facilities. In Reeves (2000) study of elite British track and field athletes Club La Santa was a regular training venue. However, a smaller related study also described a trip to the facility by a small amateur squash club for 'advanced instruction'. The members of the club all contributed towards the cost of taking their own coach with them, and they emphasized that, while the purpose of the trip was squash coaching, all ability levels could join in and benefit from the trip. Here, as with the 'learn to' element, Olympic venues have a distinct competitive advantage for advanced instruction over other sports training venues that can not offer the kudos of a link to the Olympic rings.

Similar facilities to Club la Santa exist around the world (e.g., La Manga in Southern Spain), whilst other popular sports training venues are focussed on destinations rather than a specific site (e.g., Hilton Head Island in South Carolina and San Diego in California) that have a concentration of top-class sports facilities and a favourable climate. In both cases, a significant proportion of business comes from repeat visits, particularly from elite athletes.

Sports training destinations may be in exotic locations, they may be linked to sports event venues, or they may be located where expertise exists. Of course, central to athletes' preparations for the Olympic Games is 'acclimatization' training in locations similar in climate to that where the Games are to be held. In this respect, the London Games of 2012 will see traditional ideas about warm weather acclimatization reversed, as athletes seek to acclimatize to the UK's often inclement, and always unpredictable, weather and environment. In the run up to the decision to award the 2012 Games to London, the East Midlands Development Agency estimated that Loughborough (a University town 120 miles north of London) could benefit by £5–10 million as international teams seek to utilize Loughborough University's extensive sports facilities and expertise in the 5–6 years before the Games. This may seem an excessive estimate, but the Great Britain team spent £1million on their pre-Athens Olympic Games training camp in Cyprus in 2004 (Cotton, 2005). The facilities at Loughborough have been subsidized by the UK National Lottery's Sport Fund for the specific development of elite sport (Sport England, 1999). Other sites in the UK have been similarly subsidized with some, such as the National Water Sports Centre at Holme Pierpoint, which has a 2000 m rowing lake and slalom canoe course that can and have been used for international competition, being linked to event venues. However other centres, such as the picturesque Bisham Abbey, which often hosts England hockey and football team training and is home to the

Lawn Tennis Association and English Hockey Association, are purely training venues. London 2012 will bring an unanticipated tourism spin-off for the investment in such elite sports training systems as athletes and sports governing bodies and teams from a range of countries around the world seek to use such facilities in the four years before the London Games, bringing economic benefits to both the venues themselves and the areas in which they are located.

Sports Events

As with the sports training category above, this sports tourism type is relatively easy to define. It refers to tourism where the prime purpose of the trip is to take part in sports events, either as a participant or a spectator and, of course, it is THE most obvious element in any consideration of Olympic tourism. Whilst sports events are often thought of in terms of mega-events such as the Olympics and football World Cup, the smallest of local events, such as a 5 km fun run, are also part of this category. Regardless of size or importance, all events will attract both participants and spectators (Jackson and Weed, 2003), and many smaller events may be part of Olympic-related tourism.

Much has been written about the political and economic impacts of mega events (e.g., Burbank et al., 2001; Fayos-Sola, 1998; Hall, 2001) and it would not be productive to repeat this material here – a brief discussion and reference to other sources can be found in Weed and Bull (2004). Needless to say, there will be an influx of athletes, officials and spectators during the staging of the Games themselves, all of whom will be Olympic tourists, and the details of such tourists are discussed in Chapter 3.

In order to stage an event of the magnitude of the Olympic Games, football World Cup or Commonwealth Games, partner-ship between the public, commercial and voluntary sector is required. For such major events, a country or city is nominally the provider as the named host, however this is far from the full story. Certainly government support is essentially to winning the right to stage such events, but even the most centralized of governments would not attempt to stage a wholly publicly funded mega-event. The last example of this would have been the Moscow Olympics of 1980, but at that time both world politics and the USSR's political system where very different to the present day. The commercial sector's involvement is likely to include, *inter alia*, sponsorship, management expertise, facility provision and equipment supply (Getz, 2003). In addition, the voluntary sports sector, through sports governing bodies, will be needed to oversee the technical side of the sports competition.

However, whilst the provision of such mega-events involves a complex set of partnerships among sectors, it is unlikely that the initial impetus to stage or bid for the Games will come from the commercial sector, it will usually come from the city, country or, in some cases for individual sports, the national governing body for that sport. Chapter 5 discusses at length the nature of such provision partnerships and their impacts on Olympic tourism development.

Mid-size events, such as national championships or international championships in less high-profile sports such as Judo, will generally gravitate to areas where suitable facilities exist, or to areas that have organizations that are prepared to host such events (Getz, 1997a). In many cases, mid-size events will be hosted in the run up to, and the aftermath of, mega events. The case of Sheffield (Bramwell, 1997a) highlights the way in which the facilities developed for the World Student Games in 1991 are still an important part of that city's event-based tourism strategy. As an Olympic Games approaches, previously inconsequential sports competitions in the country due to host the Games become significant international events as athletes seek to experience and acclimatize to local conditions. This will inevitably stimulate a growth in travelling sports spectators as international athletes flock to events based in a forthcoming Olympic host country, making that country the centre of international sporting competition in the 3–4 years before the Games.

While events attract commercial sponsors who get involved for the advertising and marketing benefits, it is important not to forget the importance of commerical corporate hospitality. Such hospitality may involve entertaining clients or providing incentive rewards for employees (Fraser, 1998). Corporate hospitality will obviously be most prevalent at more high profile sports and at high profile events, but to some extent corporate hospitality can exist, and can be important to providers, at many lower profile sports events (Lambton, 2001; Stewart, 1993). That a forthcoming Olympic Games is to be hosted in a particular country will, as noted above, lift the profile of many events in the run up to the Games, thus boosting the corporate hospitality sector of sports event tourism at many venues in that country.

At the more recreational level, sports participants will want to compete at venues that are or have been part of an Olympic Games. Mass participation events that take place over prospective or former Olympic courses (such as marathons and triathlons) or in Olympic venues (such as swim meets and badminton tournaments) will be likely to experience a considerable increase in prospective entrants of all abilities who wish to say they have run the Olympic course or competed at an Olympic venue.

Luxury Sports Tourism

Unlike any of the previous categories, luxury sports tourism is not defined by reference to the nature of the sport involved in the trip. Rather it is the quality of the facilities and the luxurious nature of the accommodation and attendant facilities and services that define this type of sports tourism (Weed, 2001a). Consequently it overlaps with all the other categories, as it simply caters for the luxury end of the market in each case. As such it may seem a strange category to include; however, the nature of the clientele attracted and the tourism experience provided means that it is a useful and legitimate category.

Whilst not related to the Olympics, golf and the country house hotel, are high profile examples of this type of sports tourism. In many cases, the luxury market is exploited by the addition of five star accommodation to long established and renowned facilities (Readman, 2003). Similarly, the type of recreational sailing, involving luxury motor yachts, that might be a questionable inclusion as a sport, would also fall into this category (Jennings, 2003). The luxury nature of motor yachting and sailing is defined by the exclusivity of the resorts visited, such as Monaco and San Tropez, where a marina berth would be prohibitively expensive for many aspirant tourists. Such perceptions of exclusivity are likely to be further enhanced by any destination's past or future association with the Olympic Games.

Of course, as mentioned earlier, it is perhaps in relation to skiing and winter sports provision, where the 'apres ski' experience can be important, that the clearest link with the Olympics exists in the luxury sports tourism category. In many cases this is as much a function of the exclusivity of the resort as the nature of the facilities, although five star provision is still the defining element of this sports tourism type. Winter sports resorts that have been associated with the Olympic Games will clearly appeal to those sports tourists motivated by aspects of conspicuous consumption, and such social and prestige motivators cannot be ignored in relation to this type of Olympic tourism. Such motivators and consumption will be discussed in greater detail in Chapter 2.

Luxury sports tourism can include the top end of the corporate hospitality market. The nature of the hospitality provided at many top sports events, such as the Monaco Grand Prix, would certainly put such provision into the luxury category. Of course, some elements of elite training might be also be described as luxury sports tourism, particularly for those at the very top of their profession travelling with national teams. Both of these elements are potentially part of the luxury end of Olympic tourism.

Generic tourism as an Olympic tourism product

The above discussions of the five sports tourism types identified by Weed and Bull (2004) do not quite complete the picture of Olympic-related tourism, as the Olympic Games can be used as part of strategies to generate future non-sports related tourism. Such tourism may be generated either among tourists that have visited the destination for Olympic-related reasons as detailed in the preceding discussions, or among those who have been exposed to the Olympic host destination through various written and audio-visual media. In the former instance, Weed and Bull (2004) have noted that sports events can often be used to generate repeat visits for a range of general tourist related activities. One of Manchester's policy goals in hosting the Commonwealth Games in 2002 was to promote Manchester as a broader urban tourism destination, and showcase other aspects of Manchester's tourism product, many of which had nothing to do with sport. As such the cities range of shops, cultural attractions, theatres and bars were all prominently featured in Manchester's Commonwealth Games promotional material. Olympic Games may also be used to generate positive images of host cities as potential tourist destinations through event related media broadcasts featuring the destination. Research conducted following the 1988 Winter Olympics in Calgary showed that the Games had enhanced the saliency and attractiveness of Calgary as a tourist destination (Ritchie, 1990). Such generic tourism, clearly stimulated by exposure to a destination facilitated by the Olympic Games, is a category that should not be overlooked in a consideration of Olympic tourism.

Olympic tourism – a definition

A straightforward definition of Olympic tourism that covers all the various tourism categories discussed above is:

> Tourism behaviour motivated or generated by Olympic-related activities.

This definition covers the full range of pre- and post-Games sports tourism activity discussed above, but also covers the final category, that of general tourism that has been stimulated by exposure to the Olympic host destination by various corporeal or mediated Olympic-related activities. The definition is intentionally inclusive and all-embracing and is intended to demonstrate the scope of the discussion in the remainder of the text.

Who are Olympic tourists?

The previous chapter established a definition of Olympic tourism as: tourism behaviour motivated or generated by Olympic-related activities. This broad definition comprises not only sports tourism, but also general tourism that is stimulated by Olympic-related media. In the latter case, the interest of this text is in how such generic tourism is stimulated and these issues are discussed as part of Chapter 4. In this chapter, however, the focus is on the Olympic-related sports tourist. As a background to this, the previous chapter discussed how each of the five types of sports tourism featured in Weed and Bull's (2004) Model of Sports Tourism Types might be developed as Olympic tourism products.

The discussion of Olympic tourism products in the previous chapter essentially covers the supply side of Olympic tourism. In this chapter the focus is on the demand side, the Olympic tourists themselves. A starting point for this discussion is the conceptualization that sports tourism arises from the unique interaction of activity, people and place. As such, the first part of this chapter commences with a consideration of the ways in which the behaviours of sports tourists might be understood as this is clearly relevant for an understanding of Olympic tourists. This generic discussion is followed by a consideration of three broad sports tourist profiles, each of which are discussed in respect of Olympic tourists. The second part of the chapter then outlines Weed and Bull's (2004) Sports Tourism Participation Model, before discussion the application of this model to a range of types of Olympic tourists and their associated behaviours.

Understanding the Olympic tourist as a sports tourist

In seeking to understand Olympic tourists and their behaviour, the following discussions aim to utilize perspectives from sport, tourism and sports tourism research to explore how sports tourists behaviours are derived from the ways in which people interact with activity and place. An important aspect of this inter-action is that of motivation. Both sport and tourism as separate activities involve a complex set of motivations and a consider-able literature exists which reflects this. Reeves (2000) reviews the motivational literature relating to both sports participation and tourism and there is much evidence in this review that the motivations of both sports participants and tourists share a num-ber of common traits which may offer some insights into the uniqueness of the sports tourist. According to Reeves (2000:29) it is the socio-psychological rationales that dominate the sports motivation literature and it is this perspective that 'most closely mirrors that body of literature which attempts to explain reasons for individual engagement in tourism activity' (general reviews of tourism motivation literature can be found in Ryan (2002) and Shaw and Williams (2002)). The discussions of motivations in this section are 'foundational' to the more specific discussions of Olympic tourism towards the end of this chapter and later in the text. Consequently, they are inevitably more generic discussions of sport, tourism and sports tourism.

People's motives for participating in sport are many and varied. Such activities may be shared (common) as well as unique to the individual and they are also dynamic in that they change over time. Such motivation embraces both psychological, social and philosophical perspectives. A significant amount of research on the motives behind sports participation involves the indi-vidual's characteristics – interests, needs, goals and personality (Weinberg and Gould, 1995) and is also linked to similar work on the social-psychology of leisure (e.g., Mannel and Kleiber, 1997; Neulinger, 1991). There are clearly motives which are more specifically identified with sport (rather than tourism) such as competitiveness, a desire to win, the testing of one's abilities and the development of skills and competencies, especially amongst more elite participants. However, many others might also be claimed by tourism.

This can be seen quite clearly in the classification system of the various travel motivators developed by McIntosh and Goeldner (1986) from a review of existing tourism motivation studies. Weed and Bull (2004) argued that three of their four categories of tourist motivation – physical, interpersonal, and status and prestige motivators – also have immediate relevance to sport. However, given the significant cultural importance of the Olympic Games, McIntosh and Goeldner's (1986) fourth category, cultural motivators, is also relevant in a consideration of Olympic tourists. The physical motivators include those concerned with refreshment of body and mind, health purposes and pleasure; interpersonal ones include a desire to meet people, visit friends or relatives, and to seek new and different experiences as well as the need to escape from routine experiences; cultural motivators include a desire to know more about other cultures and lifestyles; and, status and prestige motivators include personal development and ego enhancement. In attempting to consider these motivations in relation to the interaction of activity people and place, it seems quite clear that the physical motivators are related to activity and the interpersonal motivators to people. Cultural motivators can relate to aspects of all three, with views on places often being cultural appraisals, whilst activities and people each transmit cultural elements and symbols. Status and prestige motivators, however, appear to be related to the more holistic interaction of these three factors. As such, the discussion that follows will examine these four motivators in turn before discussing how a consideration of arousal theory and the concept of ritual inversion might both account for the importance of place, and link the areas together in understanding the unique attraction of the 'interactive experience' of sports tourism.

Several writers highlight the quest for health, fitness and general well-being (both psychological and physiological) as important motivations for sport (Astrand, 1978, 1987; Gratton and Taylor, 1985; Long, 1990). In sport these include such objectives as 'weight control, physical appearance and generally maintaining the body in a good physical state in order to maximize the life experience' (Reeves, 2000:35). In tourism, the emphasis is more concerned with relaxation and recuperation, giving the 'batteries an opportunity to recharge' (Cohen, 1983; Crompton, 1979; Mathieson and Wall, 1989).

Such health benefits are also inevitably linked to the idea of enjoyment, pleasure satisfaction and excitement – positive affective experiences which some, dating back to the work of Sigmund

Freud, collectively refer to as the 'pleasure principle', a feeling of well-being (Reeves, 2000) which has, in some cases, been related to physiological responses to exercise and excitement (Sonstroem, 1982; Sonstroem and Morgan, 1989; Williams, 1994). These have been claimed as important motives underpinning sports participation but they are equally relevant to tourism (Robinson, 1976; Urry, 2001). As such, 'vicarious' participation in tourism or sports tourism activities, where activities and things are experienced through others, are relevant here. More specifically, the excitement generated in spectators by performances in the 'theatre' of the Olympic Games can be important, but also the vicarious participation in Games of the past through Olympic-related museums or visitor attractions should be considered. In addition to the associated physical and psychological benefits they provide, some writers have also offered philosophical rationales to explain people's desire for pleasure in terms of a desire for a 'good life' (Kretchmarr, 1994). Sport, for example, may be perceived as an important component within a particular lifestyle and, furthermore, may also mirror developments in contemporary society and be used by individuals as a means of escaping from the pressures of everyday life. Both these motives are equally important elements within the tourism motivation literature. Holidays are now regarded as an essential component of modern lifestyles, with people prepared to forego other items rather than their annual holiday (Ryan, 2002). In addition, the sense of escapism is also seen as an important influence on tourism behaviour (Iso-Ahola, 1989; Leiper, 1984). In fact, Urry (1990:12) explicitly links the pleasure principle to escapism suggesting that tourists 'must experience particularly distinct pleasures which involve different senses or are on a different scale from those typically encountered in everyday life'. Clearly, this is of obvious relevance for Olympic tourists.

In relation to interpersonal motives, a particular strong motive for playing sport is a sense of affiliation, involving the need to belong to a team, group, club or society in general. Carron and Hausenblaus (1998) utilize theories of group cohesion to identify two main reasons to explain this need: involvement for predominantly social reasons and the subsequent satisfaction and pleasure derived from that social interaction and for task reasons, i.e., enjoyment of working with other members of the team in common pursuit of the task completion. While the latter motive may not have immediate resonance with tourism (although it would be applicable to various forms of special interest tourism such as conservation holidays) the social interaction motive involving meeting new people, visiting friends and relatives and spiritual pilgrimage is clearly relevant and is identified in the literature on tourism motivation. Several studies in fact refer to tourists as modern day pilgrims (Graburn, 1989; Hetherington, 1996; Urry, 2001) with most tourism involving people travelling in groups of one sort or other. Vicarious participation as part of a crowd at sports events is also an interpersonal motivator, and for some, trips to a major sports event such as the Olympic Games may be akin to pilgrimage. Of course, vicarious interaction need not be immediate, as people may make 'pilgrimages' to sites of previous Olympic Games, to the Olympic museum at Lausanne, or to ancient Olympia in Greece. In this case, the interpersonal interaction is virtual, as people make 'imagined journeys' (Gammon, 2002) to interact with the people and activities that are related to the site. Family bonds can also be an important part of interpersonal motivation, with parents taking their children to sporting events or sites and using the trip to reinforce family relationships around a shared interest, be this sport or travel or an interaction of the two. Finally, as Reeves (2000:34) points out, the social interaction motive 'has clearly identifiable links with the travelling or "touring" of sports teams, at all levels of participation' and Green and Chalip (1998) provide a useful illustration of this in their study of the Key West Women's Flag Football Tournament where their findings suggest 'that a pivotal motivation for these women's choice of travel and destination is the opportunity to come together to share revelry in the instantiation of their identity' (p. 286).

Cultural motivators related to seeing and experiencing 'otherness' (MacCannell, 1999) can perhaps be more widely seen in the tourism rather than the sport literature. Nevertheless, undoubtedly sport is a globalized cultural phenomenon which can also be a representation of the local. Nauright (1996) believes that sporting events and people's reactions to them are the clearest public manifestations of culture and collective identities in particular societies. Furthermore, Bale (1989) identifies sport as being a major determinant of collective and place identity. As cultural motivators relate to the desire to experience other cultures and lifestyles, it seems that sport is increasingly being seen as a representation of such local cultures and lifestyles, and is increasingly attracting the interest of the culturally motivated sports tourist. Moreover, in this context, the sports tourist is not only experiencing a sports event, but is also participating in a local cultural celebration of collective and place identity, with the resulting experience being derived from a synergistic interaction of the activity, the people and the place, with the primacy or importance of either the sport or the tourism element being redundant. As such, this is a clear manifestation of the coming together of motivations for sport and for tourism. In the Olympic context, the local (i.e., host's) interpretation of the global Olympic phenomenon is a key part of this cultural interaction. Here the presentation and interpretation of the Olympic Games is a clear manifestation of local culture, as the very different Games hosted by Sydney and Athens testify (see case studies in Chapters 7 and 8 for further details). That such cultural heritage is utilized extensively in the iconography of television coverage of the Games further highlights the importance of this local and global interaction.

Status and prestige motives are equally important for both sport and tourist activity. Goal achievement is often regarded as a key motive for sport, especially in relation to elite performance, and this is clearly relevant in relation to the Olympic Games. As Reeves (2000:35) points out, for many individuals winning provides the primary motive for participation which he suggests might be explained by Achievement Goal Theory. Here individuals who exhibit 'an ego-oriented outlook in life will tend to transfer this rationale to their participation in sport' and 'the goal or motive for such individuals is to maintain a favourable perception of their ability'. This is closely linked to the pursuit of rewards which may be tangible in the form of prizes, medals or trophies or intangible in the form of praise, encouragement, satisfaction and feelings of accomplishment. And, of course, all of this is related to the acquisition of status. Such motives are equally important for tourists. Several writers, borrowing from Maslow's hierarchy of needs, refer to the goal of self-fulfilment involving certain types of tourist achieving the ambition of 'collecting places' (Urry, 2001), or increasingly 'collecting experiences'. As such, the desire to visit Olympic sites or to experiencing the Olympic Games themselves, can clearly be linked to status and prestige motivators. Furthermore, there is also the related motive of wish-fulfilment with tourists seeking to achieve their dreams and fantasies and this is also related to status, another ambition of the sports person. Just as the sports person can achieve status through winning and achieving high levels of performance, so too the tourist can acquire status through conspicuous consumption in the form of ever more exotic and expensive holidays.

In each of the areas discussed above, it is clear that the motives of the sports participant and the tourist can be remarkably similar. Given the ideographic nature of motivation, it is likely that some individuals motivated to achieve, for example, social goals through sport, may not be similarly motivated to experience those goals through tourism. However, for others the convergence of these goals in the activity of sports tourism may result in a very powerful motivating force. It is here that the concept of optimal arousal is useful.

The view that 'leisure should be optimally arousing for it to be psychologically rewarding' (Iso-Ahola and Wissingberger, 1990:2) could be as equally applicable to sport as to tourism and could be particularly important for certain types of sports tourist. While much of the literature on arousal in sport relates to the issue of performance, arousal levels can still be achieved by participation at a less competitive level if competence motives such as skill development, or achievement motivations such as improved personal best performances are present. In fact, such participation need not be competitive at all, as arousal can be achieved by vicarious participation where some of the physical goals of excitement can be important. Such physical goals may be further enhanced by the cultural significance and the status of the event, something that is clearly relevant for Olympic tourism. Furthermore, in sporting pursuits such as skiing and various winter sports, which are often necessarily sports tourism experiences, optimal arousal levels may be achieved by the perceived level of risk involved (Carpenter and Priest, 1989; Ewart and Hollenhorst, 1994; Martin and Priest, 1986; Mortlock, 1984; Priest, 1992; Rossi and Cereatti, 1993; Vester, 1987). Important in determining arousal levels in these activities may be ideas associated with 'locus of control' (Rotter, 1966) and the perception of the extent to which the individual is able to exert control over the level of risk that exists – too little risk, and the activity ceases to be stimulating and the participation is likely to cease due to boredom, too much risk and a need to withdraw from the activity through anxiety results.

In tourism, Iso-Ahola (1980, 1982) has emphasized 'the importance of understanding intrinsic motivation within the framework of the need for optimal arousal' (Pearce, 1993:129) and subsequent work by Wahlers and Etzel (1985) has provided evidence that holiday preferences are influenced by 'the relative differences between optimum stimulation and actual lifestyle stimulation experiences' (p. 285). Those who have a high level of stimulation in their working lives will therefore seek to 'escape' stimulation on holiday while by contrast those with low levels of stimulation at work have a tendency to seek greater novelty and stimulation on holiday (see also Iso-Ahola, 1984 and Mannell and Iso-Ahola, 1987). This approach, which emphasizes the differences between 'home-life' and tourism experiences, might be considered alongside Graburn's (1983) concept of 'ritual inversion'.

One of the key motivations for tourism, according to a range of authors (Graburn, 1983; MacCannell, 1996; Reeves, 2000; Smith, 1977) is a desire to experience things that would not normally be experienced in everyday work or leisure lives. Reeves (2000:45) describes tourism as 'a vehicle for escapism which frequently allows the individual to consume outside the "normal" pattern of everyday life', whilst Graburn (1983:11) notes how:

> tourism involves for the participants a separation from normal 'instrumental' life and the concerns of making a living, and offers entry into another kind of moral state in which mental, expressive and cultural needs come to the fore.

In addition to tourism being motivated by the desire to consume outside the normal pattern of everyday life, the concept of ritual inversion on tourist trips is described by Graburn (1983:21) as a situation where 'certain meanings and rules of "ordinary behaviour" are changed, held in abeyance, or even reversed'. Consequently, the concept of ritual inversion maintains that individuals on holiday feel released to behave in ways significantly different to those in which they are expected to behave at home. Whilst for individuals who experience a high level of stimulation and arousal in their 'home-lives', this may simply relate to the freedom to relax and to not worry about tasks and activities that must be completed, for others the search for optimal arousal and the experience of ritual inversion can be a powerful motivating force for sports tourism activities.

The arousal levels felt during sports tourism participation can be significantly enhanced by the interaction of activity, people, and place. Many sports tourists may also engage in the activities undertaken whilst on tourist trips in their home environment, and as such it is likely that these activities already provide some level of stimulation. However, arousal levels can be enhanced by the addition of the place experience to the activity. The desire to take part in activities in a range of interesting and unusual places is a result of a powerful combination of the various physical and status and prestige motivators described above. When such combined place/activity experiences also take place in the company of like-minded people who share similar motives, then the experience is further enhanced by the achievement of social interpersonal goals. In a reflexive manner, the achievement of optimal arousal through these means is both likely to contribute to, and be enhanced by, the experience of ritual inversion, the 'other kind of moral state in which mental, expressive and cultural needs come to the fore' (Graburn, 1983:11). Therefore, this unique interaction of activity, people, and place is a significant factor in understanding and conceptualizing the sports tourist and, by extension, many Olympic tourists.

Sports-related Olympic tourist profiles

The largest proportion of sports tourism literature has tended to focus on its economic, social and environmental impacts and, notwithstanding the above discussions, very little has been written about the people who generate these impacts – the sports tourists themselves. Furthermore, where sports tourists are considered, they are usually presented as a homogenous group (either event- or activity-based) generating a particular type of impact. Examples of this might be the economic impact generated by visitors to sports events, or the environmental impacts of various ski and winter sports tourism. Only in very rare cases is there any detailed consideration of the behaviours and profiles of sports tourists. Even in this text, where the focus is on the specific sub-group of Olympic tourists, the discussions in Chapter 1 have shown that there are a whole range of different Olympic tourism products. The discussions above have provided a generic context relating to some of the concepts that might help in developing an understanding of the motivations of tourists consuming different Olympic tourism products. However, it is perhaps useful to take a look at sports tourist profiles in specific relation to Olympic tourism, thus establishing three broad sports-related Olympic tourist profiles.

Weed and Bull (2004) reviewed a range of previous studies in their discussion of three broad sports tourist profiles, namely: sports tourists for whom sports tourism participation is the primary reason for travel (primary sports tourists); sports tourists for whom sport is the primary reason for travel, but for whom factors other than the sport are the reason for their sports tourism participation (associated experience sports tourists); and tourists for whom sport is an interest but not the primary trip purpose (tourists interested in sport).

The first of these profiles, that of the primary sports tourist, is the most straightforward to address, as this profile perhaps comprises the 'mainstream' sports tourism market. However, as with many tourism markets and sub-markets, primary sports tourists do not exhibit an homogenous profile, and it would be very difficult to assign any common characteristics across such sports tourists, except that sport is the primary motivation for their trip. Examples of Olympic tourists that would exhibit a primary sports tourist profile might be: Olympic athletes; ski and winter sports tourists; event spectators; and participants in mass-participation sports events.

For Olympic athletes, clearly it is the status and prestige motivators related to goal-oriented behaviour (i.e., winning an Olympic medal) that is the primary motivation. However, given that the Olympic Games only take place once every four years, intermediate and secondary goals and motivations clearly exist. The importance of training in a relaxed and encouraging environment will mean that athletes will be motivated to return to places where they feel the sports training environment provides for social and interpersonal fulfilment. Furthermore, the rarity of Olympic competition means that many elite athletes are also often keen to enjoy the cultural experience of the Olympic Games, as evidenced by the number of video cameras wielded by athletes during the opening ceremonies of the Games in recent years. Such cultural motivators relate to the significance of Olympic places (in this case host cities) and to the importance of the activity (i.e., the Games themselves), which interact with people (both the best athletes in the world with which to compete, and the worldwide television audience of spectators) to make the Olympic Games the ultimate sports tourism experience for many athletes.

Goal-oriented status and prestige motivators can also be important for Olympic tourists taking part in mass participation events, such as a marathon taking place over a former or prospective Olympic course. However, here the goal-orientation is likely to be about beating personal best times rather than winning the race. Of course, the status of having raced over an Olympic course is also important, and this is partly derived from cultural motivators related to the Olympic games more generally, as is the case with Olympic athletes above. As with most Olympic tourism that involves visits to Olympic sites, courses or venues, the key cultural and prestige motivator is related to the concept of 'place collecting' and the kudos that this may afford the tourist on their return home.

Similarly, event spectators are likely to draw some motivation from any links between the events they are watching and the Olympic Games. This may be that they are watching the Games themselves, that they are watching prospective Olympic athletes preparing for the Games, or that they are watching an event at a former or prospective Olympic venue. In such cases the cultural significance of the Games may provide motivations related to vicarious participation, in which spectators feel they experience the event through the competitors, or which allows them to make an imagined journey to the actual Games themselves. The sharing of such participation and experiences with friends, relatives or those with similar interests provides motivations related to social and interpersonal goals, whilst such vicarious experiences and excitement can be seen as physical motivators. Again, there is a clear interaction here between the vicarious activity, the people with whom the experience is shared, and the cultural significance of the place in which it takes place, that contributes to the experience of Olympic-related event spectating.

Finally, ski and winter sports tourists, like each of the other examples of primary sports tourists mentioned above, are also likely to be motivated by the cultural significance of Olympic sites and the prestige associated with place collecting. However, there are also aspects of task mastery and health and fitness goals related to physical motivators, which interact with other aspects of status and prestige motivators such as the ability to tackle ski runs that have been used in the Olympic Games. Here the matching of ability and challenge is important, as skilled skiers seek a level of risk and optimal arousal that a prospective or former Olympic ski run provides. Of course, skiing and most winter sports, whilst largely being independent endeavours, often have a significant social aspect, and thus for many sports tourists social and interpersonal motivations will also be important.

The 'associated experience' sports tourist is a somewhat difficult profile to delineate. Some types of sports tourist may exhibit this profile if their primary motivation for participation relates to some aspect of the experience other than the activity itself. Mass participation sports tourists, for example, may be more interested in meeting up with old friends than in participating in the activity. In relation to Olympic tourism, it may be that some ski tourists may be more interested in the post activity experience. Consequently, the 'après' experience associated with such skiing trips makes some skiing tourists good examples of the associated experience sports tourist. Sports tourists receiving corporate hospitality at Olympic events, pre-Olympic events or Olympic venues may also demonstrate an associated experience profile.

It has been acknowledged for sometime that winter sports resorts need to concentrate as much on the 'après-ski' experience as on the sports facilities themselves. Hudson (2000:164) notes that the time skiers spend on the slopes is steadily decreasing, with the average being less than three hours a day at the start of the twenty-first century. Consequently, for many of these sports tourists, it is the experiences and activities associated with skiing that are important, rather than the skiing itself. In the Olympic context, conspicuous consumption is clearly important, and as such it is the status of the Olympic place derived from the cultural importance of the Olympics, along with the social and interpersonal nature of 'après-ski' activities, that are the key motivators. Such conspicuous consumption, of course, is dependent on the status that such associated experience sports tourists will be accorded when they return to their home environment, and as such is reliant on Olympic ski resorts having a feel of 'exclusivity' that sets those who have visited them apart from their peers. Consequently, the importance placed on status and prestige motivators means that the people and the place elements of the Olympic tourism experience are often more important for these associated experience sports tourists, than the activity itself.

Such status and prestige motivators are less important for sports tourists receiving corporate hospitality at Olympic venues than are the social and interpersonal motivators of meeting like-minded people and clients. Obviously, the status given to the venue by the Olympics is a key factor, and is likely to contribute to attracting clients in the first place, but clearly social interaction is the central goal. Consequently, while the place and the activity act as an attraction, it is the people element that is at the forefront in this type of associated experience sports tourism.

The profile of tourists interested in sport is as incidental sports tourists for whom sport is not the prime purpose of the tourist trip. However, that is not to say that sport is always irrelevant in the trip decision-making process. For many tourists interested in sport, particularly families, sports opportunities will be one of the factors considered in choosing a holiday destination. For others sports participation on non-sports holidays may be an entirely spontaneous decision that was not considered in the pre-trip period. The range of profiles of 'tourists interested in sport' are potentially huge, and might comprise any number of different types of holiday or types of tourists.

Entirely spontaneous Olympic tourists interested in sport might include those who decide to visit an Olympic-related visitor attraction or who decide to take a swim at an Olympic pool. In each case there has been no pre-planning, and so motivations might be as much related to the desire to fill a free afternoon as they are related to a real interest in sports tourist activities. However, for others there might be an underlying interest in the Olympics or sport more generally, and so it is likely to be the status and prestige and cultural motivators discussed above that drive this type of activity.

For other Olympic tourists interested in sport, Olympic-related tourism activity may have played a part in pre-trip planning, or in the trip decision-making process (as discussed under the Tourist with Sports Content heading in Chapter 1). In such cases, motivating factors will be no different to those of prime purpose Olympic tourists, the only difference is that the Olympic tourism is not the prime purpose of the trip. For example, mass-participation Olympic tourists may well combine a family holiday with the opportunity to take part in an event over an Olympic course or at an Olympic venue. While the Olympic-related tourism activity is not the prime purpose of the trip, it may well have been a differentiating factor between destinations, and the motivators will be the same as those motivating the primary purpose Olympic tourists discussed above.

The three broad sports tourist profiles vary in the extent to which sport is important in the sports tourism experience, and thus in the importance of the interaction of activity, people and place. Even when such profiles are narrowed to the sports-related Olympic tourist profiles, the range of examples of Olympic tourists identified above indicate the heterogeneous nature of both the Olympic tourist and the Olympic tourism product. Given this heterogeneity it is all but impossible to establish a workable profile of the sports-related Olympic tourist that is of any use in anything but a technical sense. However, following the preceeding discussions, it becomes apparent that there are similarities in motivations and behaviours between sports-related Olympic tourists involved in a range of different activities that might lend themselves to the construction of a 'typology' of sports-related Olympic tourist types. Such a typology for sports tourists, the 'Sports Tourism Participation Model', has been developed by Weed and Bull (2004). The discussions below outline the development of this model in more general sports tourism terms before moving on to examine its utility in understanding sports-related Olympic tourists.

The Sports Tourism Participation Model

The Sports Tourism Participation Model was developed following the recognition of a number of weaknesses of the 'Sports Tourism Demand Continuum', early versions of which were described by Reeves (2000) and Collins and Jackson (2001), before it was presented in its final iteration by Jackson and Weed (2003). The model takes its basic concept from the English Sports Council's 'Sports Development Continuum' that plots the movement of sports participants from the introductory Foundation level, through Participation and Performance, to the elite Excellence level. The Sports Tourism Demand Continuum, similarly, begins with Incidental sports participation on general holidays and moves through various levels of commitment – Sporadic, Occasional, Regular and Committed – ending with the Driven sports tourist involved in year-round travel for elite competition and training (see Figure 2.1).

Key strengths of the Sports Tourism Demand Continuum were its focus on a range of 'types' of sports tourists based on their behaviours and derived from empirical research. However, the continuum also has a number of implicit weaknesses. First, there is an implication that in moving along the continuum from Incidental to Driven participation there is an increase in sports ability. This is particularly highlighted by the conceptualization of the Driven group profile as 'elite groups or individuals'. This also

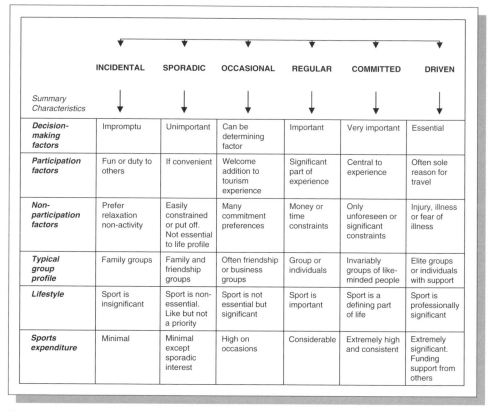

Figure 2.1
Sports Tourism Demand Continuum.
Source: Jackson and Weed, 2003 – derived from Jackson and Reeves, 1996; Reeves, 2000.

calls into question the applicability of the model to spectator sports tourists. In every other sense it appears that the continuum would apply to spectators, but the implication that levels of ability increase with movement along the continuum is difficult to reconcile with the concept of sports spectating. How would one's ability as a sports spectator be defined? The dual concept of sports tourists as both active participants and passive spectators has been one that authors have struggled with in developing models of sports tourism, and the recent proposal of 'vicarious' sports tourism participation has only added to this. The nature of participation as active, passive or vicarious often results in significant differences in behaviour patterns and motivations. In fact, this might be said of sports tourism as a whole because the range of activities often included as sports tourism make it a heterogeneous rather than a homogeneous phenomenon. This heterogeneity is what makes models based on activities rather than behaviours problematic, as it becomes increasingly difficult to include the full range of issues within a model that is simple enough to be useful.

Perhaps the most significant weakness in the Sports Tourism Demand Continuum is the assumption that for participants towards the Incidental end of the scale, sport is insignificant and, consequently, sports tourism is unimportant. Whilst this may be the case for the many people towards this end of the continuum, it fails to recognize the importance of sports tourism trips to individuals' perceived self-identity, the result being that, even where levels of participation are low, the importance placed on that participation can be significant. In seeking to address this weakness, the 'Sports Tourism Participation Model' utilizes the Sports Tourism Demand Continuum within a model that plots sports tourism participation against the importance placed on sports tourism activities and trips (see Figure 2.2).

Figure 2.2 illustrates the first stage in the development of the Sports Tourism Participation Model. Levels of participation increase along the horizontal axis, and it is here that the Demand Continuum discussed above is included. However, an important additional dimension is the inclusion of the vertical scale for the amount of importance attached to the sports tourism trip by individuals. The model illustrates that towards the Incidental end of the scale the level of importance attached to a trip may vary from a relatively high level, to little importance, or even negative importance. At the Driven end of the scale, however, both importance and participation are high. This creates a 'triangle' of participation, the size of which corresponds to the number of sports tourists at each particular level. Consequently, the model shows that there are a much greater number of Incidental sports tourists than there are Driven sports tourists. This, however, refers to numbers of participants rather than levels of activity, as those towards the Driven end of the scale will generate a much higher level of activity per participant than those at the Incidental end of the scale.

Reeves (2000), describes reluctant participation in sport on holiday that accounts for the existence of participants who attach a negative importance to sports tourism. For such people it is actually important NOT to take part in sport on holiday. Such participation is usually a result of a sense of duty to others, particularly family members such as children or partners. Participation takes place although there may be an antipathy towards it. For some participants at the other end of the importance axis at the Incidental end of the scale, sports tourism trips may be of significant importance to individuals' perceived sense of self or identity. Furthermore, for those falling into the two adjacent

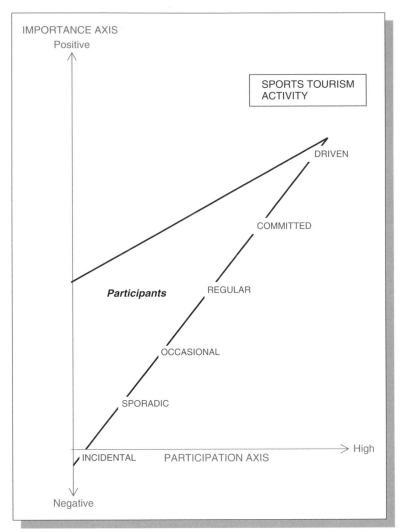

Figure 2.2
Sports Tourism Participation Model – Stage one.
Source: Weed and Bull, 2004.

types to Incidental participants (Sporadic and Occasional participants), the relatively rare sports tourism trip – or sports opportunity on a general tourism trip – may be of great importance
in shaping self-identity and perception on return from such a
trip. Consequently, although actual levels of participation may
be low, the experience is defined as much by the re-telling of
participation as by participation itself. The importance of 'returning' as a significant part of the tourism experience is described
by MacCannell (1996:4) who explains that 'returning home is an

essential part of being a tourist – one goes only to return'. Mac-Cannell believes that tourists are people who leave home in the expectation that they will have some kind of experience of 'otherness' that will set them apart from their peers on their return. This experience of otherness that can be told and re-told to peers, often based on only sporadic or incidental sports tourism participation, is what can make sports tourism important to individuals for whom actual levels of participation are low. The importance is attached to the perceived kudos derived from sports tourism experiences. In this case the level of importance is a result of extrinsic factors – the identity which is portrayed to others. For other participants towards the incidental end of the scale, and perhaps having more significance for the sporadic and occasional groups, sports tourism participation may be important for more intrinsic factors. Sports tourism participation may be an opportunity to take part in lapsed activities for which the time or opportunity for participation does not exist at home. Here significant importance may be attached to such participation because sports participation on tourist trips, no matter how low, may be the only link that such individuals have with past sports participation and, consequently, with a continued conception of themselves as a 'sportsperson'. This is something that may be of major importance to someone who has previously been a very active sports participant, but for whom other responsibilities now restrict participation. In both these cases, the contribution that sports tourism can make to individuals' perceived and self identities, means that sports tourism can be important to individuals for whom actual levels of participation are low.

As levels of participation, and broad levels of importance, increase with a move along the triangle, the quality of the sports tourism experience becomes more important. As Figure 2.1 highlights, once the continuum moves beyond the sporadic participant, sport becomes a significant factor in tourism destination choices. For such participants sport is the prime purpose of the trip, and as such a general shift has taken place in the nature of sports tourists from 'tourists interested in sport' to 'primary sports tourists', with some 'associated experience sports tourists' existing at a range of places on the scale. Consequently, the quality of the sports tourism experience becomes an important factor in choosing and planning a sports tourism trip. In this context, the nature of the place can contribute considerably to the quality of such experiences. This may be through the standard of facilities available at the destination, but also as a result of the general environment, the place ambience, the scenic attractiveness, and the presence of other like-minded people.

The significance of the unique interaction of activity, people and place would appear to increase with the move along the participation triangle. However, for some at the Driven end of the scale, the place experience may be less important than technical requirements related to the quality of facilities. Such participants are elite athletes for whom factors related to place environment – with the exception of climate which is, of course, important for 'warm-weather training' – are relatively insignificant. This, along with their elite sports ability, sets such participants apart from other sports tourists, and is a further argument for, as suggested earlier, discounting the implication that levels of sports ability increase with a move along the Sports Tourism Demand Continuum. With the exception of the elite athlete, high levels of sports ability and performance are not a pre-requisite for even the most committed of sports tourists. Furthermore, participants at this extreme of the scale may be taking part in non-competitive activities such as potholing, in which case the concept of an elite athlete is difficult to apply, or may simply have very high levels of commitment to the sports tourism experience, with all its associated environmental attractions, rather than to the technical requirements of elite sport. It is perhaps useful, therefore, to think of elite athletes as a specific group within the Driven type of participants, rather than as defining that type.

Removing the implication that elite performance is a defining characteristic of the Driven type also assists in making the model applicable to sports spectators. As mentioned above, the idea of an 'elite' sports spectator is difficult to conceptualize. Consequently, with the implication that levels of ability increase with a movement along the model discarded, the focus, again, is on participation and importance. For sports spectators this might usefully be illustrated by reference to football fans. At the Incidental end of the scale will be a vast number of people for whom identity as a football fan is of great importance, but for whom participation in live football spectating as a sports tourism experience is minimal. Similarly, there will be those who have spectated at football, but for whom it is not an important part of their identity. In fact, it is likely that, for some, it has a negative importance as participation has been out of a sense of duty to others. At the Driven end of the scale, there are those for whom participation as a football spectator is high, and for whom it is a defining part of their lives. Some of the material on football hooliganism is illustrative of this (see, e.g., Weed, 2002a), as is Bale's comparison of football fans commitment to that of a religion (Bale, 2003).

A discussion of sports spectators provides an useful avenue through which to introduce another concept into the model – that of the 'Intender'. Intenders were described in relation to arts audiences by Hill et al. (1995:43) as 'those who think the arts are a "good thing" and like the idea of attending, but never seem to get around to it'. Such a concept would also seem to be useful in relation to sports tourism, and perhaps sports spectators provide the most useful illustration. The growth in televised coverage of sport has created a vast number of sports spectators who are highly committed, and for whom watching sport is important, but who rarely travel to a live event. Many such spectators often express a desire to go to a live event, but like Hill et al.'s (1995) arts intenders, 'never seem to get around to it'. Of course, some intenders will attend the odd match, and so the boundary with incidental participation is fluid. However, this group is largely made up of those for whom watching sport is important, but for whom attending a live event never becomes more than a whimsical intention.

The Intenders categorization is, of course, equally significant in relation to active sports tourism. In the same research in which he identified holiday sports participation that takes place as a duty to others, Reeves (2000) also describes those who go on holiday with the intention of taking up some of the sports opportunities available, but never actually get round to it. The promotion of the range of sports opportunities available in hotel and resort brochures can create the intention to participate in sport on holiday, but in many cases such intention is not converted into actual participation. Even where such incidental sports opportunities may play a part in resort or hotel choice, and the intention may be described to peers pre-trip (in the same way as low levels of participation may be exaggerated post-trip as discussed earlier) as a way of boosting perceived identity, there is no guarantee that such intention will be converted into actual participation. Thus, while importance may be high, participation is very low or non-existent, and such people never become actual participants. The Intenders group is shown in the full Sports Tourism Participation Model illustrated in Figure 2.3.

The full model also shows that sports tourism participants are likely to take part in multiple activities, and although Figure 5.5 only illustrates two activities, the model can be envisaged as three dimensional with a potentially infinite number of activities 'growing out' around a central Intenders 'cone' to create a 'bowl' shape. Adding this multi-activity dimension allows for the different characteristics of individual sports tourists to be plotted in relation to their full-participation profile. Taking, as an example, the elite athlete within the Driven type of sports tourist. During warm-weather training for their main sport, such athletes are likely, within the constraints of avoiding injury (Jackson and

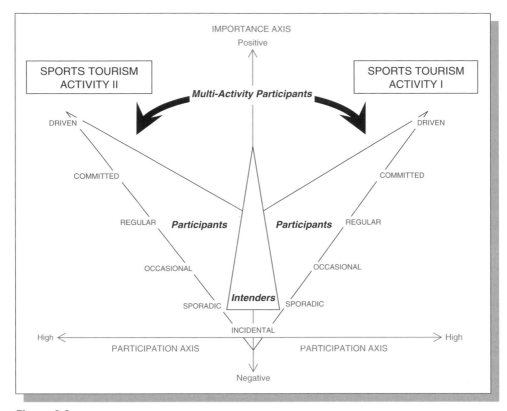

Figure 2.3
Sports Tourism Participation Model.
Source: Weed and Bull, 2004.

Reeves, 1998), to take part as Incidental or Sporadic participants in other activities for relaxation purposes whereas, in relation to some activities, they may never move beyond the Intender type. Conversely, participants in outdoor activity tourism are often Committed participants across a range of activities. The range of activities may, of course, involve active participation or spectating, or a mixture of the two, and many profiles are likely to include some classification within the Intenders group for some activities.

The inclusion of this multi-activity dimension also allows a comparison between the profiles of participants who are genuinely 'multi-lingual' in relation to sports tourism activities, and those for whom one or two activities dominate with others occurring only in an Incidental manner. Each of these types of participant is likely to have a high participation rate in sports tourism, and is likely to fall towards the Committed/Driven end of the scale, but their behaviours and needs are likely to be very different.

Types of Olympic tourists in the Sports Tourism Participation Model

The Sports Tourism Participation Model may be applied to Olympic tourists in two ways. First, the model may be applied only in relation to sports-related Olympic tourist activity and as such, a committed participant would be someone who had a high level of participation in sports-related Olympic tourist activity to which they attached a high level of importance. However, applying the model in this way would not recognize that much sports-related Olympic tourist activity will be related to other non-Olympic sports tourism activity. For example, a regular or committed event sport spectator is more likely to participate in Olympic-related sports spectating – their Olympic-related spectating is part of a wider sports spectating profile. Consequently, this second way of applying the model, which locates sports-related Olympic tourist behaviour within broader sports tourist profiles, would seem to be the best way to utilize this model.

It is perhaps useful to take the examples discussed under sports tourist profiles earlier and examine where they may fall within the Sports Tourism Participation Model. As the above discussions have indicated, prime purpose sports tourists tend to fall into the driven, committed, regular, and sometimes the occasional types. Clearly the Olympic athletes discussed earlier can be regarded as driven Olympic-tourists, with very high levels of participation in both sports training and sports event tourism related to the Olympics, to which they attach considerable importance as a result of their goal-driven status and prestige motivations, which are enhanced further as a result of the Olympics' cultural significance.

Unlike Olympic athletes, prime-purpose Olympic-related event spectators may fall anywhere between the occasional and driven types, and consequently the importance attached to such spectating may vary considerably. However, the cultural significance of the Olympics is likely to mean that even those who are participating out of a feeling of obligation to others will attach more importance to Olympic-related sports event spectating than to other types of event sports tourism. The nature of the Olympics as a rare event may also mean that some prime-purpose event-spectators may be first-time spectators who may have chosen to spectate at an Olympic-related event as a result of the cultural significance of the Olympics and what is likely to be the once in a lifetime opportunity for many to see an Olympic event. As such, the Olympics is likely to generate more one-off event spectators than other sports events, and there may be more prime-purpose spectators than is usual that fall towards the incidental end of the Sports Tourism Participation Model. The sparse number of opportunities to spectate at Olympic events may also mean that there are a high number of intending Olympic spectators, who despite attaching a high level of importance to watching sport, may never travel to spectate at an Olympic event.

For ski and winter sports tourists, the importance attached to Olympic-related ski and/or winter sports tourism may depend on whether they are prime-purpose or associated experience sports tourists. Prime purpose ski-tourists are likely to have a higher level of participation than associated experience ski-tourists, although it may be that associated experience ski-tourists attach a greater level of importance to the Olympic-related aspects of their participation due the their high level of status and prestige motivation and the emphasis on conspicuous consumption. As such, associated experience ski-tourists will fall in types towards the middle of the continuum, most likely as occasional or regular participants, but will be closer to the top boundary of the participation triangle where the importance attached to Olympic tourism is higher. Prime purpose Olympic-related ski-tourists will be more committed, and place greater emphasis on physical motivators than on conspicuous consumption. The importance of the Olympic-related aspects will be related to the opportunity to test their skills on challenging Olympic courses, although clearly there is also an important status and prestige motivation here. As the very nature of committed and driven sports tourists is that they have high levels of participation to which they attach high importance, this will be no different for prime purpose Olympic-related ski-tourists.

Many, but not all, tourists interested in sport will fall towards the incidental and sporadic end of the sports tourism participation model. Those making spontaneous decisions to visit Olympic sites or attractions will mostly have low or irregular levels of participation in sports or Olympic tourism, to which they attach little importance. However, for those tourists interested in sport for whom Olympic-related activities have played a part in the trip decision making process or in pre-trip planning, such Olympic-related participation, while relatively low, may often have high levels of importance. Such importance may be a result of the prestige attached to visiting an Olympic site or taking part in an event over an Olympic course, or it may be part of a genuine and sustained interest in sport and the Olympics and as such is more of a cultural motivator or a physical motivator related to vicarious excitement. There are of course, some tourists interested in sport who regularly take trips on which sport is not the prime purpose, but which involve some level of sports tourism activity. Such sports tourists will fall towards the middle of the continuum as regular participants, and will be more likely than most to take a general trip which involves some Olympic-related sports activity.

Conclusion

The 'Sports Tourism Participation Model' described in this chapter allows for the profiling of a range of characteristics of sports tourists and can assist in the analysis of sports-related Olympic tourist behaviour. The discussions have also examined three broad sports-related Olympic tourist profiles, as well as the basic motivational processes that underpin sports tourist (and by extension sports-related Olympic tourist) behaviour. Such discussions provide important foundational knowledge and understanding for those making policy and provision for Olympic tourism as, where appropriate, their strategies can be derived from a grounded understanding of sports-related Olympic tourist behaviour.

The foundational knowledge provided in this and the previous chapter now allows the remainder of the first section of this book to turn its attention to a more detailed analysis of Olympic tourism. While Chapter 1 has considered some broad issues relating to the nature of Olympic tourism products, and this chapter has examined the nature of sports-related Olympic tourists, there has been very little discussion of the detail of Olympic tourism. Furthermore, the focus has tended to be on the broader nature of Olympic tourism, rather than on the visits that take place to the host city or region during the Games themselves. Chapter 3 now shifts this focus to consider the detail of Olympic tourism flows to the host city/region during the Games, and then broadens the analysis, first, temporally to consider the pre- and post-Games periods, and then geographically to examine the impacts of Olympic tourism flows on the country in which the host city/region is located. Following this analysis, Chapter 4 uses both the broader motivational and behavioural concepts developed in this chapter, and the more detailed consideration of Olympic tourism flows from Chapter 3, to examine the range of leveraging strategies that might be used to capitalize on Olympic tourism. Finally, completing the first part of the book, Chapter 5 examines the role policy makers play in facilitating Olympic tourism development.

The detail of Olympic tourism

Chapters 1 and 2 have identified and discussed Olympic tourism products and Olympic tourist profiles and types, respectively, examining how sports tourism might provide the basis for such products and behavioural profiles and types. These chapters have tended to focus on Olympic tourism generated outside the period of the Olympic Games themselves, as these represent the less-obvious dimensions of Olympic tourism, rather than the visits of athletes, spectators, officials and dignitaries during the Games themselves. However, in this chapter, the analysis turns to the detail of Olympic tourism flows. The initial focus is on the Games themselves, and the tourism and other related movements of 'event-affected' people generated during the Games period. The starting point for this analysis is Preuss's (2005) work on economic impacts of major multi-sport events, where nine categories of event affected people are identified. In the initial analysis of tourism generated during the Games period, Preuss's categories are discussed in relation to the sports-related Olympic tourism profiles and types discussed in the previous two chapters. Following the discussion of the Games period, the analysis broadens to examine the movements of event affected people in the pre- and post-Games periods. Again, attempting to synthesize Preuss's work with the discussions in earlier chapters, the ways in which some of the movements during the Games have implications for the movements of pre- and post-Games general and sports-related Olympic tourists is discussed. Finally, the analysis takes a more macro-view of the long-term travel flows arising from Olympic-related activities, and Leiper's (1979) model of the tourism system is utilized to inform this discussion.

Tourism flows and other movements during Olympic Games

While previous chapters have shown that there are a range of tourism impacts of the Olympic Games that occur both before and after the Games period, clearly the starting point for any detailed analysis of Olympic tourism must be the Games themselves. Pre-Games tourism is derived from perceptions about the future hosting of the Games, whilst post-Games tourism will be significantly affected by the perceptions of the Games, both by those attending in person and by those created by the media. In fact, such perceptions can, as the following discussions will show, have an impact on tourism and travel flows during the Games themselves.

Preuss (2005) identifies nine categories of 'event affected' people in his economic analysis of major multi-sports events, of which the Olympics is clearly the largest and most significant (see Figure 3.1). Four of the categories refer to those who live in the city, namely: Residents, Home-Stayers, Runaways, and Changers. The remaining five categories are those from outside of the host city or region who are actual or potential tourists for the city/region. Four of these categories will be in the city during the Games, namely: Games Visitors, Extensioners, Casuals, and Time-Switchers. The final category, Avoiders, comprises potential tourists who do not visit. It is perhaps useful to briefly outline each of these categories in turn.

Those living in the host city/region

- *Residents* – those people who live in the city who would have stayed in the city/region at the time of the Games if the Games were not taking place, and who remain in the city/region during the Games. Essentially, these are residents who have made no changes to their plans because of the hosting of the Games.

- *Home-Stayers* – those who have decided to 'take their holiday at home' because their city/region is hosting the Games. If the Games were not being hosted, this group would have taken a holiday out of the city/region at some point during the year,

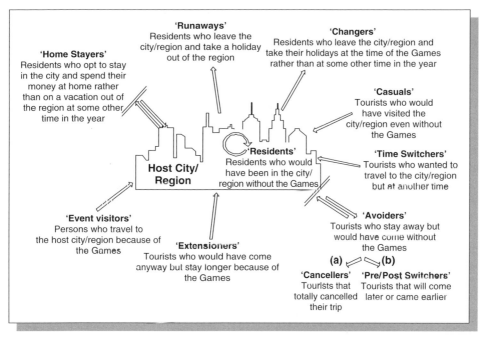

Figure 3.1
Tourism flows and other movements during the period of the Olympic Games.
Source: adapted from Preuss, 2005.

but have changed such plans to spend their 'holiday time' at home during the Games period.

- *Runaways* – local residents who plan a holiday or trip out of the city/region during the Games period. Such a trip is in addition to any holidays or trips that would 'usually' be taken, and has been specifically planned because they do not wish to be in the city/region at the time of the Games.

- *Changers* – those who change their holiday or travel plans to take a trip out of the city/region at the time of the Games. Unlike runaways, this does not represent an additional holiday or trip to that which would 'usually' be taken.

Tourists to the city/region

- *Games visitors* – those people that have made a specific trip to the city/region because the Games are being held there. This category would not otherwise have visited the city/region had it not been for the hosting of the Games.

- *Extensioners* – those people who would have been visiting the city/region as tourists regardless of the hosting of the Games, but have decided to extend their stay in the city/region because the Games are taking place.

- *Casuals* – tourists who would have been in the city/region at the time of the Games even if the Games were not taking place, and who still visit the city during the Games period. These are tourists who have made no changes to their plans because of the hosting of the Games.

- *Time-switchers* – those people who had planned to visit the city/region at a time other than that at which the Games were being held, but who have specifically changed their plans so their visit to the city/region coincides with the hosting of the Games.

Potential tourists to the city/region

- *Avoiders* – those people who would have planned to visit the city/region, but who stay away because the city/region is hosting the Games. The avoiders category falls into two sub-groups:

  a. *Cancellers* – those tourists who cancel their trip all together because of the hosting of the Games.

  b. *Pre-/post-games switchers* – tourists who do not cancel their travel plans completely, but re-schedule their trip to the city/region to avoid the Games period.

While the nine categories of event-affected people are grouped above as those living in the city/region, those visiting the city/region, and those potentially visiting the city/region, they can also be divided into those which have positive tourism impacts for the city/region, those which have negative impacts, and those which have a neutral impact. In assessing the nature of the tourism impacts of each of these groups, it is useful to consider the extent to which the various categories might be considered 'Olympic tourists', and the extent to which the Olympic Games affects their tourism behaviour.

In Chapter 1, a definition of Olympic tourism was established as: tourism behaviour motivated or generated by Olympic-related activities. Undoubtedly, Games Visitors, Extensioners and Time-Switchers fall within this definition, as they have made a specific tourist trip to the city/region, extended their trip to the city/region, or switched the time of their trip to the city/region, respectively, as a direct result of the Olympic Games. The first two of these categories clearly have a positive tourism impact for the host city/region, whilst the Time-Switchers category would appear to have a neutral impact as the tourist trip has simply been moved from one time of year to another. Conversely, the Residents category clearly falls outside of the definition of Olympic tourism as it comprises those living in the city who have not changed their behaviour as a result of the Olympic Games. This group has no tourism impact on the host city/region. However, the nature of the remaining five categories merits further discussion.

As Olympic tourism is being defined as behaviour 'motivated or generated' by Olympic related activities, the Runaways, Changers and Avoiders categories can be argued as falling within this definition. The 'runaways' group, for example, take an additional tourist trip to avoid being in the host city/region at the time of the Games. Clearly, their tourism behaviour has been motivated by Olympic-related activities, albeit in a negative sense. Had the Games not taken place in the city/region, the runaways group would not have taken this additional tourist trip. As such, this group falls within the definition of Olympic tourism. Similarly, Changers are tourists who have been motivated to modify their tourist behaviour (by taking their tourist trip out of the city/region during the Games rather than at another time of year) as a result of the Olympic Games. Finally, Avoiders, as potential tourists to the region have also modified their tourist behaviour as a result of the Olympics, either cancelling their trip altogether, or switching to the pre- or post-Games period. While these three groups have been motivated by a desire to avoid the Olympic Games, their tourist behaviour has still been 'motivated or generated by Olympic-related activity' and as such they fall within the Olympic tourism definition. Although these groups each wish to be away from the city/region during the Games, it is only the Runaways and Cancelling Avoiders who have a clear negative impact on tourism in the city/region. The Pre-/Post-Games Switching Avoiders and Changers have a neutral effect as they have simply changed the timing of their tourist trips.

The Home-Stayers category is a little more difficult. As residents of the city/region, this group will forgo a tourist trip out of the city/region to be in the city/region at the time of the Games. While their tourism behaviour has clearly been affected by Olympic-related activities, in that they do not take a trip out of the city/region that they would have otherwise taken, as residents of the host city/region, can they really be categorized as tourists? The answer depends on the view taken on the nature of tourism. A behavioural definition of tourism, like that proposed by Airey (1981:3), describes tourism as:

> The temporary short-term movement of people to destinations outside the places where they normally live and work, and their activities during the stay at these destinations; it includes movement for all purposes as well as day visits and excursions.

While this definition characterizes tourism as 'the short-term movement of people' it also emphasizes the importance of consumption 'outside the places where they normally live or work'. On one hand, this could be taken to be a geographical dimension; however, on the other hand it could be seen as a psychological dimension. A similar issue arises from the World Tourism Organization's (1991) definition of tourism, endorsed by the United Nations statistical commission in 1983, which describes tourism as: 'the activities of persons travelling to and staying in places outside their usual environment'. While this definition stipulates an overnight stay, it also proposes that a tourist is 'outside their usual environment'. Obviously, this was intended as geographical notion, but it could also refer to a psychological difference that would encourage people to partake in a range of activities that would fall outside of their usual consumption patterns. For Home-Stayers who have decided to 'take their holiday at home', the Olympic Games is likely to encourage such 'unusual' consumption patterns, and as such they will behave in a way very similar to that of tourists. However, despite this behavioural similarity, undoubtedly tourism involves 'movement of people' (Airey, 1981:3) or 'a sense of movement or visit' (Standeven and De Knop, 1999) and as such, Home-Stayers may behave similarly to other Olympic tourists, but they cannot be defined as such. Nevertheless, the fact that they have cancelled a trip away from the host city/region means that their behaviour change has a positive tourism impact.

With the exception of Residents all of the above groups have changed their planned behaviour as a result of the Olympic Games. However, the one remaining category, the Casuals, are the tourist equivalent of Residents in that the Olympic Games has not affected their planned tourist behaviour. Their visit to the city has been planned regardless of the hosting of the Games. As such they might be considered as a group with a neutral tourism impact. However, their consumption patterns once in the host city/region are likely to be affected as a result of the Games. For those Casuals who take the opportunity to become involved in Olympic-related activities, the likelihood is that their spending will increase (Preuss, 2005), and thus their tourism impact will be positive. It might be argued that some Casuals will visit the city/region during the Games and be negatively affected by the Games (i.e., they will wish to avoid the Games). However, this is unlikely as very few people travelling to a host city/region during the hosting of an Olympic Games would be unaware that the Games were taking place. If Casuals wished to avoid the Games, they would have switched or cancelled their trip like the Avoiders group. As such, Casuals' main motivation for visiting the city is not to see the Games, but they are highly likely to become involved in some Olympic-related activities while in the host city/region. Consequently, for at least part of their stay they will be Olympic tourists, and their tourism impact is likely to be, albeit in a very minor way, positive.

The view that the tourism impact of the Casuals group may be slightly positive necessitates a re-evaluation of the tourism impact of the Time-Switchers category. Time-Switchers change the time of their visit to the host city/region to coincide with the Games and, as such, the tourism impacts of such people might appear to be neutral. However, the spending of such Time-Switchers during the Games period is likely to be higher than it would have been had they visited the city/region at another time. Consequently, like the Casuals group, they have a slightly positive tourism impact on the host city/region. The impacts and nature of the various groups is summarized in Table 3.1.

Having examined the nature and impact of event-affected people during the Games period, attention now turns to how these categories of event-affected people relate to the sports-related Olympic tourism products discussed in Chapter 1 and the sports-related Olympic tourist profiles and types discussed in Chapter 2. Of the categories summarized in Table 3.1, seven can be regarded as 'Olympic tourists'. However, three of these categories – Runaways, Changers, and Pre-/Post-Games Switching Avoiders – are tourists who have left the city/region during the period of the Games. In this analysis, the interest in these groups lies in their decision to leave the city/region during the Games rather than in their behaviours once the decision to leave has been made. As such, the detail of their tourist behaviour away from the Olympic host city/region is not part of this discussion.

The remaining four categories that can be regarded as Olympic tourists – Games Visitors, Extensioners, Time-Switchers and Casuals – are each taking part in Sports Events tourism (see discussions and Figure 1.1 in Chapter 1), although there are some overlaps with Tourism with Sports Content in relation to the Casuals group, and with Luxury Sports Tourism for Games

Table 3.1
The impacts and nature of event-affected people during the Olympic Games period

	Tourism Impact?	Olympic Tourists?
Residents	Neutral	No
Home-Stayers	Positive	No, but consumption patterns will be similar to other groups of tourists
Runaways	Negative	Yes, but negatively motivated
Changers	Neutral	Yes, but negatively motivated
Event Visitors	Positive	Yes
Extensioners	Positive	Yes
Casuals	Slightly positive due to increased spending	For part of their stay, yes
Time-Switchers	Slightly positive due to increased spending	Yes
Avoiders		
(a) Cancellers	Negative	Yes, assuming the proposed trip to the host city/region has been replaced by another tourism trip to a different destination
(b) Pre-/Post-Switchers	Neutral	Yes, but negatively motivated

Visitors, Extensioners, and Time-Switchers. While the Games Visitors, Extensioners, and Time-Switchers categories will each contain people who have come to spectate at the Olympic Games, the Games Visitors category also comprises athletes, officials and dignitaries who have all clearly travelled to the host city/region as a result of the event. Many of the dignitaries will also fall into the Luxury Sports Tourism as well as the Sports Event tourism type, as their accommodation and experience is often of a luxurious nature. Some spectators in this category will also overlap with Luxury Sports Tourism as they may be part of corporate hospitality provision or may simply have paid for a more up-market product. Some Extensioners and Time-Switchers may also have paid a premium for a luxurious product, but the majority will simply be event spectators who have taken the opportunity to modify their travel plans to take part in the Olympics. Casuals will, of course, fall into both the Tourism with Sports Content and Sports Event tourism types as their tourism trip has not been planned as a result of the Olympic Games, but some Olympic-related activities will be part of their trip.

During the Games themselves, most Olympic tourists are either passive or vicarious participants. In fact, it is only the athletes and officials in the Games Visitors category that are active participants. Of course, as the Olympic Games is an elite event, all the Sports Event tourism during the Games period is elite in nature. As noted above, a corporate element may be a feature of Sports Events tourism for some in the Games Visitors category through corporate hospitality packages.

In relation to the three broad sports-related Olympic tourism participation profiles discussed in Chapter 2, Casuals can be clearly identified as Tourists interested in Sport – that is, tourists for whom the Olympic Games are interesting, but for whom it is not the prime purpose of the trip. Furthermore, Casuals will fall towards the incidental end of the Sports Tourism Participation Model (see Figure 2.1 and related discussions in Chapter 2), as any Olympic tourism participation is most likely to take place spontaneously if the opportunity arises, rather than to be a part of pre-trip planning.

Clearly, the majority of Games Visitors will be Primary Sports Tourists who have made a specific trip to the host city/region with the prime purpose being the Olympic Games. As such, regardless of whether they are athletes, officials, dignitaries, or spectators, it is likely they will attach high importance to their Olympic tourism activities. However, the Games Visitors group is likely to be distributed at a range of positions along the Sports Tourism Participation Model, with some spectators being one-off event spectators attracted by the global significance of the Olympic Games who would fall towards the incidental end of the model. Others will fall towards the middle of the continuum as regular or occasional sports tourists, while some spectators, and virtually all athletes and officials will be located at or very near the driven end of the model, attaching high importance to their high levels of sports-related Olympic tourism and sports tourism participation.

Similarly, some Time-Switchers and Extensioners will be Primary Sports Tourists. However, many others of this group may fall into the Associated Experience profile, along with some Games Visitors. In fact, it is likely that an event like the Olympic Games will attract more people who are motivated by the various status and prestige motivations that are perceived to be attached to associations with the Olympics. As such, attendance at an Olympic Games is 'conspicuously consumed' as a place or experience to be 'collected', and may be valued as much for the kudos of having 'been there' as for any intrinsic value or interest in the event itself. The major cultural significance of the Olympic Games is likely to increase the number of sports tourists showing an Associated Experience motivational profile, and for these Olympic tourists, the level of importance attached to their sports-related Olympic tourism activity is likely to be high, although in many cases their overall sports tourism participation levels may be low.

Of course, some Time-Switchers and Extensioners may, like the Casuals group, fall into the Tourists interested in Sport profile. However, unlike the Casual group, their Olympic tourism participation will have been a significant factor in the trip decision making and pre-trip planning process, but it is not the prime purpose of the trip. Olympic tourists demonstrating this profile are an important segment of the Olympic tourism market, and one that is often overlooked in providing for Primary Sports Tourists. In these cases, the Olympic Games is what has brought these tourists to the city/region, but they are interested in a broader range of tourism activities than the Olympic Games alone. Chapters 4 and 5 will consider in more detail how this, and the other groups discussed above, can best be provided for by tourism firms, organizations and policy makers.

Tourism flows and other movements in the pre- and post-Games periods

With the detail of Olympic tourism during the hosting of the Games established in the previous section, this section now extends the analysis of event-affected people to the pre- and post-Olympic Games periods. Once again, Preuss' (2005) analysis is used as a starting point, but this analysis has been extended and developed to cover a wider range of event affected people than that considered by Preuss (see Figure 3.2). The nine categories of event-affected people of interest in the pre- and post-Games periods are as follows:

Those living in the host city/region

- *Changers* – this group changed their tourism plans to take a tourism trip out of the host city/region at the time of the Games rather than in the pre- or post-Games period. Consequently, they will now be in the host city/region at a time in the pre- or post-period when they would have otherwise have been away on a tourism trip.

Tourists to the city/region

- *Pre-/Post-Games Sports Tourists* – these groups are those visiting the city/region in the pre-or post-Games period as sports tourists taking part in Olympic-related activities.

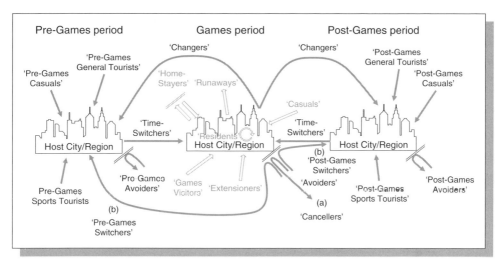

Figure 3.2
Tourism flows and other movements in the pre-, during, and post Games periods.
Source: adapted from Preuss, 2005.

- *Pre-/Post-Games General Tourists* – these groups are those who have been attracted to the city/region for general tourism as a result of the media coverage that the city/region has received due to being the host of the Olympic Games.

- *Pre-/Post-Games Casuals* – tourists whose visit to the city/region has not been influenced by the region/city's status as an Olympic host. This group would have visited the region/city in the pre-/post- Games period regardless of the hosting of the Olympic Games.

- *Avoiders: (b) Pre-/Post-Games Switchers* – these are general tourists who had planned to visit the city at the time of the Games, but switched their tourism trip to the pre- or post-Games period.

Potential tourists to the city/region

- *Pre-Games Avoiders* – tourists who avoid the city/region in the pre-Games period as they perceive that there will be a lot of construction and renovation work taking place that may affect their tourism experience.

- *Post-Games Avoiders* – this group are those who would have planned to visit the city/region, but have been put off by the images and coverage of the city/region in the media during and in the run up to the Games period.

- *Time-Switchers* – these tourists would have visited the city/region in the pre- or post-Games period, but changed their plans to take their tourism trip at the time of the Games.

- *Avoiders: (a) Cancellers* – those who have cancelled a trip to the city/region due to its status as an Olympic host.

Figure 3.2 and the above descriptors begin to illustrate the broader impact of the Olympic Games on tourism. Of the above nine categories, Changers, Pre-/Post-Games Switchers, Time-Switchers, and Cancellers have already been discussed and the nature of their tourism impact on the host city/region has already been identified. The remaining five categories, however, each have a further additional tourism impact on the host city/region in the pre- and/or post-Games periods. The Pre-/Post-Games Sports Tourists have been discussed in detail in Chapters 1 and 2 and come to the city/region specifically to take part in Olympic-related activities in the pre- and post-Games periods, and obviously have a positive tourism impact. Pre-/Post-Games General Tourists, whilst not sports tourists, have been motivated to visit the city/region as a result of images and perceptions of the city/region that have been generated as a result of Olympic-related activities, and have a positive tourist impact for the city/region. The Pre-/Post-Games Casuals group, as discussed in relation to the Games period, would have been in the city/region regardless of the Games, and may be drawn into Olympic-related activities. However, as Olympic-related activities in the post-Games period, and to a lesser extent in the pre-Games period, are not as high profile as during the Games, this group may not necessarily engage in such activities. Consequently, this group are 'potential' Olympic tourists. If they do take part in Olympic-related activities, it is likely that spending will not be higher than that which they would have otherwise spent on other tourism activities. As such, Pre-/Post-Games Casuals are likely (although not certain) to have a neutral impact on tourism in the city/region.

The Pre-Games Avoiders group have either pre-established perceptions, or have gained the perceptions through media coverage, that the city/region will be 'under construction' and experiencing disruption in the pre-Games period, and as such avoid visiting the city/region in the run up to the Games. As this group would have otherwise have visited the city/region, they can be defined as Olympic tourists because the Games have motivated them to change their tourism behaviour. This group has a negative tourism impact for the city/region. The Post-Games Avoiders group are the opposite of the Pre-/Post-Games General Tourists in that the media coverage of the Olympic Games has

Table 3.2
The impacts and nature of further event-affected people in the pre-/post-Games period

	Tourism Impact?	Olympic Tourists?
Pre-/Post-Games Sports Tourists	Positive	Yes
Pre-/Post-Games General Tourists	Positive	Yes
Pre-/Post-Games Casuals	Most likely neutral	Potentially
Pre-Games Avoiders	Negative	Yes, but negatively motivated
Post-Games Avoiders	Negative	Yes, but negatively motivated

put them off visiting the city/region. As such, this group, like the Pre-Games Avoiders, can be classified as Olympic tourists with a negative tourism impact on the city/region. The impacts and nature of these additional categories of event-affected people in the pre-/post Games periods are summarized in Table 3.2.

As in the Games period, the two groups of negatively motivated Olympic tourists (Pre-Games Avoiders and Post-Games Avoiders) are of interest to this analysis only insofar as the Olympic Games affects their decision to not travel to the Olympic host city/region. Once this decision has been made, their tourist behaviour is irrelevant to a consideration of Olympic tourism. Consequently, this leaves three groups of tourists travelling to the host city/region who will be actually or potentially taking part in, or being motivated by, Olympic-related activities. The most straightforward of these categories is Pre-/Post-Games Sports Tourists. For this group, the range of Olympic-related tourism is much wider than that undertaken during the Games which, not surprisingly, is dominated by Sports Events tourism. The Olympic tourism activities of Pre-/Post-Games Sports Tourists may include any of the five sports-related Olympic tourism products described in Chapter 1, namely: Sports Training, Sports Events, Sports Participation Tourism, Luxury Sports Tourism or Tourism with Sports Content (see Chapter 1 for examples of these). In the case of the Tourism with Sports Content product, participation in Olympic tourism activities will not be spontaneous, but will have been a part of trip decision making and/or planning, thus making the Olympic tourism element an important, although not necessarily the primary, purpose of the trip.

As the earlier discussions note, Pre-/Post-Games General Tourists are taking part in tourism behaviour that has been 'motivated or generated' by Olympic-related activities. Their tourism trip has been generated by positive images and perceptions of the host city/region gained through direct or mediated engagement with Olympic-related activities. The trip may have been generated by media coverage, or through perceptions of the city/region gained during a previous Olympic-related visit. While the purpose and motivation of their trip is clearly not Olympic-related, once in the city/region they may engage in some Olympic-related tourism activities. Consequently, as well as taking part in generic tourism generated by Olympic-related activities, they may also take part in Tourism with Sports Content. Therefore, in addition to being 'actual' tourists generated by Olympic-related activities, this group may also 'potentially' fall into the Tourism with Sports Content form of Olympic-related sports tourism described in Chapter 1.

Pre-/Post-Games Casuals are, like the previous category, general tourists. However, their trip has not been motivated or generated by Olympic-related activities, and as such they are 'potential' rather than 'actual' Olympic tourists. If they do become Olympic-tourists, they will also fall into the Tourism with Sports Content category as the prime purpose of their trip is general rather than Olympic-related tourism.

Clearly, of these three categories, only the Pre-/Post-Games Sports Tourists may have the Primary Sports Tourist profile discussed in Chapter 2, whilst some of this category may be Associated Experience Sports Tourists and in some cases Tourists interested in Sport. Pre-/Post-Games General Tourists and Pre-/Post-Games Casuals, if indeed they become sports tourists at all, will have a Tourists interested in Sport profile, with any Olympic-related sports tourism being a spontaneous rather than a planned participation decision.

Pre-/Post-Games Sports Tourists, as noted above, may be consuming any of the sports-related Olympic tourism products, and as such both their activities and motivations will be widely varied, from a visit to see an event at an Olympic site on a trip with other prime purposes, to an Olympic athlete taking part in a training or preparation camp (see discussions under Sports-related Olympic tourist profiles in Chapter 2). As such, Pre-/Post-Games Sports Tourists may fall at any place on the Sports Tourism Participation Model, with a range of combinations of participation levels and levels of importance attached to such participation. It is perhaps worth noting, however, in drawing to a close the discussions of tourism movements in the pre- and post-Games periods, that the number of sports-related Olympic tourists demonstrating an Associated Experience profile is likely to be lower in the pre- and post-Games periods than during the Games themselves. This is because the status and prestige motivations of conspicuous consumption and place-collecting are not as well provided for by visiting an Olympic site in the pre-/post-period as by 'being there' during the Games. Consequently, while undoubtedly still existing, the Associated Experience sports tourist profile is less prevalent in the periods before and after the Games.

A broader consideration of travel flows generated by Olympic-related activities

The above discussions of event-affected people represent a 'micro' analysis of Olympic tourism. However, it is useful to now broaden this discussion further to a consideration of travel flows between cities, regions and countries that might be generated by the Olympic Games. Of course, these broader flows will both be affected by and have an effect on the 'micro' behaviours described above, and as such there is a recursive relationship between them. The discussion of travel flows that follows utilizes the concept of travel propensity and Leiper's (1979) model of the tourism system.

Whilst there are a wide-range of individual motivations to travel, travel propensity is a macro concept relating to the propensity of a population to travel (Boniface and Cooper, 2001:13). Travel propensity is usually understood to refer to national populations, but the concept can be applied to any population that exhibits similar characteristics, or that is subject to similar influences. Consequently, a local area's travel propensity might be examined, or the travel propensity of particular subcultures or groups considered.

Travel propensity is a function of contextual, personal, and supply factors (Boniface and Cooper, 2001:14). Contextual influences relate to levels of economic development and affluence, population characteristics and, political and/or power relations. More personal influences are related to variations in lifestyle, life-cycle, and personality. Finally, supply factors relate to the availability and perceived availability of tourism opportunities and include such influences as technology, price, frequency, and speed of transport, as well as the characteristics of accommodation, facilities and travel organizers.

The travel propensity of a particular population will clearly have an effect on the tourism flows between the regions in which such populations live. As such, travel propensity, and the factors which influence it, are a key consideration in the model of the tourism system (adapted from Leiper, 1979) which illustrates the 'flow' of tourists between regions (see Figure 3.3).

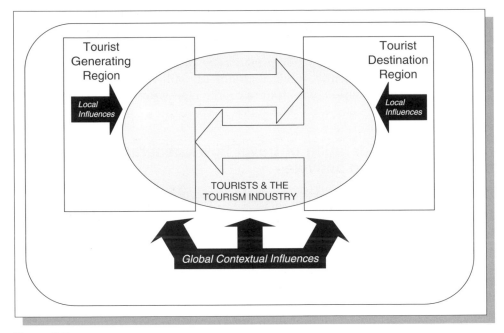

Figure 3.3
The tourism system.
Source: Weed, 2005c – adapted from Leiper, 1979.

The model of the tourism system shown in Figure 3.3 illustrates not only the 'flows' of tourists between regions, but also the factors that influence such flows. The travel propensity of the tourist generating region is influenced by local contextual and personal factors, by contextual, personal and supply factors local to the tourist destination region, and by global contextual influences. Such global influences also play a part in shaping local influences in both the tourist generating and destination regions. The tourism flows that are a result of these influences are a form of macro spatial interaction between regions (Boniface and Cooper, 2001:5). Such flows are highly complex and, as the model outlined here has begun to indicate, are influenced by a wide variety of interrelated variables.

In an analysis of the impact of Olympic-related activities on the model of the tourism system, the host city/region will be both a tourist destination region (for those travelling to the city/region for Olympic-related activities) and a tourist generating region (for those leaving the city to escape Olympic-related activities). Obviously, some of the major influencers on Olympic-related travel flows are contextual, personal and supply factors in the host city/region. However, clearly the global nature of the Olympic Games means that broader global contextual influences will both impact on travel flows and on Olympic-related local contextual, personal, and supply factors.

The global environment and global contextual influences

Much has been written about globalization processes in recent years (Houlihan, 2003; Maguire, 1999), focussing on the growing international interconnectedness of societies, economies and cultures, alongside considerations of the extent to which a dominant global culture is emerging. The Olympic Games is an oft-cited example in relation to globalization processes, and the Olympic Rings are undoubtedly the most recognizable not-for-profit 'brand' in the world. Research conducted by the International Olympic Committee in eleven countries around the world found the attributes to be most important and most associated with the Olympics were: friendship, multiculturalism, globality, participation, and fair competition (IOC, 2004). The Olympics is a global brand and attributes associated with that brand influence and reinforce its global nature. Of course, a central factor in the global character of the Olympic Games is the high-profile worldwide media attention it receives. Such media attention, like Olympic tourism, is not confined to the period of the Games themselves, but spread across a lengthy pre- and post-Games period. From the decision to bid for the Olympic Games until the Games become a fading memory, host cities/regions can expect around 10–12 years of international media coverage. While some of this media coverage will inevitably be negative (e.g., corruption allegations, inability to deliver facilities), it still develops a global awareness of host cities and regions over a long time period.

In addition to coverage of host cities/regions, the Olympic brand more generally enjoys constant global media exposure, with the focus often being on attributes such as fairness, multiculturalism, and friendship noted above. The existence of this generally positive perception of the Olympic Games is certainly a key global contextual influence on travel flows to Olympic host cities/regions.

There are, of course, a range of non-Olympic geo-political global influences that affect travel flows. The ongoing conflict of the Cold War affected travel flows to the Olympic Games in Moscow in 1980, not only due to the US led boycott, but due to the negative perceptions that many potential Western travellers had of these former Communist bloc countries in general, and of the USSR in particular. The Beijing Games in 2008 may have to overcome some trepidation from potential Olympic tourists from the West as many tourists have a general fear of unfamiliar destinations (see Chapter 9). In addition, there may continue to be negative media coverage in relation to human rights issues that puts off such tourists and thus affects travel flows. For many countries in the West, the population's propensity to travel to a "culturally distant" (Hofstede, 2001) destination such as Beijing is likely to be much lower than that to more familiar and psychologically 'safe' destination such as Athens or Sydney. The process at work in this instance is a dominant set of perceptions, generated by a global media, that impacts upon local influences in tourist generating regions and negatively affects propensity to travel to the tourist destination region. Such processes highlight the clear connection between global contextual influences and local influences in the tourist destination and generating regions, to which the discussion now turns.

Olympic host cities/regions as tourist destination and generating regions

As destinations for Olympic tourism, Olympic host cities/regions are, as noted above, subject to global influences which affect travel flows. However, there are also a series of local influences in the destination region that will impact upon travel propensities in tourist generating regions and thus upon travel flows. The previous discussions noted that global perceptions of Olympic host countries can affect travel flows, and while this is partly generated by global media coverage, it is also a result of contextual and supply factors in the destination region. Perceptions of potential Olympic tourists to a host city/region are affected by contextual factors such as the nature of the local culture and, of course, a wide range of supply factors such as the nature of the tourism product on offer. In relation to Olympic tourism, the way in which a host city/region interprets and presents 'their' Olympics will be an interaction of local contextual and supply factors. This interaction will result in an Olympic tourism product that will then be interpreted in tourist generating regions, according to personal and supply factors in such regions relating to the nature of both the Olympics and the host city/region, and will consequently affect travel propensities. Of course, supply factors such as the nature of Olympic tourism products offered, and broader local contextual factors such as the way in which host cities/regions choose to present the Olympic Games, can largely be managed and controlled by host cities/regions, whereas global contextual influences cannot. As Chapter 4 will show, there are a range of 'leveraging' strategies that can be employed by host cities/regions to try to positively affect the travel propensities of potential tourism generating regions, both in the short and the long term. Of course, such strategies, as well as being aimed at positively influencing broader travel propensities, will also be targeted at the various types and categories of Olympic tourist discussed earlier in this chapter.

The analysis earlier in this chapter highlighted that the Olympic Games will also have a negative impact on tourism in the host city/region, thus generating travel flows out of the city/region, and consequently this analysis also must consider Olympic host cities/regions as tourist generating regions. As an Olympic-affected tourist generating region, host cities/regions are generating Olympic tourism that is negatively motivated by a desire to escape the Olympic Games. Consequently, the process is fairly simple. Among 'Olympic-averse' tourists, travel propensity is entirely derived from contextual, personal, and supply factors in the generating region with these factors, quite simply, being the hosting of the Olympic Games in the city/region. As a result the travel propensity among these groups is to leave the generating region rather than to visit a destination region. While this is clearly a negative impact for the host city/region, the fact that such travel propensities are affected largely by factors local to the host city/region means that strategies can be employed that attempt to lessen such propensities, and these are discussed in Chapter 4.

Olympic host countries as tourist destination regions

The discussions so far in this chapter have focussed on the immediate host city or region as the unit of analysis for Olympic tourism. However, as some of the discussions in Chapter 1 indicated, aspects of Olympic tourism may also need a broader consideration of the host country as a tourist destination region. In fact, some of the strategies for leveraging Olympic tourism that will be discussed in Chapter 4 will include those aimed as spreading Olympic tourism beyond the immediate host city or region to the host country as a whole. This may include the hosting of Olympic acclimatization training camps (sports Training tourism) or events (sports Event tourism) throughout the country in the years approaching the Games, or encouraging those visiting the host city/region for the Games to also explore other areas of the country as part of their stay. The key factors influencing the way in which host countries as well as host cities/regions are successful as tourist destination regions will be supply factors local to the destination region, and the way in which the Olympic destination can be presented as the country as a whole rather than just the host city/region.

Linking this analysis to the consideration of event-affected persons earlier in the chapter, it is possible that a consideration of the country rather than the city/region as the destination region may impact upon those Olympic tourists motivated to leave the host city/region while the Games is taking place. If the unit of analysis is seen as the host country, and these tourists can be persuaded to remain in the country, then travel flows on a national level will not be adversely affected. This highlights the *stratified geography* of tourism flows in which the level of analysis can change the effect of the flows. This means that a trip from the host city/region to a region elsewhere in the host country to escape the Games will be a negative flow for the host city/region, a positive flow for the other region, and a neutral flow for the country as a whole. An understanding of the stratified geography of Olympic tourism flows is essential for those responsible for leveraging and making policy for Olympic tourism, and is discussed in these respects in Chapters 4 and 5, as well as throughout Part 2 of the book.

Conclusion – the utility of the analysis

The discussions in this chapter have outlined in some detail the range of event-affected people both during the Olympic games and in the pre-/post-Games periods, as well as considering the broader issue of travel flows to and from Olympic host cities, regions and countries. The discussions were linked to the analyses of types of sports tourism that may be generated by Olympic-related activities from Chapter 1 and to the types of sports tourist that might be motivated by Olympic-related activities from Chapter 2. While these discussions may be interesting in and of themselves, their broader utility is in informing an understanding of the strategies that might be employed to 'leverage' Olympic tourism, maximizing the incoming flows and minimizing the outgoing flows from an Olympic host city, region, and country. As has been argued elsewhere, strategies aimed at providing for tourists and sports tourists need to be underpinned by a full and detailed knowledge of the behaviours of such tourists (Downward, 2005; Weed, 2005a), and this is no different in relation to Olympic tourism. While Chapters 1 and 2 utilized more generic perspectives from sports tourism to inform an understanding of Olympic tourism, this chapter has taken

Preuss' (2005) more specific analysis of major multi-sport events as its starting point. However, this micro-analysis has been integrated with the more generic sports tourism material, before being located within the macro framework provided by Leiper's (1979) model of the tourism system. The perspectives generated by these discussions are now used in Chapter 4 to inform the analysis of strategies aimed at providing for and 'leveraging' Olympic tourism.

Leveraging Olympic tourism

A recent special issue of *European Sport Management Quarterly* (Vol.5, No.3, 2005) focussed on 'Sports Tourism Theory and Method'. The issue addressed a broad range of concerns relating to the theoretically informed and methodologically robust study of sports tourism and included the paper by Holger Preuss (2005) which provides the basis for much of the discussion of the detail of Olympic tourism in Chapter 3. One of the key themes of the issue was the need for policy and strategy to be underpinned by a detailed knowledge of the motivations and behaviours of participants (Downward, 2005; Weed, 2005a). The first three chapters of this text have endeavoured to provide this detailed understanding of such motivations and behaviours, and it now falls to the remaining two chapters in the first part of the book to examine ways in which this knowledge might be applied to the development of strategy and policy in relation to Olympic tourism. Chapter 5 examines policy considerations for Olympic tourism, but the focus of this chapter is on the development of effective provision strategies and, in line with current research and practice in the field, this requires a consideration of the concept of leveraging.

Leveraging, quite simply, refers to the processes through which the benefits of a particular business opportunity or investment are maximized (Boulton et al., 2000; Slywotsky and Shapiro, 1993). In the recent literature on sports events, it has been proposed that decisions to host events should not be based simply on the potential projected impacts, but on the extent to which strategies can be developed to effectively leverage or maximize those impacts (Chalip, 2006). This is the result of an increasing recognition that the benefits of hosting sports events do not just materialize, they must be planned for and strategies must be employed to ensure they are realized. This is particularly true of the Olympic Games, and especially of the pre- and post-Games periods. As the discussions of the Sydney Games in Chapter 7 will show, the 2000 Olympics were the first in which clear strategies were developed to leverage the benefits of Olympic tourism, and the approaches employed have provided the model for more recent attempts at leveraging not just the Olympics, but sports events in general.

Chalip (2004) has developed a general model for sport event leveraging, and the discussions in this chapter are based on a model derived and developed from Chalip's (2004) work that has been specifically adapted to assess the leveraging strategies that need to be employed to fully capitalize on Olympic tourism opportunities. Chalip's (2004) general model for sport event leveraging includes a consideration of strategies to develop long-term business relationships and to retain expenditure locally through supply-chain management (Gibson et al., 2005). However, as the focus of this text is on Olympic tourism and the maximization of tourism benefits, these broader economic development goals for sports events are not discussed here (an excellent discussion of such economic development goals can be found in O'Brien, 2006).

The discussions in this chapter, in line with those in earlier chapters, extend Chalip's (2004) model both temporally and geographically. The temporal dimension is extended to incorporate an analysis of the leveraging opportunities in the pre- and post-Olympic Games period as well as during the Games themselves. The geographic dimension is extended to a consideration of the host country and regions within that country, as well as the immediate host city/region. Consequently, the stratified geography of the Olympic 'destination' is considered on a local, regional and national scale. The model for Olympic tourism leveraging is shown in Figure 4.1.

The model identifies the Olympic Games as a leveragable resource. However, as earlier chapters have noted, the potential impacts of the Olympic Games do not just occur during the Games period, but for several years before and after. As such, the Olympic Games as a leveragable resource includes all the

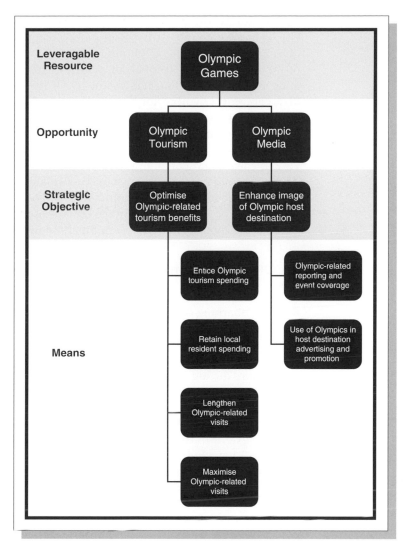

Figure 4.1
Model for Olympic tourism leveraging.
Source: adapted from Chalip, 2004.

potential opportunities to develop the range of Olympic tourism products that were identified in Chapter 1 and which fall under the broad definition of Olympic tourism as 'tourism behaviour motivated or generated by Olympic-related activities'.

Olympic tourism, however, is one of two 'opportunities' identified in the model for leveraging the Olympic Games. The other is Olympic media, by which is meant, first, Olympic-related media coverage of the host city, region or country and, second, opportunities to incorporate Olympic-related material into host city, region or country advertising and promotion. The strategic objective in leveraging Olympic Media is to enhance the image of the Olympic host destination, which in turn will help to generate further future tourism business. As the strategic objective of leveraging Olympic tourism is to optimize Olympic-related tourism benefits, the opportunities to leverage Olympic tourism and Olympic media have very similar long term goals. Perhaps a crude way of looking at the two leveraging opportunities is to view the leveraging of Olympic tourism as referring to immediate strategies to generate tourism business related to the Olympics, wheras the leveraging of Olympic Media is part of a longer term strategy for host destination image enhancement that is aimed at stimulating more generic tourism business in the future.

The role of the Olympics in trip decision, planning, and behaviour

Before embarking on a detailed examination of the ways in which the Olympic Games might be leveraged for tourism benefit, it is useful to consider the role of the Olympics in tourists' decisions to take a trip, in their planning for a trip, and in their behaviours during a trip. This is because a knowledge of the way the Olympics affects tourists' decisions, planning and behaviours is important in developing a range of appropriate leveraging strategies. For most Olympic tourism, the Olympics will feature to some extent in the trip decision making process. However, as Chapter 3 has shown this may either be in a positive way (i.e., a decision to visit an Olympic host destination) or in a negative way (i.e., a decision not to visit, or to get away from, an Olympic host destination).

Taking, first, those tourists for whom the Olympics has a positive influence on the trip decision. This group may be further sub-divided into those for whom the Olympics is the reason for the trip, and those for whom the Olympics has influenced the trip destination or timing. For example, in the consideration of Olympic tourism flows in Chapter 3, many Games Visitors will be making a specific trip to visit the Olympic Games. For such tourists, the Olympics provide the main reason for their trip. Conversely, the Olympics may not be the main trip purpose for some other tourists falling within the Games Visitors category, the main purpose may be a family holiday. However, the hosting of the Olympics has meant that these tourists have decided to visit the host city/region for their holiday, rather than another destination. While visiting the Olympic Games is not the main reason for their trip, it has affected their trip decision making.

Similarly, Time-Switchers will have changed the timing of their trip to incorporate the Olympics, and as such the Olympics has influenced their trip decision, but has not provided the reason for their trip.

Whilst the positive influence of the Olympics for many tourists may occur at the trip decision making stage, it may also (as discussed below) occur at the trip planning or behaviour stage. However, the negative influence of the Olympic Games occurs almost exclusively at the trip decision making stage. This is because there is little that can be done at the post-decision trip planning stage, or at the post-arrival trip behaviour stage to avoid the Olympics if the decision has already been made to take a trip to an Olympic host city/region (although this may be less true of the pre- and post-Olympic Games periods). Therefore, for the categories of Olympic tourist identified in Chapter 3 as being negatively motivated such negative motivation manifests itself at the trip decision-making stage. For example, Cancelling Avoiders will decide not to take a trip they might otherwise have taken to an Olympic destination because the Olympic Games are being hosted there. Similarly, Runaways and Changers will decide to leave the Olympic host city/region during the Games period. Each of these tourist flows, which have been negatively motivated by the Olympics (i.e., by a desire to avoid the Olympics) originate from the trip decision-making stage.

Once tourists have made the decision to take a trip to a particular destination, there is often a certain amount of pre-trip planning that takes place. For those Olympic tourists for whom the Olympics is the prime-purpose (or a very significant part) of their trip, such planning will largely be about what events to visit and when to visit them. However, for those Olympic tourists who exhibit the Tourists interested in Sport profile discussed in Chapter 2, it is at the trip planning stage that the Olympics may have a more significant influence, particularly if the visit is in the pre- or post-Games period when there are likely to be many more visitors for whom the Olympics has not been part of their trip decision. For example, many Post-Games Sports Tourists as identified in Chapter 3 will exhibit the Tourists interested in Sport profile discussed in Chapter 2. Such tourists, whilst not having considered the Olympics in their trip decision, may, once they know they will be visiting a former Olympic host city/region, plan as a core part of their trip a visit to former Olympic facilities or to Olympic-related visitor attractions. Similarly, Pre-Games Sports Tourists may plan a visit to a pre-Olympic Games warm-up event. In each case, the Olympics has not influenced the trip decision-making process, but it has influenced the pre-trip planning process.

The final stage at which the Olympics might influence tourists is at the post-arrival trip behaviour stage. Of course, many trip behaviours are the result of the original trip decision, or the post-decision trip planning stages. However, there are also some trip behaviours that are spontaneous, or that are decided upon after arriving at the destination. In the Games period this may take the form of tourists in the Casuals category identified in Chapter 3 deciding to get involved in Olympic related events or activities once they are at the destination, whilst in the pre- or post-Games period it may take the form of Tourists interested in Sport, taking spontaneous decisions to visit Olympic warm-up events, sites or visitor attractions. The key here is that such behaviours were not a result of the trip decision-making process, nor were they planned for pre-trip, but they took place as a result of spontaneous decisions made after arrival at the destination.

The discussions above have incorporated a temporal dimension, in that they have considered the role of the Olympics in the trip decision, in trip planning and in trip behaviours in the pre- and post-Games periods as well as during the Games themselves. However, as with other aspects of this analysis, the geographic dimension is also important. As such, trips outside of the immediate Olympic host city/region may also be a part of trip decision-making, of trip planning and/or of trip behaviours related to the Olympic Games, and must also be considered in the development of appropriate leveraging strategies. Each of these dimensions are considered in the remainder of this chapter, first in relation to leveraging Olympic tourism and, secondly, in relation to leveraging Olympic media.

Leveraging opportunities for Olympic tourism

The strategic objective for leveraging Olympic tourism opportunities is, simply, to optimize Olympic-related tourism benefits. While this obviously includes strategies to maximize the numbers, lengths of stays and spending of Olympic-related visitors, it also comprises strategies to minimize the potential negative impacts of those wishing to 'escape' Olympic-related activities. This is reflected in the 'means' for leveraging Olympic tourism shown in Figure 4.1.

Leveraging strategies may be macro strategies employed by destination wide agencies, such as marketing consortia, tourist boards or the public sector or, indeed, partnerships of such agencies. However, at the micro level, individual businesses or small groups of businesses can consider leveraging strategies that might maximize the benefits of the Olympics for such businesses. An example of the former might be a decision to host an Olympic festival of arts and entertainment in the pre-Games period, wheras an example of the latter might be a decision made by an individual restaurant to have an 'Olympic Menu' or by a group of businesses in the same street to get together to develop a coherent Olympic-related theme for their business precinct (cf. Chalip and Leyns, 2002).

Strategies for leveraging Olympic tourism in the pre-games period

In the pre-Games period, leveraging efforts will focus on four of the categories of Olympic tourist identified in Chapter 3: Pre-Games Avoiders, Pre-Games General Tourists, Pre-Games Casuals, and Pre-Games Sports Tourists. However, as Pre-Games General Tourists represent a category whose presence will be the result of a trip decision influenced by Olympic media, this category will be discussed later in the chapter when the leveraging of Olympic media is addressed. Any strategies aimed at leveraging the spending of this group post-arrival will be the same as those aimed at Pre-Games Casuals because once they have arrived at the destination their behaviours and interests are very similar.

Of the four means of leveraging Olympic tourism identified in Figure 4.1, the most significant in the pre-Games period will be strategies aimed at enticing Olympic tourism spending and those aimed at maximizing Olympic-related visits. Strategies aimed at the former are targeted at influencing pre-trip planning and post-arrival behaviours, whilst those aimed at the former arc targeted at influencing the trip decision-making process. Generally, strategies aimed at maximizing Olympic-related visits will focus on potential Pre-Games Sports Tourists, while strategies aimed at enticing Olympic tourism spending will focus on both Pre-Games Sports Tourists and Pre-Games Casuals.

In the Olympic host city/region, strategies for maximizing Olympic-related visits in the pre-Games period should focus on sports tourism activities related to the Olympic Games. This requires a consideration of the range of sports-related Olympic tourism products discussed in Chapter 1, namely: Sports Training, Sports Events, Luxury Sports Tourism, Sports Participation Tourism, and Tourism with Sports Content. Specifically, Olympic host cities/regions need to consider the types of provision they might make to attract Pre-Games Sports Tourists and what their particular target markets might be. Key products are likely to be Sports Events and Sports Participation Tourism, as well as a range of incidental Tourism with Sports Content products. While it might be expected that an important part of provision for an Olympic host city/region might be Sports Training tourism, previous experience has shown that Olympic-related training camps in the years running up to the Games are more likely to take place in regions adjacent to the host city/region than they are in the host city/region itself.

The key attractions of an Olympic host city/region in the pre-Games period are the places in which the Games themselves will take place. Such places may be potential sites for Sports Participation Tourism, as Pre-Games Sports Tourists may wish to take part in activities in future Olympic facilities. Here the importance of vicarious participation becomes important, as participants can make an imagined journey to the Games themselves and put themselves in the places of their favourite athletes competing in the Olympic arena. As such, it is not just the opportunity to use Olympic facilities that is important in making provision in this area, but the opportunity to see places that will become Olympic sites. As such, key parts of provision can be festivals of sport in and around the Olympic arenas, with opportunities to use those facilities that have been constructed, and opportunities to see the way that those facilities yet to be constructed will look. Easily accessible plans, and computer generated imagery of such facilities are an important part of this type of provision, as are such things as 'Countdown to the Games' boards and lists and sets of images of sports people who have visited the site. The status and prestige motivators discussed in Chapter 2 should not be overlooked in this respect, as those who have visited Games facilities and sites in the pre-Games period will enjoy telling their friends and associates as they watch the Games (either live at the events, or mediated back home) about the construction miracles that have taken place, or that 'I've been there!'.

Of course, there is considerable overlap, and a fuzzy boundary, in the pre-Games period, between Sports Participation Tourism and Sports Events. Many of the opportunities for pre-Games participation at Olympic sites and facilities may be through fairly low-level or informal events. However, other such pre-Games Sports Events may be more formal, with Pre-Games Sports Tourists wishing to run the Olympic marathon course, for example, and such behaviours are likely to be motivated by similar status and prestige factors as discussed above. At the more elite end of the spectrum, events at Olympic facilities in the years approaching an Olympic Games are likely to attract a significant number of very high level international athletes, who will want to be familiar with the Olympic facilities. A key factor for Olympic athletes is to feel 'at home' during an Olympic Games, and such a feeling is more likely to be engendered if they have competed at Olympic facilities before they compete in the Games themselves. In addition, the opportunity to spectate at what will essentially be

Olympic warm-up events in the few years before the Games will be a particularly attractive one for sports enthusiasts, especially as they will know that the competitors at such events will often include the top athletes in the world. As such, a key strategy in maximizing Olympic-related visits for the host city/region will be to consider what opportunities exist to host events. This is likely to include close partnerships between public sector bodies, commercial sector providers or facility managers, and national governing bodies of sport (see discussions in Chapter 5) to ensure that maximum benefit is achieved and that the full range of opportunities for event hosting are fully exploited.

Further opportunities to maximize Olympic-related visits in the pre-Games period relate to providing for Olympic-related Tourism with Sports Content, and thus in attracting Pre-Games Sports Tourists exhibiting the Tourists interested in Sport profile discussed in Chapter 2. A host city/region should ensure that there is an ongoing series of events and attractions that will appeal to the Tourist interested in Sport that might encourage them to take a break in the host city/region in the pre-Games period, rather than a tourist trip to another destination. As such, the forthcoming Olympics should be seen as an opportunity to add value to a host city/region's tourist offer. Therefore, along with the types of provision discussed above in relation to Sports Participation Tourism and Sports Events, efforts should also be made to ensure that the Olympic theme is carried into other aspects of the city/region's tourist product. Examples might include special exhibitions on Olympic history in the city/region's museums or displays of Olympic-related art in local galleries. Of course, such provision is only part of the leveraging process, leveraging Olympic media to fully market and promote Olympic tourism in the pre-Games period is a further key activity, and this is discussed later in the chapter.

In order to entice Olympic tourism spending, leveraging strategies should be aimed at affecting the pre-trip planning of Pre-Games Sports Tourists, and the post arrival behaviours of Pre-Games Casuals and Pre-Games Sports Tourists. The nature of provision in affecting pre-trip planning in this area will be much the same as discussed above for maximizing Olympic-related visits, whilst some more specific leveraging strategies can be employed in attempting to affect post-arrival behaviours.

Much of the leveraging effort aimed at affecting post-arrival behaviour will attempt to entice tourists to the region who have not considered the Olympics in their trip decision making or pre-trip planning, to spend additional money in the area by providing opportunities relating to the Olympic Games. Of course, such efforts also need to consider 'aversion' markets (such as those in the Pre-Games Avoiders category), and to ensure that pre-Games Olympic related themes and provision does not overwhelm aspects of the tourism product that has attracted those who are not interested in the Olympic Games. Chalip (2004) suggests a range of questions that should be considered in attempting to entice visitor spending, with those that are relevant to the pre-Games period of Olympic tourism leveraging being:

- Who should co-ordinate leveraging efforts?

- What promotions will appeal to pre-Games visitors?

- Which areas would benefit from Olympic theming?

- How should Olympic theming be designed?

- How can accompanying and aversion markets be catered for?

The key aim of leveraging Olympic tourism spending by affecting post-arrival behaviour in the pre-Games period is to encourage visitors to spend money they would not have otherwise spent by visiting attractions or areas they would not have otherwise visited. This can be somewhat difficult, as much Olympic-related spending among Pre-Games Casuals is likely to be replacement spending. This means that in taking part in Olympic-related activities, such tourists are simply replacing non-Olympic-related tourist behaviour, in which they would also have spent money. Consequently, such leveraging strategies need to focus largely on creating an Olympic 'buzz' or feel in the host city/region that makes it feel like an exciting place to be. However, such a 'buzz' needs to be carefully managed, as it could potentially have a negative effect on tourism if positively motivated Olympic tourists spend only on replacement activities, and aversion markets (for example, Pre-Games Avoiders) spend less or take their money out of the host city/region.

Of course, an Olympic 'buzz' is something that a country containing a future Olympic host city/region can expect to experience in the years following the decision to award the Games, and this will have an effect on the country's broader tourism product, with Olympic theming being a key part of national tourism strategy in the years before and after an Olympic Games. However, there are specific opportunities for regions outside of the host city/region in the years before the Games and these are largely presented by Pre-Games Sports Tourists, Pre-Games Casuals and, to a certain extent, Pre-Games Avoiders. For Pre-Games Sports Tourists and Pre-Games Avoiders, strategies will largely be related to maximizing Olympic-related visits, whilst strategies targeting Pre-Games Casuals will tend to focus on enticing Olympic tourism spending.

While opportunities related to Pre-Games Sports Tourists relate to the sports-related Olympic tourism products outlined and discussed in Chapter 1, in the country outside the Olympic host city/region, it is likely to be Sports Training and Sports Event tourism that provide the greatest opportunity to maximize Olympic related visits in the pre-Games period. While these product types will attract Primary Sports Tourists in terms of people who have specifically travelled to train, compete or spectate, Sports Events also allow for Tourism with Sports Content and as such may provide a trip activity for Tourists interested in Sport. In each of these cases, as the aim is to maximize Olympic-related visits, leveraging strategies are targeted at the trip decision stage.

As noted above, previous experience indicates that Sports Training tourism in the form of Olympic-related training camps in the years running up to the Games are more likely to take place outside the host city/region than within it. Such training camps, therefore, present a real but limited opportunity for regions outside the host city/region. There is often a misconception that Olympic-related training camps are only likely to take place in the year or so before the Games; however, opportunities to host such camps exist in the four years preceding a Games as once the previous Olympic Games has finished, athletes and national sports organizations are starting to prepare for the next Games, even though it may be four years away. This preparation includes physical acclimatization to climate and conditions, but also cultural acclimatization to local customs, language, and social infrastructure. As such, places seeking to host such Olympic-related training camps need to ensure not only that top class sports facilities and support are provided, but also that opportunities for cultural acclimatization are provided in an atmosphere that is relaxing and away from the glare of the Olympic media. It may often be these latter opportunities, as much as the availability of sports facilities, that means that Olympic-related Sports Training touris takes place away from the host city/region.

Sports events outside the host city region in the pre-Games period can also provide many of the physical and cultural acclimatization opportunities for elite athletes that training camps provide. However, they add the further dimension of competition in conditions likely to be very similar to those of the forthcoming Games. The need to compete in local conditions akin to those expected in the Games themselves is likely to mean that existing small and minor sports events around the host country will become much more significant in the four years preceding the Games and present opportunities for regions around the host country to leverage Olympic-related sports tourism. Such events will attract a much more high profile line-up which, in turn, will attract more spectators, either those travelling specifically for the event (Primary Sports Tourists), or those taking in the event as part of a wider trip (Tourists interested in Sport). While a forthcoming Olympics may mean that a country may stage more than its usual share of World and European championships or events, it is likely that few additional events will need to be hosted, rather the strategy should be to expand current events in the years before the Games. This is a more sustainable long-term strategy for Sports Event tourism after the Olympic Games have come and gone.

A strategy of capitalizing and building upon existing events is something that should also be part of provision of the Cultural Olympiad, which commences four years before the start of the Games, as soon as the preceding Games has ended. Such Olympic-related cultural events are likely to entice Olympic tourism spending among Pre-Games Casuals who are in the area in any case, but who may wish to attend such Olympic-related events and festivals. However, the provision of festivals and other events in the Cultural Olympiad should both capitalize on current cultural provision, and carry a flavour of local interpretation of Olympic-related ideas. In this way, the work put into developing such festivals is likely to result in a continuing event after the Olympic spotlight has turned elsewhere.

A final issue for regions outside of the host city/region to consider is the potential tourist trade they may be able to attract among those people who are put-off visiting the host city/region because they feel it will be 'a building site' in the pre-Games period (Pre-Games Avoiders). While the potential to attract avoiders may be greater during the Games period itself, there are still opportunities to market other areas of the country to ensure that potential inbound tourists still visit, albeit a different part of the country. Such opportunities, of course, will depend on the motivations of such Pre-Games Avoiders, and the extent to which the host city/region has a unique product that is differentiated from that of the rest of the country.

Strategies for leveraging Olympic tourism during the period of the games

As Chapter 3 showed, the Games period is when Olympic tourism flows are most complex, with inward, outward, and temporal (i.e., trips for which the timing has changed) tourism flows taking place. Equally, each of the four means of leveraging the

strategic objective of optimizing Olympic-related tourism benefits shown in Figure 4.1 are relevant during the Games period.

The most obvious category of Olympic tourist during the
Games period is Games Visitors, those tourists who are visiting the host city/region because of the Olympic Games, and
would not have made the trip if the Games were not taking place
there. It would be expected that the attraction of these tourists
would derive from strategies aimed at maximizing Olympic-
related visits. However, many of these tourists will travel regardless of leveraging strategies and they will often exhibit the 'sports
junkie' profile described by Gibson (1998). The general media
coverage of the Games will often be enough to attract such visitors and, as such, further leveraging strategies aimed at maximizing Olympic-related visits have less potential to 'add-value' to
tourism benefits than efforts in other areas. Consequently, while
this means of leveraging is relevant, during the Games period it
is less so than the other three leveraging means highlighted in
Figure 4.1.

Of course, while Games Visitors is the only category of
Olympic tourist to have made a specific trip to see the Games,
other categories (Extensioners, Time-Switchers, and Home-
Stayers) have each considered the Games at the trip decision-
making stage. Consequently, for Games Visitors, Extensioners,
and Time-Switchers leveraging strategies aimed at lengthening
Olympic-related visits are important (Home-Stayers, of course,
cannot have their visit lengthened). Chalip (2004:235) highlights
four questions that should be considered in lengthening visitor
stays, each of which may be relevant to Olympic tourism:

- What new event components can we add to increase the number of days over which the event takes place? How will the
  market respond to these components?

- What entertainments might be added in the lead up to the
  event to create a lengthened festival atmosphere around the
  event? How will the market respond to those entertainments?

- What post-event social spaces and activities can we create
  through which event visitors can revel in their shared subcul-
  tural identities? What is required to make those spaces and
  activities particularly appealing to event visitors?

- What activities or tours can we offer as part of event package bundles? Which activities and tours will be particularly
  attractive to the event's market segments?

Of course, some of these questions have very different implications for Olympic tourism than for a general consideration of

Sports Event tourism. For example, the second question relating to how a lengthened festival atmosphere can be created may seem a little superfluous, on a macro-level at least, because, as noted earlier, the Olympic 'festival' can last for years rather than just the period of the event itself. However, on a micro-level of extending trip visits, the question remains relevant as a festival atmosphere around the event itself may contribute to the decision to take an extended visit.

As strategies aimed at lengthening visits are targeting the trip decision making stage, it will be the perception that there will be an ongoing festival around the event that will cause tourists to plan a lengthened stay. In this respect, tangible markers of a lengthened event need to be promoted. As Chalip (2004) notes, this may be pre-event parties or post-event festivals. In respect of the Olympics, a multi-sport event that lasts 16 days, the challenge of lengthening stays may be related to enticing visitors to stay longer than the period for which they have specific event tickets, rather than the 16-day period of the entire event. As such, the provision of big screens in public places, showing the action and continuing the party may be a way in which stays may be lengthened.

The provision of big screens may be a consideration for regions outside of the host city/region, and may link the second and fourth of Chalip's (2004) questions in an Olympic context. Chalip asks what activities or tours might be offered or bundled with the event. It may be that Olympic tourists who have seen the specific events for which they have tickets may wish to both continue the party, but also spread their wings and visit other parts of the host country. As such big screen festival areas, akin to the Fan Fests that were so popular in Germany during the 2006 World Cup, in locations and regions around the country can allow tourists to both visit a broader range of areas and continue to feel part of the Olympic party. A further consideration for regions outside of the host city/region is the extent to which Olympic tourists can be encouraged to take non-Olympic-related trips around the rest of the country after the Games have finished. Chalip's consideration of post-event tours largely relates to the host city/region. However, with an event as large as the Olympic Games there may be an anti-climatic element of 'post-event hangover' in the host city/region itself. As such, there may be opportunities for other regions to offer explicitly non-Olympic activities to extend Olympic tourists' stays.

In addition to lengthening visitor stays, leveraging strategies for all categories of Olympic tourists producing positive flows in relation to enticing Olympic tourism spending are very similar to those in the pre-Games period. As such, the questions posed earlier in the chapter in relation to the co-ordination of Olympic promotions and themes remain relevant in the Games period. Such questions are posed to affect post-arrival behaviour in encouraging visitors to engage with tourist activities that are related but peripheral to the Games themselves. Many of these strategies revolve around the creation of a festival atmosphere in which tourists feel they are enjoying a unique, once-in-a-lifetime experience on which it is worth spending money.

While the above strategies may be useful in respect of 'positive flow' Olympic tourists, chapter three also highlighted a number of tourism flows out of the host city/region, or aversion markets, during the period of the Games. Of these markets, some are temporal flows (i.e., the timing of the trip is changed rather than the trip itself) which have a neutral tourism impact (Changers and Pre- and Post-Games Switchers). However, others (Runaways and Cancellers) are negative flows for which strategies should be considered to minimize impacts. Such negative flows may, in fact, be exacerbated by strategies to maximize or lengthen visits, and this should be borne in mind when developing such strategies.

Strategies to minimize the effect of negative Olympic tourism flows during the Games need to be considered within the 'stratified geography' of such flows noted at the end of Chapter 3. If an Olympic host city/region is considered within the context of a host country, three geographical levels may be identified: the host city/region, the rest of the country, and the country as a whole. This stratified geography results in a different impact of tourism flows at different geographical levels. For example, if there is a flow of residents out of the host city/region during the Games period, then that is a negative flow for the host city/region, but if this flow is to another region in the country, then that is a positive flow for that region. However, the net flow for the country as a whole is neutral. Consequently, the Runaway category represents a negative effect for the host city/region, a potential opportunity for other regions throughout the country, and a challenge to ensure that the effect is neutral for the country as a whole. This, of course, implies that there may need to be very different Olympic tourism strategies at national level, at non-host regional level and in the host city/region (see discussions of the planning for the London 2012 Games in Chapter 10). In this respect, the host city/region will need to examine strategies to persuade Runaways to stay, which may mean toning down some of the other suggested leveraging strategies. Other regions might wish to consider opportunities that the Runaway aversion markets provide. Chalip (2004:231), for example, notes that during the Olympic Games in 2000 some rural regions outside the host city of Sydney enjoyed a booming tourist business by promoting themselves as Olympics-free zones. It falls, of course, to national tourism organizations to examine the best way to ensure that the national impact of aversion markets is as close to neutral as possible. This may involve persuading the host city/region to advertise other regions in the country that provide an escape from the Games, otherwise Runaway flows may go out of the country.

A similar set of considerations applies to potential Cancellers, a sub-set of the Avoiders category. One strategy is to attempt to change these negative flows to temporal (and therefore neutral) flows by persuading Cancellers to switch their trip to the pre- or post-Games period. Other strategies would be to persuade Cancellers to make the trip, or to travel to another region in the country. In considering the Cancellers sub-category it is useful to extend the analysis of the 'Games period' to the months around the Games, and to illustrate this with a particular example, that of the conference/exhibition sector of business tourism. Experiences from previous Games indicate that there is often a feeling that Olympic host cities/regions are 'closed for business' during Olympic year, and consequently much conference/exhibition business may go elsewhere. The challenge here for host cities/regions is to persuade such potential Cancellers that they can still be accommodated within the city in the months around the Games, while the opportunity for other regions is to suggest that such conferences/exhibitions would be better served by taking their business to other areas of the country because the host city will be too busy and too focussed on the forthcoming Games. Again, the role of national tourism organizations is to ensure that the country as a whole retains the business by attempting to strike a balance between these two strategies.

Strategies for leveraging Olympic tourism in the post-games period

As Figure 3.1 in chapter three shows, Olympic tourism flows in the post-Games period comprise inward positive flows of Post-Games Sports Tourists, Post-Games General Tourists, and Post-Games Casuals, inward temporal (neutral) flows of Post-Games Switchers (Avoiders) and Changers, outward temporal (neutral) flows of Time-Switchers and outward negative flows of Post-Games Avoiders. As with the pre-Games period, Post-Games General Tourists represent a category whose presence will be the result of a trip decision influenced by Olympic media. Similarly, the decision of Post-Games Avoiders not to travel are also influenced by Olympic media. As such, these categories will be discussed later in the chapter when the leveraging of

Olympic media is addressed. Of the temporal flows, Changers (who changed their holiday away from the host city/region from a post-Games period to the time of the Games) and Time-Switchers (who changed their trip to the host city/region to coincide with the Games) will have already made their trip decisions and taken their Olympic-related tourism trips, and as such need not be considered in this section.

Consequently, the relevant Olympic tourist categories to be considered in leveraging post-Games tourism are the positive flows of Post-Games Sports Tourists and Post-Games Casuals, and the neutral temporal flows of Post-Games Switchers (Avoiders). As in the pre-Games period, the most significant means of leveraging Olympic tourism (see Figure 4.1) are those aimed at enticing Olympic tourism spending and at maximizing Olympic tourism visits, with the former aiming to influence pre-trip planning and post-arrival behaviour and the latter aiming to influence the trip decision. Generally strategies will focus on maximizing visits among Post-Games Sports Tourists, and on enticing the spending of both Post-Games Sports Tourists and Post-Games Casuals.

Both in the host city/region and in other regions around the country, strategies aimed at maximizing post-Games Olympic tourism (as opposed to generating tourism through Olympic media which is discussed later in the chapter) will largely revolve around sports tourism. Returning, again, to the range of potential sports-related Olympic tourism products discussed in Chapter 1 (Sports Training, Sports Events, Luxury Sports Tourism, Sports Participation Tourism, and Tourism with Sports Content), it is likely that key products in the host city/region will be Sports Events, Sports Participation Tourism and Tourism with Sports Content. As such, much provision is analogous to that for the pre-Games period discussed earlier in the chapter. Post-Games Sports Tourists will wish to take part in activities in venues that have hosted Olympic events, either as a core part of the trip (Sports Events or Sports Participation Tourism) or as a supplementary activity (Tourism with Sports Content). As in the pre-Games period, vicarious participation is important, as are status and prestige motivators relating to having visited or competed in Olympic venues or along Olympic courses.

Vicarious participation may also be important in developing visitor attractions relating to the Games. The exact nature of these may depend on the events that take place during the Games themselves, but 'iconic' performances or stories may play a central part in any such attractions. However, such attractions, particularly with the passage of time, are more likely to be part of the destination package (see later discussions relating to Olympic media) than to comprises the prime trip purpose, and should be planned with the purpose of attracting Tourists Interested in Sport, be they Post-Games Sports Tourists or Post-Games Casuals.

An obvious strategy, for both the host city/region and other regions throughout the country, is to build on both the Olympic Games themselves and the range of sports and Cultural Olympiad events that have been developed in the pre-Games period to develop a continuing portfolio of events. Such strategies will largely be dependent on having carefully constructed a sustainable planning approach to events in the pre-Games period. The rewards of such an approach should be a range of sports and cultural events in the host city/region that can continue to trade on the Olympic association. Furthermore, sports and cultural events that took place outside the host city/region in the pre-Games period will have had around a four year period to become established as significant events in their own right as a result of the pre-Games Olympic spotlight. If such events were organized well and ran smoothly in this pre-Games period, there is good reason to expect that they will be able to survive in their own right once Olympic attention has turned elsewhere.

While on the surface it would seem unlikely that there would be any Olympic-related opportunities in the Sports Training tourism area in the post-Games period, it may be that regions and facilities that hosted Olympic-related training camps for major teams or gold medal winning athletes can continue to benefit from this association. Ongoing provision for Sports Training might continue to be at the elite level, but provision may also be made for non-elite athletes and clubs to take part in more recreational Sports Training tourism, or for 'learn-to-play' courses to take place. The draw of a venue that has hosted gold medal winning individuals and teams will be significant for those sports tourists driven by status and prestige motivators. As such, former venues of Olympic-related training camps (and, indeed, regions in which such venues are situated) should ensure that the Olympic association is capitalized upon in any post-Games marketing (see Olympic media discussions later in the chapter).

Of course, in each of the cases described above, there is the potential for a more upmarket offer that would locate such sports-related Olympic tourism products as Luxury Sports Tourism. Hosts of sports such as sailing and tennis might consider how opportunities to take part in or watch sport at these Olympic venues might be packaged with top-class luxurious accommodation and services to attract the premium that many of those seeking Luxury Sports Tourism are prepared to spend. A further element of post-Games Olympic tourism, a significant proportion of which might be at the luxury level, is that of conference and exhibition tourism. The added value that former Olympic event or Olympic training venues can add to this market is significant.

A final note of caution for the host city/region must be sounded in relation to the Post-Games Switchers category. These tourists, which are a sub-category of Avoiders, have been negatively motivated by the Olympic Games to take their trip to the host city/region at a later date to avoid the Games. Host cities/regions must ensure that the core tourism product that existed prior to the Olympic Games is not displaced by efforts to attract Olympic tourists, otherwise Post-Games Switchers may change their plans and become the other Avoiders sub-category – Cancellers. Attention, therefore, must be paid by destination marketers and managers, to ensuring that Olympic tourism products are carefully integrated into the more longstanding tourism products that the host city/region offers.

Leveraging opportunities for Olympic media

The purpose in leveraging Olympic media is to identify means to maximize the positive effects that the Games can have on the image of the host city/region and country projected into both domestic and international markets. Brown et al. (2002) note that media leveraging strategies are derived from the association of the host city/region with the Games, and the meanings that are attached to that association. As such, strategies aimed at leveraging Olympic media focus on the trip decision stage (rather than the trip-planning or trip-behaviour stages) of the trip decision making process – i.e., such strategies seek to influence destination choice. Drawing on Leiper's (1979) model of the tourism system discussed in Chapter 3, the leveraging of Olympic media attempts to increase the propensity to travel to the Olympic host city/region and country (the tourist destination region) among populations in key tourist generating regions for Olympic tourism. In this respect, one of the goals in leveraging Olympic media is to increase the extent to which the Olympic host is thought of as a potential tourist destination region, and thus it is almost a pre-decision stage that is targeted. Furthermore, as strategies aimed at leveraging Olympic media focus on increasing general travel propensities, rather than promoting specific Olympic tourism products (as discussed in the previous part of this chapter), it tends to be tourists to the host city/region and country in the pre- and post-Games periods that are targeted, be they sports tourists or generic tourists. As such, the key Olympic tourism categories (discussed in Chapter 3) for strategies aimed at leveraging Olympic media are Pre- and Post-Games

General Tourists, Pre- and Post-Games Sports Tourists and Pre- and Post-Games Avoiders.

As Figure 4.1 shows, there are two clearly differentiated means by which Olympic media might be leveraged, namely: Olympic-related reporting and event coverage and the use of the Olympics in host destination advertising and promotion. The former is outside of the control of destination managers and marketeers and, as such, strategies aimed at leveraging reporting and event coverage are less straightforward than those that utilize the Olympics within destination marketing strategies. As these respective means of leveraging Olympic media are very different, the following discussion takes each of them in turn.

Strategies for leveraging Olympic-related reporting and event coverage

As has been noted in a number of previous places in this text, the spotlight of Olympic-related media coverage is turned onto an Olympic host as early as the bid period, before the Games have even been awarded. From this point onward the coverage intensifies through the pre-Games period and during the Games themselves. However, such coverage largely ceases with the closing ceremony as coverage then intensifies on the next host. As such, strategies aimed at leveraging Olympic-related reporting and event coverage are most important in the pre-Games period and during the Games. That is not to say that Olympic-related reporting and event coverage does not have an implication in the post-Games period. In fact, it is likely that the majority of trips generated by the leveraging of Olympic-related reporting and event coverage will take place in the post-Games period.

The goals of leveraging Olympic-related reporting and event coverage are to enhance images and perceptions of the Olympic host city/region and country through coverage provided by others. Chalip (2000) notes that this requires active media management strategies, and cites the Sydney Games as providing an example of how such strategies can have a significant impact on the way in which the image and perception of the host is portrayed in both domestic and international markets. Of course, as the discussions in Chapter 3 (and the discussions of Beijing in Chapter 9) have shown, it is possible for tourists to be put-off by Olympic-related coverage. Pre-Games Avoiders, for example, may have considered visiting an Olympic host city/region in the pre-Games period, but develop negative perceptions as a result of Olympic-related coverage, and decide not to visit, thus creating a negative flow as a result of Olympic media. The discussions on Beijing in Chapter 9 suggest that coverage of alleged human rights violations in China may have such an effect on potential Olympic tourism to Beijing.

There is a range of Olympic-related reporting and event-coverage that might be envisaged. In the pre-Games period there are likely to be general Olympic stories across a range of issues. These might range from negative stories about corruption (e.g., Salt Lake City, 2002) or escalating budgets (e.g., Athens, 2004; London, 2012) to more positive stories about the positive economic and social impacts of the Games or the completion of Games venues. Other stories might be those 'planted' by Games hosts. In early 2007, for example, the organizers of the London Olympic Games released a number of features to celebrate '2012 days until London 2012'. There is also the potential for coverage of Games-related events in the pre-Games period. This might include sports events that are seen as warm up events for the Games, visits for training camps of high-profile teams or athletes, and events taking place as part of the Cultural Olympiad. Linking pre-Games and Games coverage are likely to be stories relating to particular athletes and teams and their preparations and participation in the Games. Such coverage may overlap with coverage of pre-Games events and, obviously, with coverage of the Games themselves, but may also include a more long-term human interest coverage of the athletes 'road to the Games'. During the Games, there will obviously be coverage of the competitions (rowing, swimming, athletics, and so on) but, again, there are also likely to be background or human interest stories that may cover athletes, officials, volunteers, or spectators. All of these types of Olympic-related reporting and event coverage can be capitalized upon by leveraging strategies.

Chalip (2004:240), in discussing his general model of sport event leverage, suggests five sets of questions that should be considered in building strategies to showcase the host destination in event-related media, and these have been adapted here for the Olympic context:

- What aspects of the host city/region and country are likely to appeal to those interested in the Olympic Games and the Olympic movement? How can these be built into Olympic-related reporting and event coverage?

- How can journalists be assisted to locate and research background stories or anecdotes about the Olympic host city/region and country. What stories ad anecdotes are likely to be appealing? What supporting materials can be provided?

- How can Olympic-related events be constructed to showcase the destination? How should photographers and/or television cameras be placed to provide the most favourable destination backdrop shots of such events?

● What elements representing the host destination can be designed into various Olympic and event logos?

● How can sponsors be prompted and assisted to use host destination mentions and imagery in their advertising and promotions?

A number of authors have noted that there will be a link between an event and the city, region or country that hosts it. In particular, that the host's destination image will become linked with the image of the event (Chalip, 2004; Gwinner and Eaton, 1999; Simonin and Ruth, 1998). In the case of the Olympic Games the significance of this link is magnified considerably. Chapter 6 notes how the Swiss ski resort of St Moritz still benefits from the association with the Winter Olympic Games, even though it has been almost 60 years since the Games was last staged there. Furthermore, as an Olympic host has an association that spans a number of years before and after the main event, there is a macro link between the Olympics and the host, but also a number of micro-links between Olympic-related events and a number of cities and regions within the host country. So, the first question listed above will be of concern to host cities/regions, but also to other regions in host countries that may be hosting Olympic warm-up events, training camps and aspects of the Cultural Olympiad. Of course, the audience for much Olympic-related reporting will be those that are already interested in the Olympics. As such, it may be more likely that messages in such coverage will be targeted at Pre- and Post-Games Sports Tourists and may focus on promoting the sporting credentials of destinations. However, this may not always be the case. Aspects of the Cultural Olympiad and some more general Olympic stories may appeal to a wider audience and coverage of such events and issues may have a role to play in attracting Pre- and Post-Games General Tourists (particularly in attracting Post-Games General Tourists during the Games themselves when media coverage is all pervasive), or in putting-off Pre- and Post-Games Avoiders. These latter two categories are important to consider and should not be overlooked in media management strategies. In particular, while the first question in the list above highlights the importance of identifying which aspects of the host will appeal to potential Olympic tourists, it is also important to identify those stories that will not appeal, or even be disturbing, to potential visitors. Extreme examples of such stories may be those mentioned earlier relating to corruption and the Salt Lake City Winter Games of 2002 and the alleged human rights abuses in the preparations for Beijing 2008.

The second question listed can be important for both the host city/region and other regions in both the pre-Games and Games periods. Stories relating to visits for training camps for high profile teams and athletes can showcase destinations outside the host city/region in the pre-Games period, but can also provide a background story to the performances of individuals and teams during the Games themselves. If a particular region can establish a link with a successful team and/or athlete, this can provide useful avenues to promote the area, particularly if archive footage of the team's/athlete's visit to the area is made available. Chalip (2004:241) notes that the strategies related to this question are derived from standard public relations techniques and cites the Sydney example:

> In the years leading up to the Sydney Olympics, for example, the Australian Tourist Commission (ATC) ... worked with journalists by helping them to find stories about Australia, by facilitating familiarisation visits and by providing the necessary introductions to enable stories that showcased the country. During the Olympic Games, they provided press conferences to journalists to help them write interesting stories about Sydney and Australia. Before, during and after the Games, the ATC provided event broadcasters with video postcards (short visuals of Australian icons) that could be inserted into telecasts.

Following Sydney's lead, the Athens organizers developed 10 short films promoting Greece and the Olympic Games, covering a range of traditional cultural and historical subjects, from Greek music to classical Greece, to the treasures of Athens and the islands, which were distributed to broadcasters for use in their coverage.

Linked to the second question listed is the third relating to how Olympic-related events might be structured to showcase destinations. As above, such events may be the Games themselves or events in the pre-Games period. Perhaps the most well-known image of any Olympic Games in this respect is that from the diving competition at the Barcelona Games in 1992 (which features on the front cover of this book). Here the only feature in the forefront of the image to which the Barcelona cityscape provides the backdrop is a lone athlete taking off from the high-diving platform. Similarly, routes for the Torch Relay and the Marathon can be constructed to allow the best coverage of iconic place images.

Chalip (1990) notes that post-event evaluation showed that international audiences perceptions of Seoul and South Korea were enhanced as a result of the coverage of the Marathon at the 1988 Olympics, the route for which was designed to showcase the city, its parks and the Han River. Whilst these examples relate to the Games themselves, the same principle applies to pre-Games sports events, training camps, and the Cultural Olympiad.

The fourth question concerns the more specific issue of the Games and associated events logo. Research has shown that event logos, as a result of the length of time they are on-screen during the event, are a useful way of promoting iconic destination features (Green, Costa and Fitzgerald, 2002). The logo for the Sydney Olympics, for example, featured the peaks of the Sydney Opera House. However, logos for a high profile event such as the Olympics can often be the subject of close scrutiny and intense criticism. The London 2012 logo, launched in June 2007, has been criticized for failing to incorporate anything distinctive to London or the UK, apart from the word London in fairly small lettering.

The fifth and final question relating to leveraging Olympic-related reporting and event coverage relates to the way in which hosts might benefit from sponsors' promotion of their sponsorship of the event. Specifically, how a host's relationship with a sponsor might lead to the utilization of host destination images in sponsors advertising campaigns. Such a relationship is beneficial to sponsors as it can help to combat the problem of 'ambush marketing' as noted by Chalip (2004:243) in relation to Visa's longstanding sponsorship of the Olympics:

> For many years American Express ambushed Visa by airing television commercials featuring Olympic host cities, thus giving the impression that American Express, rather than Visa, was an Olympic sponsor (Card Watch, 1992; Sutton, 1993). By the time of the Sydney Olympics, the lesson had been learned: It is not sufficient for a sponsor to advertise its association with an event; the sponsor must also link itself to the event's host destination (Chalip, 2000).

The Sydney example is picked up in greater detail by Graham Brown in Chapter 7, where he outlines the range of relationships between Olympic sponsors and the Australian Tourist Commission.

As noted earlier, strategies for leveraging Olympic-related reporting and coverage can be complex because Olympic hosts are attempting to encourage positive coverage of the city/region and country as a destination in the coverage of others rather than generating their own advertising. Furthermore, with an event of the size and interest of the Olympic Games, the potential to experience negative coverage is significant. However, an effective Olympic media leveraging strategy can play a central role in attempting to maximize the positive aspects of the coverage. Of course, such a strategy also includes the use of the Olympic Games in the destination's own advertising material where, as discussed in the next section, the destination is in control of the messages.

Strategies for leveraging the Olympics in host destination advertising and promotion

As noted above, strategies for leveraging Olympic-related reporting and event coverage may have success in targeting Pre-Games and Post-Games Sports Tourists as a consequence of the fact that sport-oriented individuals are likely to form a significant proportion of the audience for Olympic-related reporting and coverage. In contrast, and notwithstanding the potential to target sports tourism market segments, the audience for host destination advertising and promotion is likely to be a more general one and, as such, attempts to use the Olympics in such promotions need to be carefully balanced. On one hand, the use of the Olympics in host destination advertising and promotion may attract Pre-Games and Post-Games General Tourists (and, indeed, some Pre-Games and Post-Games Sports Tourists); but, on the other hand, the use of the Olympics in such advertising may increase the size of the Pre- and Post-Games Avoiders categories. However, attempting to leverage the Olympic in this way differs from leveraging Olympic reporting and event coverage in two ways: first, such advertising and promotion is wholly controlled by destinations and, second, the Olympics can be used in host advertising and promotion long after the Games have taken place. In fact, as time progresses after the hosting of an Olympic Games, the leveraging of Olympic tourism products (as discussed in the earlier part of this chapter) becomes less significant, and the use of the Olympics evolves into a becoming a part of the general destination profile. Consequently, over time there should be a change in emphasis from advertising the range of Olympic tourism products (as discussed in Chapter 1) in the pre-Games period to using the hosting of the Olympics to say something about the attributes of the destination in the post-Games period. If this is done effectively, the Post-Games General Tourist category can be maximized and the numbers of Pre- and Post-Games Avoiders can be minimized. The key to strategies attempting to leverage the Olympics in this way is an understanding of the relationship between destination and Olympic association sets. Again, Chalip (2004:244) has provided some useful questions for destinations to consider, and they are reproduced here in an Olympic context:

- How do the host city/region's and country's target markets view the destination? What are their association sets for the host city/region and country?

- How do the host city/region's and country's target markets view the Olympics? What are their association sets for the Olympics?

- What elements from the Olympics association set does the host city/region and country want to use strengthen or change its image?

- How can Olympic associations be best used to emphasize the desired aspects of the host city/region's and country's image?

Brown et al. (2002) are cited by Chalip (2004) as providing two key insights into the relationship between event images and destination images from their work on the Sydney 2000 Olympics. First, it is noted that images and associations are multi-faceted. An Olympic host city/region and/or country is likely to be associated with a range of characteristics (e.g., weather, attractions, etc.) and with emotional responses (e.g., stimulation, relaxation, etc.), whilst the Olympics itself has similar associations with features (e.g., elite competition, fair play) and emotions (e.g., pride). Second, the key to effective leveraging is to identify the Olympic associations that the host city/region and country wishes to develop as part of its image, and develop strategies to transfer those associations from the Games to the host city/region and country (Chalip, 2004).

In the pre-Games and Games periods, a key aspect of this strategy of association is for Olympic hosts to decide on the way in which they are going to interpret aspects of the Olympic Movement, history, and ideology to match their characteristics. The Athens Games of 2004, for example, focussed on the link between ancient and modern. A key part of the Olympic Games is its link to its ancient history, but it is also a global phenomenon that represents the pinnacle of modern sport. Athens wished to draw on this association to promote the value of its ancient culture and history to tourists, but to also show that it was a modern country with a high-quality tourism infrastructure. Similarly, the forthcoming Games in London in 2012 have linked the international nature of the Olympic Games (each of the Olympic rings represents one of the World's continents) with the multicultural nature of London, its population, and its tourism product. Such local interpretations of Olympic themes by host cities/regions and countries should be a clear and consistent part of marketing strategies in the pre-Games and Games periods. The important aspect of such strategies is to use the Olympics to portray messages and associations that are relevant to more general tourists, rather than associations specific to those interested in the Olympic Games. In focussing on more generic associations, hosts are less likely to alienate 'aversion markets' who are put-off by the Games themselves, thus helping to minimize the size of categories such as Pre- and Post-Games Avoiders.

Similar principles apply in attempting to leverage the Olympics in post-Games destination advertising and promotion. Over time there should be a gradual move away from advertising Olympic tourism products (such as sports events and attractions) towards using Olympic themes to reinforce destination images. One such theme might be to focus on quality. A number of previous Olympic hosts have successfully used the association of the Olympics with top-quality sport to promote the high-quality of tourism services and products. Similarly, the size of the Olympics, and the infrastructure needed to host an Olympic Games, can be harnessed to promote a modern and efficient tourism and transport infrastructure, which an event of the size of the Games demands. Chapter 9 describes Beijing's efforts to promote itself as a modern and progressive global city, and its hosting of the Olympic Games is a key part of its strategy to show itself in this light to a global audience. Beijing sees the Games as a route to developing tourism and trade links with key Western markets. Other hosts have used the Games to develop the lucrative business and conference tourism market. Graham Brown's discussion of Sydney in Chapter 7 notes that the Sydney Convention Centre generated Aus$530 million worth of business in the four years following the Games in 2000.

A key consideration in leveraging Olympic media is the extent to which messages which may have positive impacts on one category of Olympic tourist (e.g., Post-Games Sports Tourists) may have negative spin-offs for another (e.g., Post-Games Avoiders). However, unlike strategies aimed at leveraging Olympic-related reporting and event coverage, the leveraging of the Olympics in host destination advertising and promotion is under the control of destination managers and marketers. Therefore, whilst balancing promotional strategies to cater for the complex range of categories of Olympic tourist outlined in Chapter 3 is not simple, the strategic planning to successfully achieve such a balance is within the capacity of such managers and marketers.

Conclusion

This chapter is perhaps the pivotal chapter in the book, as it attempts to draw together the discussions of the range of Olympic tourism products in Chapter 1 with the discussions of the motivations and behaviours of a range of sports-related Olympic tourist profiles and types in Chapter 2 and the examination of the detail of Olympic tourism flows and categories in Chapter 3 to inform a discussion of the strategies that might be employed to leverage Olympic tourism. The discussions throughout this book have been concerned to extend the scope of analysis beyond the Games themselves, both temporally (i.e., across the pre-, during, and post-Games periods) and geographically (i.e., across the host city/region, other regions in the host country, and the host country as a whole). Such an extended scope has led to the discussions in this chapter, by necessity, being illustrative rather than comprehensive, although an attempt has been made to cover as wide a range of issues as possible. Chapter 7 will now discuss the way in which policy-makers in sport, tourism and other sectors might facilitate and support Olympic tourism. Like the scope of the analysis in this book, the structure of policy-making for Olympic tourism needs to cope with both temporal and geographical differences in terms of the development of appropriate policies and the inclusion of appropriate organizations. That the sport and tourism sectors have shown themselves to be reluctant to work together in a range of countries around the world in the past could be a significant impedance to Olympic tourism policy, and such issues are a key part of the discussions in the next chapter.

CHAPTER 5

Planning for Olympic tourism

As the final chapter in the first part of the book, this chapter provides the final piece of the jigsaw of an understanding of Olympic tourism. The book commenced with an overview of the relationship between sport, tourism, and the Olympic Games, in the process reviewing a number of Olympic tourism products and establishing a definition of Olympic tourism as tourism behaviour motivated or generated by the Olympic Games. Having established the range of Olympic tourism products in Chapter 1, Chapter 2 discussed the nature of the sports-related Olympic tourist, examining motivations, behaviours profiles and types. These first two chapters provided the background for a detailed examination of travel flows generated by the Olympics during, before and after the Games in both the immediate host city/region and in the wider host country in Chapter 3. Drawing on this material, Chapter 4 then examined a range of strategies that might be used to capitalize on, or leverage, Olympic tourism. This chapter will now discuss the issues that might be experienced by a range of agencies in developing policy and planning for Olympic tourism.

In the broader sport and tourism area, Weed (2001b; 2005b) and Weed and Bull (1997a; 1998) have suggested that there are few examples around the world of effective and sustainable policy partnerships between agencies responsible for sport and for tourism. This lack of liaison has been attributed to, *inter alia*, government policy (Weed and Bull, 1997b), organizational culture (Weed, 2002b), the different histories, cultures and structures of the respective policy communities for sport and for tourism (Weed, 2001b), and the perceptions of key individuals in policy-making agencies (Weed, 2006c). However, it has also been suggested that there are ways in which such barriers to liaison can be overcome (Weed, 2003a), and the later part of this chapter examines the extent to which the prospect of the Olympic Games, and the range of benefits it might bring both to sport and to tourism, can stimulate policy partnerships that would not otherwise have emerged. The chapter also examines the potential for such partnerships to sustain beyond the hosting of an Olympic Games, as well as discussing the most effective ways to organize Olympic-related policy development and planning. However, first, the range of issues that any policy partnerships for the Olympic Games might be expected to address are examined.

Olympic tourism policy areas

In their first work on policy development for sport and tourism, Weed and Bull (1997a) conducted a review of regional policies for sport and tourism. A framework was required for this review, and so a Policy Area Matrix for Sport and Tourism was compiled. This Policy Area Matrix was intended to illustrate those areas where it might reasonably be assumed that policy-makers responsible for sport and for tourism should collaborate. In relation to Olympic tourism, some of the issues contained in the matrix (such as those relating to Environment, Countryside, and Water Issues) are less relevant, whilst there is also a need to allow for general tourism generated by an Olympic Games. Consequently, the Matrix has been adapted into a set of *Olympic Tourism Policy Rings* (see Figure 5.1), where the central ring relates to policy considerations for the six core Olympic tourism products described in Chapter 1 (Tourism with Sports Content, Sports Participation Tourism, Sports Training, Sports Events, Luxury Sports Tourism, and General Tourism). The central ring of Olympic tourism products is shown as overlapping with four further broad Olympic tourism policy areas, which each themselves overlap. The four further broad policy areas are: Facility Issues, Information and Lobbying, Resources and Funding, and Policy and Planning. The five Olympic Tourism Policy Rings are further sub-divided into 20 sub-areas. The overlapping nature of the rings is intended to show that there are a wide range of links across the areas and

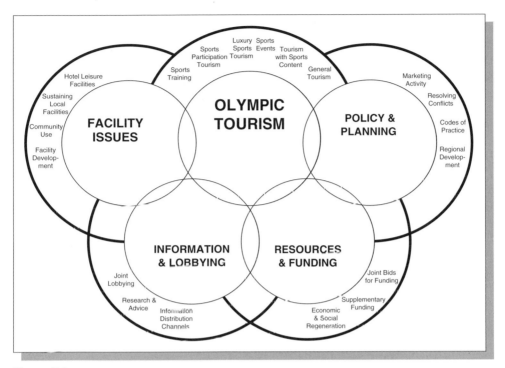

Figure 5.1
Olympic Tourism Policy Rings.
Source: derived from Weed and Bull, 1997a.

sub-areas. For example, collaboration on 'Facility Development' under 'Facility Issues' is linked to policy considerations for a range of Olympic tourism products (e.g., 'Sports Events' and 'Sports Training') under the central 'Olympic Tourism' area.

Like the original Policy Area Matrix for Sport and Tourism, the Olympic Tourism Policy Rings aim to summarize those areas in which agencies responsible for developing policy for Olympic tourism might reasonably be expected to collaborate. As such, it is useful to examine some examples from around the world of both successful and less successful policy collaborations. Such examples might usefully be considered in the context of the nature of sports-related Olympic tourism as being derived from the interaction of activity, people and place, with many policy initiatives focussing on the place element. Perhaps the most obvious examples from the Olympic tourism product policy ring are in relation to Sports Event tourism. Whilst the focus is usually on maximizing the economic contribution of such events, a further consideration relates to the post-event use of major arenas and specialist facilities constructed for such events. The athletics stadia used for the Atlanta Olympics (1996) and the Manchester Commonwealth Games (2002) incorporated temporary stands which allowed for the adaptation of the facilities for the long term use of the Atlanta Braves Baseball team and Manchester City football club, respectively. In each of these cases the experience of place generated by and associated with athletics is different to that required for both baseball and football. Consequently, modifications to these stadia were made to ensure their long term use, where a different group of people would expect a different place experience in watching a different type of activity. An example from the Facility Issues ring is provided by Calgary, who had mixed success in ensuring that the facilities constructed for the 1988 Winter Olympic Games were suitable for dual use for both spectator events and general casual community sport. Here the requirement was for places that would be capable of adaptation to produce different place experiences for different people participating in or watching a range of different activities. On one hand, the Canmore Nordic Ski Centre, in addition to continuing to host events, provided for 40,000 recreational cross-country skiers in its first year of post-Olympic operation. On the other hand, the luge and bobsled track, the ski-jump tower, and the indoor speed-skating oval have not attracted nor been adaptable for community use, although events such as World Cup Speed Skating continue to be hosted (Granson, 2005; Whitson and MacIntosh, 1993; 1996).

Securing and using Resources and Funding to promote and develop Olympic tourism is a key policy ring where collaboration between sport, tourism and a range of other interests could develop much further than is presently the case. Whilst the channelling of resources into projects that use high profile sport to regenerate communities has been a feature of city marketing in the USA for some time, there is often extended debate about the use of resources for an Olympic Games, particularly if costs appear to be continually rising and policy planning and partnership is seen to be lacking. In this respect, some of the concerns expressed in the run up to the Athens Olympic Games of 2004 provide a useful example (see also Chapter 8). In the context of a rising budget and a perceived lack of planning, the President of the Athens Hotel Owners Association claimed that while hotel owners were investing over 500 million Euros in modernizing hotels, they were being let down by the government who were squandering resources on 'sloppy solutions' such as the accommodation of Olympic tourists on islands coupled with the organization of day trips to Athens to watch the events (Sports Business, 2002). The lack of resources allocated to proper planning structures was also criticized by the Managing Director of the Greek Association of Tourism Enterprises, who condemned the government for not doing 'anything all these years to formulate a marketing strategy that would make the Olympics the pole attraction for millions of foreign visitors to Greece.' (Yannopoulos, 2003). Such a marketing strategy, had it been developed (as it has in other cases – see discussion of the Winter Games in Turin in Chapter 6), could have served to attracting new people to the area through the packaging and promotion of a range of new and existing activities. The aim is that new people and activities will serve to revitalize the place and consequently improve both the Olympic tourism experience and the lives of local residents. The unfortunate aspect of the Athens case is that there was a desire to do this as illustrated by both Buhalis (2001) and the Greek Minister of Culture, who each refer to a desire to use the 2004 Games to develop the Greek tourism product beyond a straightforward resort-based beach tourism destination to a more diversified offer that would include urban and cultural tourism.

Related to such marketing strategies and initiatives are areas in the Policy and Planning ring such as the development of codes of practice. In Wales, where activity tourism is an important market, the Wales Tourist Board established an Activity Holidays Advisory Committee to supplement the work of the British Activity Holidays Association, through which it liaises with the Sports Council for Wales to develop and maintain codes of practice to ensure the safety of activity holidays. Such aspects of sports tourism might be utilized as part of a policy to provide opportunities to 'escape' from the Olympic Games for those minded to do so (see discussions on Olympic tourism flows in Chapter 3). Finally, in relation to the Information and Lobbying policy ring, Gunn (1990) describes a collaborative initiative in South Africa relating to research and advice. The South African Tourism Agency and the Recreational Planning Agency collaborated on a joint research programme to identify tourism strengths in relation to sports and recreation facilities and resources. As such, a key role for regional policy makers outside of the Olympic host city/region is in assessing the product strengths that their region can utilize to capitalize on the Olympic Games (see discussion of Olympic tourism products in Chapter 1 and the London 2012 Games in Chapter 10). These examples highlight the ways in which the sports tourism experience might be enhanced by collaborative accreditation and research initiatives that ensure that people use the most appropriate places in the most effective and safest ways for the most appropriate activities.

What the examples above show is that policy collaborations relating to Olympic tourism are not always successful in delivering the strategies required to fully leverage the opportunities that exist. As such, it is useful to turn to a consideration of the issues that might impact upon Olympic tourism policy development and collaboration and Weed's (2001b) Model of Cross Sectoral Policy Development as applied to the sport and tourism sectors. Weed (2001b, 2003a) discussed the range of factors that mitigate against cross-sectoral policy partnerships, identifying the structure and culture of the respective policy communities for sport and for tourism, ideologies, definitions, regional contexts, government policy, organizational culture and structure, and individuals as being the key influences. The following section examines each of these factors in turn and discusses the way in which they may manifest themselves in relation to Olympic-related policy partnerships between sport and tourism.

Influences on Olympic-related policy partnerships

Six influences on policy liaison between sport and tourism interests were identified by Weed (2003a), and these each have the potential to impact upon Olympic-related policy partnerships. However, a further factor, namely the structure of the policy communities for sport and for tourism (Weed, 2001b), also wields an influence in providing the context within which policy liaison takes place. Consequently, such policy structures and cultures are discussed in the first section below, thus providing a context for the subsequent sections which discuss in turn how ideologies, definitions, regional contexts, government policy, organizational cultures and structures, and individuals may affect Olympic-related tourism policy development.

Policy structures and cultures

In many countries around the world the agencies and structures that exist for developing sport and tourism, respectively, have been established and have developed entirely separately. This separate development is often compounded by a significantly different 'culture' or 'ethos' in the two sectors. There is often a tradition of public sector support, subsidy and/or intervention in the sports sector (the exception, perhaps, being the USA, where the United States Olympic Committee, although granted a role via legislation, receives no public sector funding), whilst the tourist sector is largely seen as a private sector concern, and agencies are often limited to a marketing or business support role. These factors are further complicated by the different levels at which responsibility for policy development lies. Organizations may exist at national, regional and/or local level, and in countries such as the USA or Australia, which have federal systems of government, the significant role of state governments also needs to be considered. The respective responsibilities of these agencies can mean that in some instances liaison needs to take place not only across sectors, but also between levels.

Such problems are illustrated in Weed's (2001b) Model of Cross Sectoral Policy Development that combines the policy community models suggested by Rhodes (Rhodes and Marsh, 1992; Rhodes, 1981) and Wilks and Wright (1987). This combination allows for an analysis of the way in which the structure of the policy communities at the sectoral level (e.g., sport, tourism, arts, etc.) might affect the development of policy networks at the sub-sectoral level (e.g., sport-tourism). The model sets the sport and tourism policy communities within a broader leisure policy universe that includes other interests such as the arts, heritage, and countryside recreation. Policy communities themselves are characterized as existing on a continuum from a close-knit policy circle, to a much more loose and open issue zone. The structure of such communities is seen as affecting the potential for sub-sectoral policy networks to emerge to deal with more specific areas of policy such as the sport-tourism link, or in this case, Olympic-related tourism issues. An analysis of sport and tourism policy communities around the world shows that sports policy communities generally tend to have a primary core, comprising key organizations and incorporating central government, which is fairly closed to the rest of the community, and a more open secondary community. Tourism policy communities, on the other hand, tend to be altogether more open. Although in relation to tourism policy communities, sports policy communities tend to be more tightly formed, and thus are perhaps more able to exclude tourism interests than vice-versa, both communities are unable to insulate themselves from other, more politically important policy areas.

In the usual course of events, the more politically important policy areas that the policy communities for sport and for tourism might find impinging on their work might include law and order, foreign affairs or economics. In each of these cases it is likely that the interests of such policy areas will take precedence over those of sport and of tourism. However, the hosting of an Olympic Games elevates sport and tourism interests to a much more significant place on the political agenda, and this obviously has implications for policy development.

As the discussions of the London Olympic Games in 2012 in Chapter 10 highlight, there has been considerable activity among policy making agencies in preparing for the London Games. A number of agencies have been established with a remit that is entirely focussed on the Olympic Games (e.g., the Olympic

Delivery Authority), while a number of other agencies that would usually have little input or interest in the relationship between sport and tourism have, understandably, taken a lead role in policy discussions and developments (e.g., the London Mayor's Office). In addition, agencies that have had previous input into the development of sport and of tourism, and in some cases of sports tourism, such as the Regional Development Agencies, have established 'Task Forces' and 'Working Groups' to examine the potential impact of the London Games on their region and the ways in which they can capitalize on it. To facilitate this, a 'Nations and Regions Group' has been established to examine ways in which the benefits of the London Olympic Games can be spread around the UK. Clearly, in the London case, an 'Olympics policy community' is taking shape, and such policy communities have operated in the past in other Olympic host countries (see discussions of specific Olympic Games in part two of the text). However, while an Olympic policy community clearly focuses attention on issues associated with sport and with tourism in relation to the Olympic Games, the way in which it emerges and its membership will determine the nature of its long-term impact. Undoubtedly, the role of any Olympic policy community will be to effectively plan for, deliver and leverage the Games, but an important secondary role should be to establish legacy policy development benefits.

It is usually the case that discussions of the long-term or legacy impact of the Olympic Games relate to economic, tourism and sports development gains. However, in policy development terms, the Olympic Games has the potential to bring together agencies from both the sport and the tourism policy communities that have, in the past, shown considerable reluctance to work together (Weed, 2003a). Consequently, the policy development benefits of an Olympic Games could be to establish long-term sustainable policy collaboration and liaison mechanisms and relationships between sport and tourism policy communities that can exist long after the Olympic Games has come and gone. Such partnerships, stimulated by the mutual interests of sport and tourism in relation to the Games, can potentially continue and broaden in scope to become long-term 'legacy' collaborations dealing with the full range of issues on which it might be expected that sport and tourism agencies might collaborate as outlined by Weed and Bull (1997a) in their Policy Matrix for Sport and Tourism, from which the Olympic Tourism Policy Rings discussed earlier (Figure 5.1) were derived. However, such legacy policy development benefits will only be realized if an Olympic policy community incorporates those agencies and interests that play key roles in the sport and the tourism policy communities. As an Olympic policy community inevitably has a fixed life-span, it will be those agencies that will outlast the Olympic policy community that will be the key players in any legacy collaborations between sport and tourism. Consequently, if the key players in an Olympic policy community are agencies such as (in the London example) the Olympic Delivery Authority and the Nations and Regions Group, with agencies from the sport and the tourism policy communities playing a minor role, it is unlikely that any legacy liaison benefits will be realized as sport and tourism agencies will not have had the opportunity to 'learn' how to work together. The need for sport and tourism agencies to learn how to work together is clearly highlighted by the range of previous research noted earlier that describes the various barriers to liaison between sport and tourism interests. The impact of these influences in an Olympic context is discussed further in the sections below.

Ideologies

Ideologies can influence policy development at all levels of the policy process. They may be derived from political beliefs, professional frameworks, or they may be more personal ideologies that are not necessarily professional or political. Ideological problems in the development of policy for sport and tourism have often been the result of different professional ideologies across the sport and tourism sectors, of inconsistent political ideologies relating to the strategic development of sport and/or tourism, or a clash between political goals (which may often reflect expediency) and the often longer-term goals of sport and tourism professionals. The awarding of an Olympic Games to a city (and thus to the country in which the city is located) will often result on the politicization of decisions and, indeed, policy areas as a whole, in which deliberations usually take place largely out of the political arena. In both the sport and tourism policy areas most policy and strategic decisions, while sometimes influenced by government at the general level, are usually taken by supposedly de-politicized bodies such as National Tourism Organizations and National Sports Development or Olympic Agencies. An impending Olympic Games will make many of the decisions made by these agencies national political issues, and certainly the resources made available to fund pre-Olympic development in the areas of both sport and tourism, and the source of such funding, will be the subject of national political debate. Consequently, ideological questions that are more usually part of education and health policy discussions, such as who benefits, who pays, and who decides who benefits and who pays, become important issues in the areas of sport and tourism as a country plans for an Olympic Games.

Regional contexts

In their discussion of policy development for sport and tourism, Weed and Bull (2004:111) identify regional contexts as 'perhaps one of the most significant influences' on sport-tourism policy. They note that historical contexts, geographical resources, administrative structures, economic activity and development, political structures and a whole host of regional influences can impact upon the development of policy for sport and tourism. Of course, in developing policy for Olympic issues in general, and Olympic tourism in particular, one of the prime concerns will be the proximity of the region to the Olympic host city. Certainly in terms of the way in which policy makers perceive the potential benefits, the locality (or not) of the Olympic Games themselves is a prime consideration. However, also key are the perceived strengths of the region in relation to potential Olympic tourism products. Some regions, for example, may feel that they have particular product strengths in relation to Sports Training, whereas others may feel they have the ability to benefit from hosting Sports Events in the few years before the Olympic Games. Of course, an appreciation of the product strengths of a region in relation to potential Olympic tourism requires a knowledge of the nature of both Olympic tourism and sports tourism and this, in turn, is dependent on the ability and desire of policy makers from different sectors and traditions to come together to consider such issues. In this respect, regional historical, cultural and administrative factors may either facilitate or constrain such developments.

A further 'regional context' for consideration, linked to the discussions of ideology above, may be the traditional or historic relationship between the Olympic host city/region and other regions of the country. If regions outside the host city/region believe that the host city/region has traditionally been economically dominant in the country as a whole, then there may be some objections to central government money being spent on an event that some regions may believe will benefit only one area of the country. The political imperative in some regions may be to say: 'what are the benefits for us of this event, and why should tax-payers in this region contribute to paying for it?'.

Definitions

Linked to some of the discussions above, is the influence of organizational and individual definitions of sport, tourism, sports tourism and Olympic tourism. A more narrow definition of sport, focussing only on formal competitive activities, obviously reduces the scope for liaison with tourist agencies. Similarly, if tourism is defined as involving an overnight stay, then this excludes a vast range of sports day trips. Such definitions may be actual (in that a sports agency may adhere to a narrow definition of sport) or perceived (in that a sports agency may perceive that a tourist agency is only interested in travel involving an overnight stay). Work on the impact of such definitions on sport-tourism policy (Weed, 2006b) has found that there are often misconceptions about the roles and remits of potential partner agencies across the sport and tourism sectors, and consequently this results in a rather narrow perception of the nature of sports tourism, and a lack of appreciation of the potential impacts and range of the area. It is likely that there may be a similar effect with Olympic tourism. Part of this may be directly related to the lack of understanding of the extent of sports tourism discussed above, and of the extent and range Olympic tourism products as discussed in Chapter 1. A narrow perception of Olympic tourism may be that it comprises tourist trips to an Olympic host city/region during and after an Olympic Games. There is much talked about the 'legacy' tourism benefits of an Olympic Games, but policy-makers are often unaware of the 'pregnancy' tourism benefits (i.e., potential tourism prior to the Olympic Games). An example of this is provided by a projected impact study of the London 2012 Olympic Games by Pricewaterhouse Coopers for the Department for Culture, Media and Sport in the UK (Pricewaterhouse Coopers, 2005). This study makes economic projections for the potential impact of the Games on tourism during and after the Games period, but assumes there will be no impact in the pre-Games period. This is somewhat strange because, as Chapter 4 on leveraging has shown, the potential for increased media coverage of an Olympic destination is by far the greatest in the four years leading up to and including the Games. A further misconception of Olympic tourism by policy makers may be a failure to consider the full range of tourism flows discussed in Chapter 3, particularly those that have a negative tourism impact. As Chapter 4 shows, such negative impacts can be ameliorated if appropriate strategies are put in place in both the Olympic host city/region and in the country as a whole. However, a lack of appreciation of the wide-ranging nature and impacts of Olympic tourism, and a failure to understand the stratified geography of Olympic tourism flows (see Chapters 3 and 4) may result in policy-makers overlooking such considerations.

Organizational culture and structure

In an initial consideration of the factors that might influence policy development for sport and tourism, Weed and Bull

(1998) discussed organizational culture and structure separately. However, in more recent writings they have, as a result of further empirical investigations, come to the conclusion that 'culture and structure evolve together and are inextricably interlinked' (Weed and Bull, 2004:112). Organizational structure refers to the formal structure of an organization, whereas organizational culture refers to the informal ways in which people work within that structure. While in some cases culture might subvert structure, the two are dialectical and have a reciprocal influence on each other. Structural and cultural issues relating to the development of policy for sport and tourism have often been related to the imposition of initiatives on organizations, and of potential resistance to such initiatives from within the organization. Similarly, this may be the true for Olympic tourism, with organizations, particularly those in the tourism sector working in regions outside the host city/region, feeling that there are more important aspects of their work than that concerned with Olympic tourism. Conversely, a challenge for some organizations will be in adapting to the imposition of new structures that might comprise an 'Olympics policy community' as discussed earlier in the chapter. Organizations will have to adapt as the result of such structures as they are required to either engage with an Olympics policy community or fight for their position or inclusion within it. This may require changes to the ways in which priorities are decided within organizations and will inevitably, as noted above, encounter some inbuilt resistance to change.

Individuals

The influence of individuals is felt at all levels of the policy process. In some cases, individual influence will be the result of a the position an individual holds, such as a Minister for Sport in national governments. In other cases, individuals will wield influence as a result of their personal standing, regardless of the position they hold. In relation to the London Olympics, Lord Sebastion Coe, a former double Olympic champion, whilst being Chairman of the London 2012 bid and organizing committee, holds influence beyond that accorded by his position as a result of the esteem in which he is held within the Olympic movement more generally. Consequently, individuals can be influential as a result of positional or personal 'power'. This can be both positive and negative for the development of policy for Olympic tourism. If such a key individual does not have a full appreciation of the nature of Olympic tourism (as discussed under definitions) or is motivated by political expediency (as discussed under ideology), or has a particular axe to grind about the allocation of resources (as discussed under regional contexts), a single pronouncement from such an individual can alter significantly the direction of policy. In these cases, this will likely have a negative effect on the development of Olympic tourism. However, an influential individual with a full understanding of the issues can have a very positive effect. Regardless of the direction of the effect, the key consideration is that influential individuals have the potential to have a significant impact on policy development, and in many cases can be more influential than many of the other factors discussed above. This is particularly so when an issue is high on the political agenda and in the media spotlight, as is the case with the Olympics.

Government policy

Government policy can be both the cause and the result of some of the problems and issues discussed in this chapter so far. In relation to sport and tourism policy, government policy for sport (such as a narrower focus on competitive sport) can have unintended impacts on sport-tourism policy development (in this example, such a narrower focus would make liaison with the tourism sector less likely). However, as noted above, government policy for sport, for tourism, and in very few cases for sports tourism, is usually not a big political issue. However, the impending hosting of an Olympic Games changes this, and heightens public, political and media interest in sport and tourism policy development. In such an atmosphere, government policy initiatives have a greater than usual impact upon sport, tourism, sports tourism, and Olympic tourism policy development, because they will be more detailed and more extensively resourced. Furthermore, government initiatives aimed directly at Olympic tourism have the potential to overcome some of the issue raised in the previous sections. For example, government initiatives could provide resources for the development of initiatives to spread the tourism benefits of an Olympic Games around the regions of a country outside of the Olympic host city/region. However, as with the previous sections, such initiatives, whatever they may be, require a full understanding of the nature and potential of Olympic tourism. As such, a key role of governments in this area should be related to information collection and dissemination to ensure that policy makers at all levels have full knowledge of the potential benefits (and potential negative impacts) of Olympic tourism in their area.

The operation of Olympic policy communities

Weed and Bull (2004) discuss the potential operation of sport-tourism policy networks. Unlike such networks, which exist at the sub-sectoral level, Olympic policy communities will largely exist at a level that is multi-sectoral, or even supra-sectoral (in that they will work above and across sectors), and Olympic tourism will be one issue among a range of Olympic-related affairs that an Olympic policy community will consider. However, the factors that Weed and Bull discuss in relation to the potential operation of sport-tourism policy networks are also pertinent for the operation of Olympic policy communities, not least because they each involve actors from more than one sector. Weed and Bull (2004:113) draw on the work of Wright (1988) to examine 'rules of the game' in the operation of policy networks and communities; such rules act as an unwritten constitution, guiding the behaviour of actors within the community. In the Olympic context, a further dimension is added by the multi- or supra-sectoral nature of some of the issues under consideration. In the case of sport-tourism networks, complications arise as a result of the partnership between two sectors, in the Olympic case, there are multiple sectors involved and this further complicates some of the issues discussed below. Furthermore, as Olympic tourism will not be the sole concern of an Olympic policy community, there may be a range of interventions from other sectors. This is one of the considerations in the discussions below, that examine the impact that the operation of Olympic policy communities may have on the development of Olympic tourism.

The first of Wright's (1988:609–610) 'rules of the game' is mutuality. Members of policy communities accept and expect that mutual advantages and benefits will result from their participation in the community. It is therefore necessary that the multitude of agencies involved in Olympic policy discussions, such as those interested in, *inter alia*, sport, tourism, health, culture, economic development, local government, and regional development, believe that there are potentially positive outcomes from the hosting of the Olympic Games and that they each stand to benefit from it. Although there are doubters, the potential for the Olympic Games to have a range of positive impacts in a range of sectors is generally accepted. This is in contrast to the operation of sport-tourism policy networks discussed by Weed and Bull (2004:113) who note that sport and tourist agencies are often not aware of the full extent of the benefits of linking sport and tourism, and thus they believe that mutuality will not exist within sport-tourism policy networks. However, of relevance to the development of Olympic tourism are Weed's (2006b) findings that sport and tourism agencies often do perceive that there are potential benefits arising from the hosting of major events. This would seem to suggest that such agencies would be more positively oriented to accepting that mutual benefits will arise from their involvement in an Olympic policy community. However, as earlier discussions in this and other chapters have shown, there can often be differential benefits in different regions as a result of the stratified geography of tourism flows between the host city/region, other regions in the host country, and the host country as a whole. Furthermore, some of these flows result in a positive impact for one region at the expense of another (e.g., a flow of tourists away from the host city/region to other regions, or the displacement of tourists from other regions to the host city/region). As such, some strategies aimed at leveraging regional development outside the host/city region may be in competition with those that attempt to leverage the benefits of Olympic tourism to the host city/region. Consequently, rather than mutuality, in some cases there may be perceptions of 'mutual exclusivity'. The challenge for Olympic policy networks is to ensure that strategic national actors, such as central government departments or national tourism organizations, are aware of areas of potential mutual exclusivity and examine ways in which they can be effectively mediated.

The second of Wright's (1988) rules of the game discussed by Weed and Bull (2004) relates to consultation, both the willingness of an agency to consult within the network and the expectation by agencies that they will be consulted. Weed and Bull noted that in the case of sport-tourism, where the policy network draws its membership from two different policy communities, some issues are seen by the sports policy community as falling exclusively within their 'territory', whilst the tourism policy community will feel that certain issues fall exclusively within their territory. This obviously creates problems for consultation within the policy network. However, Jordan and Richardson's (1987:55) discussion of the extent of organizations' territory is helpful in addressing this issue:

> each organisation has a notion of its own 'territory', rather as an animal or bird in the wild has its own territory, and it will resist invasion of this territory by other agencies. There is not a precise definition of exactly where the territory ends. For example, there is territory which is at the periphery of the bureau influence and where it has some, but not great influence and there is territory which is quite 'alien' to the bureau and where it has no influence. On the other hand, it has its heartland which is quite alien to any other bureau and which it will defend with great vigour and determination.

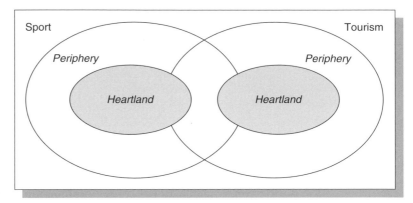

Figure 5.2
Sport and tourism policy communities: Heartland and Periphery.
Source: Weed and Bull, 2004.

Figure 5.2 shows that, in a sport-tourism policy network, the majority of policy deliberations fall within the policy periphery of both the sport and tourism policy communities, and this means that problems relating to organisation territory are limited. However, Figure 5.3 shows that the emergence of an Olympic policy community complicates this picture considerably Here there are a range of Olympic-issues that not only cut into the heartland of both sport and tourism agencies, but that are also likely to cut into the policy heartland of agencies in other sectors both within and without the leisure policy universe. In the simpler (although still complex) picture that exists within sport-tourism policy networks, Weed and Bull (2004:114) suggest that the issue of organisational territory can be resolved through accepting that neither a sport nor a tourist agency can provide permanent leadership in a sport-tourism policy network as allocating permanent leadership would result in the invasion of 'policy space'. Consequently a joint or floating leadership initiative is necessary, with one of the sports agencies leading the network on issues falling within their policy heartland whilst one of the tourist agencies leads on predominantly tourism issues. Major conflict is avoided because the policy heartlands of the two communities do not overlap and thus a flexible, floating network leadership allows the full range of issues pertaining to sport-tourism to be addressed.

However, as Figure 5.3 shows, the situation in relation to Olympic policy is much more complex, with a range of sectors with actual and potential overlapping policy heartlands being involved. To a certain extent this can be resolved by considering leadership. The discussions of the London 2012 Games in Chapter 10, for example, describe the establishment of Olympic sub-groups (e.g., arts, media, economic development, education, sport, tourism, transport, and health) in many regions to deal with 'sectoral' issues in which agencies that 'own' the policy

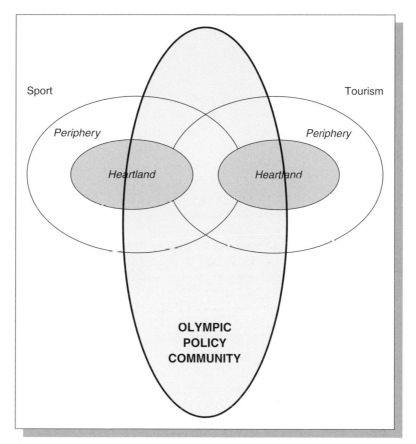

Figure 5.3
The Olympic policy community.

heartland take the lead, and in such situations tourism organizations are most often those which lead on Olympic tourism issues. However, this does not address the issue of co-ordination and overall leadership, and to do this it is useful to consider a further 'rule of the game', that of recourse to higher authority.

Wright (1988) notes that it is generally accepted that, as far as possible, policy communities will resolve issues within the community, and this is a third rule of the game. As such, the recourse to higher authority, be that the courts or the state, or the opening up of an issue to wider debate involving those outside the policy community, will be avoided wherever possible. This is generally because the opening up of an issue to wider debate outside the policy community will result in other organizations impinging on the network's 'territory'. Consequently, as far as is possible, policy communities attempt to resolve issues within the community. There are two issues here in relation to an Olympic policy community: first, it may be all but impossible to avoid opening many Olympic issues up to wider debate as the press and media interest in such Olympic issues is intense throughout the preparation, during, and in the aftermath of an Olympic Games. Second, the concept of a 'higher authority' outside of an Olympic policy community is to a certain extent a misnomer as 'the state' as one such higher authority is incorporated within, and often provides overall leadership on, Olympic policy issues. It is this aspect of Olympic policy communities that gives them their 'supra-sectoral' dimension, that of the state (often the head of the government and the executive), which exists at the supra-sectoral level, taking an overall lead or at least giving overall direction to Olympic policy. The implications of this for Olympic tourism development may be that in certain circumstances, the needs of Olympic tourism development may be seen as secondary to the needs of another sector in the Olympic policy community as assessed by an incorporated supra-sectoral 'higher authority'. This is because the recourse to higher authority, often an undesirable occurrence for policy communities, is a fundamental feature of Olympic policy communities as a result of their multi- and supra-sectoral nature.

A fourth 'rule' identified by Wright (1988) emphasizes informality within policy networks and communities. It is therefore expected that the officers of agencies in the various sectors involved in Olympic policy would feel able to communicate with each other on an informal basis. Evidence from the UK (Weed and Bull, 1998) in relation to sport-tourism collaboration suggests that informal contacts can be vital to the development of sport-tourism policy networks. In one example from the English regions, the departure of one member of staff led to the cessation of informal contacts and the failure of an emergent sports tourism initiative to move beyond an initial joint policy statement. Other examples describe the contribution of informal networks, often sustained outside of the work context, to the success of initiatives. These examples serve to re-inforce the importance of key individuals discussed earlier, and their ability to communicate effectively with people from other sectors. As such, the development of informality can be assisted by Wright's (1988) fifth and final rule: that policy issues are discussed in a commonly accepted language. However, this has been shown to be problematic in the more straightforward bi-sectoral sport-tourism policy network, where actors often come from distinctly different backgrounds and cultures which use different modes of communication and specific technical languages. This is only likely to be exacerbated in an Olympic policy community, where the number and range of the sectors involved is much wider. On a more basic level, as the discussions of definitions above have suggested, there may be different perceptions of definitions of sport, tourism, the arts, economic development, education and so on which, if communication is already minimal, can lead to problems through misunderstanding or misconception. However, Wright (1988) indicates that if a set of policy issues are important enough, and the policy community has a strong shared purpose and identity (through the acceptance of the rules of consultation and mutuality), then it is likely that this will lead to informality and a commonly accepted language. In the case of Olympic policy communities the commonly accepted language is likely to be, as noted above and in contrast to some sport-tourism policy networks, a discourse that emphasizes the potentially positive nature of Olympic-related outcomes, and a commitment to leveraging such outcomes.

Conclusion

This chapter has concluded the generic discussions of Olympic tourism by focussing on planning for Olympic tourism. It has both examined the potential scope of policy development for Olympic tourism, and explored the issues and problems that might affect Olympic tourism policy development, including the way in which policy for Olympic tourism relates to broader aspects of Olympic policy. As such, the discussion of the nature of Olympic tourism is now complete, and in summary:

- Olympic tourism largely comprises, but is not limited to, sports tourism, and a range of Olympic tourism products (which each contain a range of sub-products) can be identified (see Chapter 1)

- Olympic tourism is an heterogeneous phenomenon in which a range of motivations drive behaviours, and as such a range of sports-related Olympic tourist profiles and types can be identified (see Chapter 2)

- Olympic tourism comprises a range of tourism flows both before during and after the Games, the impact of which may vary depending on the level of analysis (host city/region or host country) (see Chapter 3)

- A consideration of Olympic tourism products, Olympic tourist profiles and types and Olympic tourism flows is important in informing strategies to leverage the positive benefits of Olympic tourism (see Chapter 4)

- In planning for Olympic tourism, a wide range of substantive issues need to be considered in addition to understanding the problems of organizational and policy collaborations in relation to Olympic tourism in particular, and Olympic policy in general (see discussions in this chapter).

The remainder of the book now turns to illustrating these issues in the substantive contexts of previous and prospective Olympic Games in the 20th century.

PART 2

The Winter Olympic Games

Although sharing the name 'Olympic Games' with the summer event, the Winter Games are a very different animal. Their organizational requirements, the economics of hosting the Games and the nature of their tourism impacts vary considerably from the Summer Games. Holger Preuss, in his seminal examination of the economics of hosting the Olympic Games recognizes this and, in fact, believes that the Summer and Winter Games are so different that they do not bear comparison: 'They [the Winter Games] are an independent event and, in this book, are considered only occasionally' (Preuss, 2004). Essex and Chalkey (2002) note that there has been far less research into the Winter Games than that which exists for the Summer Olympics. In fact, it is probably fair to say that there is a dearth of academic analysis of the Winter Games. This is somewhat surprising because, although the Winter Games might exist in the shadow of the Summer Olympics, they are still a significant event in their own right, with substantial economic and, more importantly in the context of this book, tourism implications. As such, it is perhaps useful to examine the historic development of the Winter Olympic Games and their relationship to their summer counterpart as a context for a consideration of the tourism implications of more recent editions of the Games.

A separate Winter Olympic Games was not organized until nearly 30 years after the first Summer Games, prior to which some winter sports were included in some of the Summer Olympics (e.g., figure skating in London 1908 and Antwerp 1920; ice hockey in Antwerp 1920). However, despite some objections that a Winter Games would negatively impact on a range of traditional Scandinavian sports festivals (e.g., Nordic Games), the Paris Summer Games of 1924 saw a separate 'winter sports week' being held at Chamonix six months prior to the Games. Following the success of the Chamonix event, the IOC officially created the Winter Olympic Games in 1925, and retrospectively designated Chamonix as the first Winter Olympics. However, until the Second World War, the Winter Games were tied to the summer event in that the country that hosted the Summer Games also hosted the winter event. A separate competition to host the Winter Games was instigated after the war, with St Moritz, much as London had done for the Summer Games (see Chapter 10), stepping into the fray to host the first post-war Winter Olympics in 1948. The Winter Games continued to be hosted in the same year as the Summer Games until 1992, when concerns about the overshadowing of the Winter Games by the summer event, alongside a desire to maximize the value of the Olympic name and brand throughout the four year 'Olympiad', saw the Winter Games being switched to being held two years prior to the Summer Olympics. As such, to facilitate this change, the 1994 Winter Games in Lillehammer were held two years after the 1992 Winter Olympics in Albertville.

The IOC identifies three 'types' of organizing cities for the Winter Games (IOC, 2001), and these Games are listed in Table 6.1. The table shows that the early hosts of the Winter Games were all already established winter sports resorts which already had the requisite infrastructure to host the Games. Although the IOC does not recognize this, it may be that the choice of such resorts to host the Games in the early years may have been due to the need for a host of the Summer Games to find a 'ready made' location for the winter event in their country where the organizational costs would be low. As such, if 1948 is discounted as a post-War anomaly, on only three occasions since the host for the Winter Games has been chosen separately has a winter sports resort hosted the Games. The separate bidding process for the Winter Games, therefore, appears to have resulted in the focus shifting to major cities, or to wider regions which have designated their main town as the 'host city'. However, such towns and cities still need to be located in mountainous areas, with 'ice events' tending to be focussed in the host town or city, and 'snow events' located, often some distance away, in mountain locations. As such, post-war Winter Olympic Games have tended, in reality, to be 'two-centre' events (see later examples).

Table 6.1
Hosts of the Winter Olympic Games

Date	Host	Winter Sports Resorts	Major Cities	Regionally Significant Small Towns
1924	Chamonix	X		
1928	St Moritz	X		
1932	Lake Placid	X		
1936	Garmisch-Partenkirchen	X		
1948	St Moritz	X		
1952	Oslo		X	
1956	Cortina d'Ampezzo	X		
1960	Squaw Valley	X		
1964	Innsbruck		X	
1968	Grenoble		X	
1972	Sapporo		X	
1976	Innsbruck		X	
1980	Lake Placid	X		
1984	Sarajevo		X	
1988	Calgary		X	
1992	Albertville			X
1994	Lillehammer			X
1998	Nagano		X	
2002	Salt Lake City		X	
2006	Turin		X	
2010	Vancouver		X	

Source: IOC, 2001.

In seeking to explain the move from winter sports resorts, which would seem to be natural hosts for the Winter Games, to major cities or regional towns as hosts, it is useful to turn to Essex and Chalkey's (2002) consideration of the changing infrastructural requirements of hosting the Winter Games. Essex and Chalkey (2002) identify four phases in the development of the event:

- *1924–1932: Minimal Infrastructural Transformations*
  In this period, the Winter Games were small-scale events, with between 250 and 500 athletes taking part, and the combined populations of the first three hosts being only 9,400 people. Unsurprisingly, the event was seen as part of tourism development strategy for such resorts, and both Essex and Chalkey (2002) and Preuss (2004) note that St Moritz, which staged the Games in both 1928 and 1948, developed very rapidly and still

benefits today as a leading winter sports resort as a result of having been an Olympic host. However, the development of these resorts was as a result of the marketing benefits gained rather than as the result of any major infrastructural developments. Essex and Chalkey (2002) note that the skeleton run constructed for the 1928 Games in St Moritz was a huge and expensive white elephant, being used by less than 30 people after the Games. Consequently, the skeleton event was omitted from the Olympic programme for future Games and only re-instated at Salt Lake City in 2002. There were also very few accommodation developments for these early Games, with the focus being on the use and/or 'winterization' of existing hotel and cottage accommodation.

- *1936–1960: Emerging Infrastructural Demands*
  With the exception of Garmisch-Partenkirchen in 1936, the largest of the pre-war winter sports resort hosts (population 12,600), all of the Games in this phase were in the post-War period. In many cases the 'two-centre' nature of the ice and the snow events meant that large numbers of athletes and spectators needed to be moved around, and this required investment in new transport infrastructure, including that at the competition sites (e.g., Ski lifts). This was a particular feature of the Oslo Winter Olympics, the first of the major city hosts, which was also the first Winter Games to build an Olympic Village (with post-Games utilization as student accommodation, a hospital and a residential care home). However, this period also saw two small winter resorts with populations of less than 5,000 hosting the Games, but there were still infrastructural plans (Essex and Chalkey, 2002). At Cortina d'Ampezzo in 1956, local hoteliers blocked plans for an Olympic village, fearing post-Games competition from increased accommodation provision. By 1960, the small local community of Squaw Valley could not provide the required accommodation for the rapidly expanding Winter Games, and so the construction of an Olympic Village was a necessity. However, with the exception of Lake Placid in 1980 (which had hosted the Games previously) the 1960 Games at Squaw Valley were the last time a small winter resort would be able to cope with hosting the Winter Olympics.

- *1964–1980: Tool of Regional Development*
  The growing scale of the event meant that the Winter Games were recognized as a regional development tool from the 1960s onwards (Essex and Chalkey, 2002). Generally, hosts were now significant in size (four out of five in this phase having populations over 100,000, with one having more than one million) and

thus had the capacity to accommodate the growing demands of the event, as well as to make good use of facilities after the Games. Generally, Olympic Villages were used as apartment blocks or university halls. An indication of the success of this approach is that the Olympic Village built for the Innsbruck Games in 1964 was no longer available when the Games were again staged at Innsbruck in 1976 as it had become occupied as a residential suburb of the town. Transport infrastructure development was an inevitable feature of hosting the Games in major cities, as such cities could not provide for the snow events. At Grenoble in 1968 the development of motorway links acted as a catalyst for the post-Games development of Grenoble as a major conference centre. Transport infrastructure was not only to transport athletes and spectators between Olympic sites, but also to access the host cities in the first place. At Sapporro in 1972, for example, infrastructure investment included two airport extensions. Obviously, while these investments have long-term benefits, they also incur significant costs over a relatively short period of time. As such, an illustration of the arguments against investment in a Winter Olympic Games was provided by the residents of Denver, who voted in a referendum against providing state funding for the Winter Games of 1976, with the result that Denver had to withdraw from hosting and the 1976 Games were staged at Innsbruck at short-notice.

- *1984-present: Large-scale Transformations*
  The Winter Games from 1984 onwards mirrored the Summer Games in growing significantly in size. Money from television rights, although first being a revenue stream in the 1960s, increased significantly after 1980. Still larger host cities were needed, and at least two Olympic Villages were provided to cater for ice and for snow events, with a further village often being provided for the media. The focus had shifted from 'development' to 'transformation', with the Yugoslavian government seeing the Sarajevo Games in 1984 as an opportunity to modernize the city, whilst both Calgary (1988) and Lillehammer (1994) hosted the Games with the intention of reviving the local economy. Seventeen years after the hosting of the 1988 Calgary Winter Games, the *Alberta Venture* carried a feature claiming that 'Almost overnight, the cowpoke image of the prairie city was transformed into a vibrant and colourful urban centre, showcasing its standard of living, cultural diversity and world-class recreational facilities'. Lillehammer in 1994, staged the Games utilizing temporary facilities and accommodation, but secured a major economic legacy for the

region by the post-Games use of the media centre as a major centre for telecommunications training along with all the associated business tourism and conference benefits that this continues to bring (Collins and Jackson, 1999).

Of course, while the picture painted in the development of Essex and Chalkey's (2002) four phases discussed above is one of an ever increasing size of Winter Olympic host, Winter Games host cities are still dwarfed by the size of hosts for the Summer Olympics. This is because, despite the trend towards major cities, Winter Games hosts still need to be located near to mountainous terrain to provide for the ski events. It is for this reason that, despite continuous growth in the size of Winter Games hosts, the average population size of Winter Olympic cities is still less than one tenth (236,000) of the average size of Summer Games hosts (2,840,000). There are a number of implications that emerge from this. While the cost of the Summer Games since 1984 has always been higher than that for the winter event, the Winter Games are far more costly on a per-capita basis (Preuss, 2004 – see Table 6.2). Furthermore, because Winter Games host cities, notwithstanding their growth over time, tend to be smaller with less capacity to attract commercial funding for development (Essex and Chalkey, 2002), the burden of investment tends to fall on the public-sector

Table 6.2
Respective costs of Summer and Winter Games

Olympiad	Host Cities	Total Cost (US$million)	Cost per capita (US$)
XIV	WINTER: Sarajevo, 1984	179	400
	SUMMER: Los Angeles, 1984	412	121
XV	WINTER: Calgary, 1988	628	981
	SUMMER: Seoul, 1988	3,297	326
XVI	WINTER: Albertville, 1992	767	38,350
	SUMMER: Barcelona, 1992	9,165	5,578
XVII	WINTER: Lillehammer, 1994	1,511	65,695
	SUMMER: Atlanta, 1996	2,021	5,129
XVIII	WINTER: Nagano, 1998	3,412	9,451
	SUMMER: Sydney, 2000	3,438	929
XIX	WINTER: Salt Lake City, 2002	1,330	7,628
	SUMMER: Athens, 2004	–	–

Source: Preuss, 2004.

(although as noted below, there is a long-standing link with the ski industry). While the Summer Games have increasingly attempted to follow the commercial model adopted by the Los Angeles Games of 1984, only the Calgary Winter Games (1988) has had any success in following this approach.

The staging, therefore, of a Winter Olympics can yield varying benefits, with gains often being specific to host cities and to the stage of development of the city/region at the time. Preuss (2004) reinforces this, noting that a city's unique characteristics and the economic conditions at the time are largely responsible for relative successes. However, that is not to downplay the potential opportunities of the Winter Games for which, as they are hosted in much smaller cities than the Summer Games, 'effects can be proven much more easily because the economic impact to the host city is comparatively larger' (Preuss, 2004).

Essex and Chalkey (2002) list the potential legacies of Winter Games as:

- The construction or refurbishment of sports stadia and facilities

- The provision of hotel accommodation and/or housing

- The development of a modernized transport infrastructure

- The creation of a new global image for the host centre

Each of these legacies can and have contributed to the development of a winter tourism industry. As noted previously, the early Winter Games were hosted by winter sports resorts and these resorts reaped considerable promotional and marketing benefits at a relatively low cost (compared to current Winter Games) from hosting the Winter Olympics. This promotional element did not go unnoticed by the IOC, with Avery Brundage (the IOC president from 1952 to 1972), a staunch supporter of the amateur ethos, finding it particularly distasteful. In fact, Chappelet (2002) notes that Brundage considered cancelling the Winter Games permanently on more than one occasion, considering that they were 'too closely linked to the ski industry in terms of both the equipment that was blatantly highlighted and the booming real estate around skiing areas'. Certainly the geographic distribution of the hosts for the Winter Games – with the exceptions of Sapporro and Nagano in Japan, exclusively in Europe (13 times, mostly in the Alps) and North America (6 times) – reflects the global distribution of the ski industry. In fact, Chappelet (2002) notes that the resort of Squaw Valley, the host in 1960, did not even exist when it was awarded the Winter Games on the basis of plans alone. Espy (1979) believes that Brundage hoped that the problems leading to Denver's withdrawal as the host for the

1976 Games would result in the 'burial' of the Winter Games, with Chappelet (2002) arguing that had Brundage still been IOC President at the end of 1972 when this happened, he would have attempted to permanently cancel the Winter Games.

Chappelet (2002) singles out the 1988 Games in Calgary as the point where the emphasis shifted from tourism promotion to economic development. The fact that Calgary was able to follow the Los Angeles model can be attributed to the fact that the petrochemical industry in Alberta subsidized the Games in an effort to attract inward investment, and the city grew to a population of almost 700,000. Notwithstanding the continued presence of tourism promotion as a goal of the Winter Games, not least in Lillehammer, where the coverage of the small Norwegian ski resorts in the region on the world stage as worthy competitors with Apline countries was significant, such promotion is now but one among a number of goals for Winter Olympic host cities.

Long-term evaluation – The XVth Winter Olympic Games in Calgary

Gratton, Shibli and Coleman (2006) in tracing the development of the literature on the economics of major sports events identify Ritchie's in depth study of the 1988 Calgary Winter Games (Ritchie, 1984; Ritchie and Aitken, 1984, 1985; Ritchie and Lyons, 1987, 1990; Ritchie and Smith, 1991) as the first sustained examination of the economic impacts of an Olympic Games. As this examination coincides with Chappelet's (2002) view that these Games marked a shift to economic development goals from tourism promotion, it is useful to consider here briefly some of the lasting legacies of the 1988 Games.

The road to the hosting of the XVth Winter Olympic Games in Calgary was not a smooth one. Previous attempts to secure the Winter Games for the Banff National Park in 1968 and 1972 failed, in large part, due to the objections of conservationists who argued the Games were contrary to the original purpose of National Parks (Weed and Bull, 2004). Certainly the 1988 Games resulted in some costly and underused facilities, with the luge and bobsled track and the ski-jump tower requiring refrigeration and snow making capacity. Together with the indoor speed skating oval, these facilities have required ongoing public subsidy and have not attracted or been adaptable for local community use (Whitson and MacIntosh, 1996), although they have hosted further major events such as World Cup Speed Skating (Granson, 2005). However, at the other end of the spectrum, the Canmore

Nordic Ski Centre attracted 40,000 cross-country skiers in its first year of post-Olympic operation (Whitson and MacIntosh, 1993).

Studies have shown that awareness of Calgary has improved significantly as a result of the Games, particularly in the key tourism markets of Europe and the USA. In the year running up to the Games (1987/1988), 'unaided' awareness of the region went up from 12 per cent to 40 per cent (Ritchie and Smith, 1991), and although awareness has dropped by 10 per cent since the Games, the number of non-Canadian visitors to the wider state of Alberta has never dropped below pre-Olympic numbers (Ritchie, quoted in Grenson, 2005).

In 1999, the Utah Division of Travel Development invited the leader of the Calgary studies, Brent Ritchie, to discuss the Calgary experience and its potential applications to the 2002 Winter Olympic Games in Salt Lake City. Many of the comments in his advice, 'Turning 16 Days into 16 years' (Ritchie, 1999) reflect the issues discussed in the first part of this book, and are a useful lead in to discussions of the Winter Games in the 21st century:

- *'A successful event and successfully marketing the host city are distinctly different concepts'*
  Leveraging strategies and a knowledge of potential tourism are required for the successful development of Olympic Tourism. This bears little relation to the organization of the Games. However, a successful Games will assist with the leveraging efforts, but it will not in itself lead to successful tourism development

- *'The focus of Olympic attention can create new resort communities in very short time-frames'*
  Canmore, which hosts the Nordic Ski Centre mentioned above, now has a population of 10,000, compared to just a few thousand in the pre-Games period, and is starting to rival Banff (Canada's mountain icon) as a visitor destination.

- *'Building alliances can greatly enhance the total success of the Games'*
  Ritchie claims that the key to spreading the benefits beyond the immediate host is 'sharing without diluting'.

- *'Olympic Campaigns to promote the host destination should build on and enhance existing appeals'*
  Put simply, the Olympics are not an end in themselves in terms of tourism development, they are a means to promote and develop existing product strengths. Any marketing campaigns

should also be consistent with residents views of themselves and the destination, as it is residents who will be the core of the product once the Olympics have been and gone.

- *'Extensive and detailed planning is essential'*
  Furthermore, such planning should include as core partners those bodies/agents that will responsible for the development and promotion of tourism after the Games have taken place.

The Winter Olympic Games in the 21st century

The XIXth Winter Olympic Games, the first of the 21st century, took place in Salt Lake City in the US state of Utah in 2002. The image of these Games had suffered considerably when, at the end of 1988 Swiss IOC member Marc Hodler alleged that some IOC members had taken bribes to vote for Salt Lake City as the 2002 Winter Olympic host city. In the following year, he suggested that Salt Lake City might not be able to fulfill its contract with the IOC to stage the 2002 Games, because the bribery scandal would make it more difficult to raise the finance for the Games. However, following expulsions from the IOC and a wholesale re-organization of the Salt Lake City organizing committee, the 2002 Games went on to be the most financially successful so far, returning a higher profit than any previous Winter Olympics.

Prior to the 2002 Games, Salt Lake City and Utah were very much domestic tourism destinations – of the 17.8 million visitors to Utah in 2000, 96 per cent were US residents (Inter Vistas Consulting, 2002), and Travel Utah's 1,000-day plan reflects this. The plan, seen as long-term, covered the 150 days leading up to the Games and the 850 days after the Games. In doing so, it appears that opportunities to capitalize on the Olympics in the pre-Games period may have been missed as Travel Utah considered that the 'window of opportunity' was only two years. One of the main goals of the 1,000 day plan was to capitalize on the 'awareness bonus' of the Winter Olympics and, whilst trying to improve awareness among Europeans, to focus on the link between Utah's brand values of 'Discovery and Recovery' with Olympic values and memories among the core American market (see discussions on leveraging Olympic media in Chapter 4).

As noted earlier, Salt Lake City had tried to draw on lessons from Calgary in building a strategy for Olympic-related economic development and tourism. In taking this and the experiences of other past Winter Olympics, Travel Utah (2002) discussed the six key lessons that they had drawn from former Olympic hosts:

1. *Context:* Each Games is unique and has its own political, social and economic circumstances which, combined with external events, greatly influence future tourism activity in an Olympic region.

2. *Post-Games Marketing:* Increases in tourism are not a direct function if hosting the Games or of Olympic media – such increases need to be effectively leveraged.

3. *Economic Returns are Uneven:* Tourism growth is most likely in areas directly involved with the Games – outlying areas should consider ways in which they can associate themselves with an Olympic area.

4. *Focus Strategies:* Leveraging strategies are most likely to be successful if they are targeted – holistic approaches can dilute resources and messages.

5. *Sustainable Development:* Normal (i.e., 'without Olympic') growth patterns should guide expectations and development to avoid excess capacity which can destabilize the host region in the post-Games period.

6. *Preserve Networks:* The people and organizations responsible for the presentation of the Games should also be those involved in leveraging the post-Games environment.

Many of these issues have been raised in the first part of the book. The need for non-host regions to create Olympic associations – either through direct linkages with Olympic areas or through, for example, the hosting of training camps (see Chapters 3 and 4), and the need to ensure that those responsible for developing Olympic tourism policy are those who will remain responsible for capitalizing on such tourism development long-after the Games (see Chapter 5) are two such issues. Whilst such lessons largely relate to the longer-term development of tourism, it is useful to look at Travel Utah's (2002) immediate post-Games analysis of the winners and losers in Olympic year (see Table 6.3).

In relation to the impact of Olympic media (see Chapter 4), Travel Utah (2002) estimated that the value of print media that focussed on tourism related themes during the Games was US$22.9 million. This comprised:

- US$22 million – National and syndicated stories

- US$89,100 – Features from Sports Illustrated 'Dailies'

Table 6.3
Winners and losers from the Salt Lake City Winter Games

WINNERS	LOSERS
• Hotels	• Business Services
• Restaurants	• Finance, insurance and real estate
• Retailers (particularly Olympic Vendors and 'Made in Utah' products)	• Ski resorts
	• Transportation
• Olympic Travellers	• Construction
	• Business and Ski Travellers

HOTSPOTS: Olympic Venues, Park City & Downtown Olympic District

EMPTY: Businesses outside Downtown Olympic District

Source: Travel Utah, 2002.

- US$89,800 – USA Today Stories
- US$420,300 – US Daily Newspapers from major markets
- US$367,600 – Southern Utah Stories

Given the Travel Utah strategy of focussing on the USA tourism market, this represents a very useful return. What is not clear, however, from the Travel Utah report, is what leveraging strategies (if any) were employed to generate these stories, and how 'tourism-related themes' are defined. Nevertheless, the generation of US$22.9 million worth of print media alone is a significant achievement given the problems of attempting to get tourism/destination themes into media coverage (Chalip and Leyns, 2002).

A clear feature of Olympic host-cities in the 21st century is a desire to learn from previous hosts, particularly hosts that might have transferable experiences. As noted above, Salt Lake City turned, in particular, to the last North American Winter Games (the Calgary Games of 1988) for assistance in developing its tourism strategy. In this respect, Turin, the host of the XXth Winter Olympic Games in 2006, would appear to have a wealth of previous European hosts from which to seek assistance and advice. However, the previous two European hosts had been regional towns rather than major cities (Albertville, 1992; Lillehammer, 1994) and the previous European host before then was Sarajevo (1984), which was located in the former communist bloc. Consequently, the last even marginally comparable Winter Olympic host to Turin was Innsbruck in 1976, and 30

Table 6.4

Turin 2006 – lessons regarding impact and benefits for tourism

	BIDDING	PRE-GAMES	GAMES	POST-GAMES
INVESTMENTS	Advertising	Infrastructure Media Interest	Visitor services	Promotion and avoiding the 'intermediate effect'
EFFECTS	Image positioning Increase in popularity	Peak in market interest Creating new 'cathedrals' Increase in infrastructures	Customer satisfaction Media publicity Increase in number of tourists	Avoiding drop in occupation Increase in business tourism Long-term image growth
EXAMPLES	Sion 2006 Andorra 2010 Saltzburg 2010 Beijing 2008	Salt Lake City 2002 Sydney 2000	Sydney 2000	Barcelona 1992 Sydney 2000

Source: Turismo Torino, 2004.

years of global economic and sporting development meant that such comparisons were of limited utility. Turin, therefore, had to attempt to apply more recent generic Olympic knowledge to its specific modern European city context. Table 6.4 shows the complex range of lessons that Turismo Torino (2004) had attempted to draw from previous Olympic Games, both summer and winter, in the bidding, pre-Games, Games, and Post-Games periods.

In fact, if there was a 'role model' for Turin, it was the 1992 Summer Games in Barcelona (Bondonio and Campaniello, 2006). Turin, like Barcelona, sought increase its ranking as a tourist destination on the world stage, but also within its own country:

> [Torino] . . . envisions a tourist mecca that would finally marry its historic centre – and all of its elegant cafes and museums – with the rustic Alps. 'When people think about northern Italy, they think Milan,' said Cosmo Perrello, a manager of the Amadeus Hotel, a 26-room local fixture just off the grand Piazza Vittorio Veneto. 'Torino has been a last stop in Italy. It has always been a town of working people. We hope now that it will become a first stop for Italy.' (USA Today, 2006)

Given that Turin, like many other major-city Winter Games, is a two centre Games, with Turin itself only able to host the 'arena' ice events, many venues were located outside the city in the 'Olympic Valleys' at distances of up to 60 miles away. This has generated high costs for transportation, road construction, communications networks and two Olympic Villages in the valleys (Bondonio and Campaniello, 2006), but it has also left an infrastructure that links the Apline areas with the city, and thus allows the city to develop as a gateway for not only winter sports tourism, but also for summer sports such as canoeing, rafting, cycling and hiking, and for general 'lakes and rivers' tourism.

Turismo Torino, unlike Travel Utah (Salt Lake City) which developed only a 1,000 day plan for tourism, considered the tourism impacts of its Winter Olympic Games from bidding to well into the post-Games period. In doing so it considered some of the issues surrounding tourism flows discussed in Chapter 3, noting particularly in the pre-Games period that there was potential to displace and crowd out tourism, and that strategies were needed to address this, both in terms of general tourists, who may have felt that the city would be a 'building site' and business tourism organizes, who may have felt that the Olympic Games would have caused price rises for conferences and meetings (Turismo Torino, 2004). This is reflected in the objectives for the Turin Games as laid out in their Olympic tourism strategy, which covered the pre-Games (2002–2005), Games (2006), and post-Games (2006–2008) periods:

- Avoiding a decrease in the tourist flow in the years preceding the celebration of the Olympic Games

- Projecting the image of a city and an area under transformation that are evolving thanks to the Olympic Games

- Achieving perfect co-ordination to promote both the Turin 2006 Olympic games and Turin before, during, and after the Games

- Promoting the Olympic Games of Turin 2006 so as to create internal support and awareness, attracting the widest audience and the support of the tourist sector.

Among the strategies that Turin employed was an 'Olympic Turin' promotion programme that focussed on generating positive stories about Turin in the non-sports media in the pre-Games period, thus seeking to leverage the image benefits of Olympic media. While the success of this programme does not appear to have been evaluated, it is a clear attempt to move towards the leveraging approach discussed in Chapter 4.

In February 2007, Turismo Torino reported on 'Turin 2006: One Year On' in which they noted that Turin's Olympic facilities have already hosted 20 sports events, including the Winter University Games and the World Fencing Championships (showing that Winter Olympic arenas need not exclusively be used for winter sports) as well as over 40 non-sporting events (rock concerts, exhibitions, etc.). Turismo Torino's estimated figures claim an estimated increase of 100,000 to 150,000 tourists per year to the Olympic area following the Games. Providing for such visitors is a local guidebook, 'Turin, A Local's Guide to the Olympic City', a nice touch in leveraging the post-Games Olympic effect. Organizationally, the *Fondazione XX Marzo Foundation* has been established to run seven of the former Olympic sites and to optimize the legacy of the Games – an indication that Turin recognizes that legacy benefits, like most other Olympic impacts, need to be leveraged.

A leveraging focus is something that has been a key part of Vancouver's preparations for the 2010 Winter Games from the very start of its bid. Eight years before the Games, Inter Vistas Consulting (IVC) were commissioned by British Columbia to report on the economic impacts of hosting the 2010 Winter Olympics in Vancouver, and a central part of this study was a recognition that:

> In order to achieve the higher tourism growth scenarios and capitalise on long-term opportunities, British Columbia's tourism industry will require significant marketing resources and a co-ordinated effort. (IVC, 2002)

Vancouver is fortunate in that it is able to draw on the recent experiences of a Winter Games in the North American Context, namely that in Salt Lake City in 2002. However, like Turin 2006, Vancouver consider that the potential tourism impact of the Games extends beyond the 'two-year window of opportunity' that Salt Lake City sought to capitalize on. The IVC study (2002) for Vancouver 2010 drew up four 'visitation scenarios': low, medium, medium/high and high. In all but the high scenario, pre-Games Olympic tourism was assumed to commence in 2008 and the 'tail' of post-Games tourism was assumed to end in 2015. However, in recognizing that the lessons from Salt Lake City do not 'represent the best outcome that British Columbia can achieve', largely because Salt Lake City's marketing efforts did not commence until five months before the Games, the 'high visitation' scenario assumes that pre-Games Olympic tourism will be induced prior to 2008, but note that this is dependent on pre-Games marketing efforts commencing 7 years in advance of the

Games. Similarly, the 'high visitation' scenario for post-Games tourism includes post-Games tourism through to 2020, but once again this assumes that tourism marketing organizations use the Olympics as part of a long-term growth strategy and, more importantly, that the funds and will exists to develop a marketing programme that has a positive impact on international visitors both before and after the Games. IVC's scenarios for incremental (i.e., additional) economic impact of Games visitors and tourists are:

LOW	CA$ 920 million	(circa US$ 787 million)
MEDIUM	CA$ 1,295 million	(circa US$ 1,108 million)
MEDIUM/HIGH	CA$ 2,228 million	(circa US$ 1,906 million)
HIGH	CA$ 3,145 million	(circa US$ 2,690 million)

In providing a composite estimate of these numbers for the more concentrated two years before and two years after period, Jane Burns, the Director of British Columbia 2010, claimed that there would be approximately 1.1 million additional international (including US and overseas) visitors to British Columbia across 2008–2012. (Burns, 2005). Burns' estimate was given to a USA Senate sub-committee hearing on the potential impact of Vancouver 2010 on Oregon and the Pacific North West. Submissions to these hearings demonstrate that regions around British Columbia (in this case, those in another country) have been considering the range of Olympic tourism products discussed in Chapter 1 and the nature of Olympic tourism flows discussed in Chapter 3. Todd Davidson, the Director of the Oregon Tourism Commission identified four opportunities arising from Vancouver 2012 for Oregon:

1. Acting as a training site for Olympic athletes seeking to acclimatize

2. Reaching out to non-accredited media that attend Olympic Games to generate lifestyle stories

3. Exploring the potential to develop travel packages to bring athletes and spectators through Oregon and to encourage the extension of visits to include time in Oregon

4. Promoting Oregon at Olympic venues to build awareness.

Similarly, Dave Riley, the General Manager of Mount Hood Meadows Ski Resort in Portland, Oregon, but only 75 miles from

Vancouver, noted that a key opportunity for his resort, and for Oregon more generally, would be to capitalize on the numbers of skiers and snowboarders that would be avoiding Vancouver and Whistler during and in the run up to the 2010 Games (see discussions of Olympic tourism flows in Chapter 3). He identifies the key opportunity as 'taking advantage of the displaced visitors who would otherwise have gone to Whistler by developing the amenities on Mount Hood between now and 2010 that are necessary to influence their destination choice' (Riley, 2005).

Planning for Olympic tourism in and around Vancouver appears to be far in advance, in terms of the understanding of the nature of Olympic tourism, of that of previous Winter Games. In particular, the explicit recognition that investment and coordination in terms of tourism marketing are key to leveraging the tourism potential of the Games has been a core part of the planning process even before the Games were awarded to Vancouver. The recognition of this in the IVC study commissioned by British Columbia is a lesson for all future Olympic hosts: '[Tourism] benefits will not materialise automatically. They must be earned by a focussed, adequately funded and skilfully executed marketing programme' (IVC, 2002).

Conclusion

Undoubtedly the Winter Olympic Games differ from their summer counterparts. They are smaller and less costly, although often more costly per resident of the host city/region, but are still a highly significant event in their own right that can bring significant economic and tourism benefits. While academic research on the Winter Games is limited, it appears that the Winter Games of the 21st century are far more strategic in terms of planning and investment than previous editions of the Games.

In terms of Olympic tourism, there is a long history of an association between the Olympic Games and the ski industry, with the early editions of the Games often having a spin-off in terms of promoting the winter sports resorts in which they were staged. In fact, the nature of the Winter Games is such that there is a much more significant 'active' sports tourism legacy (in terms of Sports Participation Tourism and Luxury Sports Tourism – see Chapter 1) than for the summer event where the sports tourism legacy is much more clearly centred on 'passive' or 'vicarious' sports tourism linked to Sports Events tourism. Of course, hosts of both the Winter and Summer Games attempt to leverage Olympic media to generate positive images of themselves as a general tourism destination, and in this respect they both benefit from an association with the Olympic Rings.

CHAPTER **7**

The Games of the XXVII Olympiad in Sydney (2000)

by Graham Brown

Every Olympic Games is different and presents distinctive opportunities for the host country. Two years after winning the bid to stage the 2000 Games, a Standing Committee of the Australian Federal Government predicted that tourism would be one of the biggest beneficiaries of the Sydney Olympics (Industry, Science and Technology, 1995). At the completion of the Games, the significance that had been accorded to tourism was acknowledged by the Director of Marketing for the International Olympic Committee (IOC):

> Tourism has joined sport, culture, and the environment as an important dimension of the Olympic Games. Australia is the first Olympic host nation to take full advantage of the Games to vigorously pursue tourism for the benefit of the whole country. It's something we've never seen take place to this level before, and it's a model that

> we would like to see carried forward to future Olympic Games in Athens and beyond. (Payne, 2000, cited in Brown, 2001)

This chapter will describe some of the elements of the 'model' that made it possible to achieve tourism benefits. It will focus primarily on examining the rationale for, and success of, strategies that were implemented by the Tourism Olympic Forum and by the Australian Tourist Commission (ATC), and as such relates to much of the discussion in Chapter 5. Prior to this discussion, some of the factors that influenced the nature of Olympic tourism in Sydney will be examined.

Olympic tourism in Sydney: a contextual analysis

As indicated by Michael Payne's comment above, tourism planning for the Olympics in Sydney had to be developed without the benefit of prior experience. There were few examples of how tourism had been managed at previous Games. A review by the ATC concluded that the Seoul Olympics in 1998 had left a legacy of new railroads and an upgraded airport but public relations had been oriented internally, to Korea's domestic population, rather than to an audience in the rest of the world. The development of tourism infrastructure and Barcelona's enhanced credibility as an international tourist destination were noted as outcomes of the 2002 Games in the Catalan capital (ATC, 1998). Tourism impacts in Barcelona have been recognized to a greater extent more recently, as certain trends have become more apparent. A review by the Director General of Turisme de Barcelona concluded that the Games 'provided the impulse for Barcelona to become a leader in many respects, but especially in tourism' (Duran, 2005:89). He noted that Barcelona had been named as the best world urban tourism destination in 2001 by Condé Nast Traveller magazine and described the dramatic growth in the number of cruise ships that now called at the port and of product launches, particularly for new car models, that had been held in the city. These developments were attributed to the way Barcelona's image had been positively affected by the Games (Duran, 2005).

In contrast to the benefits gained by Barcelona, an assessment of Atlanta's performance judged that 'the city missed out on a golden opportunity for future tourism. Local attractions suffered substantial down turns in visitors, day trips were non-existent, and regional areas suffered. Neighbouring states took out ads telling people to stay away from Atlanta and the city suffered' (ATC, 1996). These findings served to reinforce what needed to be done in Sydney to ensure different outcomes.

A temporal framework associated with preparations for the Millennium Games required tourism activities to be responsive to the needs of the different phases associated with the event:

- the period of the bid
- the pre-Games period
- the Games period
- the period following the Games

Some businesses and organizations had important roles to play at particular times, linked to a certain phase. For instance, Qantas Airways offered a range of services in support of the bid but did not become the official airline of the Games. For those businesses that supported the bid and continued to be involved through to the Games, their period of involvement lasted at least ten years. During the Games, some businesses had to change the timing of operational practices. For instance, deliveries could only be received by some hotels at particular times due to constraints imposed by the Sydney Organizing Committee for the Olympic Games (SOCOG). Some hotels also found it necessary to reschedule meal times in response to the distinctive pattern of behaviour exhibited by people attending Olympic events.

The intensity of involvement for a business varied throughout the different phases of the Games and was partly determined by the nature of the relationship between the business and the Olympics. This relationship can be categorized according to businesses that were:

- Olympic sponsors
- Contractual suppliers to SOCOG
- Providers of services to Games visitors
- Involved in destination planning and activities that supported the host city

The implications of these relationships were complex and often produced a mix of both positive and negative outcomes for the business. Sponsors such as Ansett Australia (the official airline) were able to take advantage of new business opportunities by networking with other sponsors and to develop the brand through promotional activities linked to the Olympics (Brown, 2000). However, the title of official airline brought with it considerable responsibilities to meet the needs of SOGOG and the International Olympic Committee (IOC) and was accompanied by a high level of risk and uncertainty that impacted on other areas of the airline's activities. Prior to the Games, the airline's Olympics Manager expressed fears that 'whilst Sydney would be very busy with Olympic traffic, there was the potential that the rest of the network would be in real need of help to keep load factors up. People would avoid Sydney and regular international wholesale business may not visit Sydney at all because they could not get hotel rooms' (McLean, 1998).

Businesses under contractual agreements to provide resources such as hotel rooms or buses to SOCOG experienced similar problems and were unable to meet the needs of traditional markets. This placed strains on relationships with key distributors. The Sydney Convention Centre was not available for a considerable period before and during the Games but the resultant loss of business could be set against the increase in forward bookings attributed to the success of the Games. More than 86 events, worth A$530 million, were won by the Sydney Convention and Visitors Bureau (SCVB) for the period from October 2000 until 2005 (Hutchison, 2000).

Throughout this time, many businesses changed their business practices. Some established relationships with new players, such as sports marketing companies who were responsible for organizing sponsor hospitality programs. The Games brought some businesses into contact with government agencies, such as Austrade, for the first time. Unusual collaborative relationships were formed. For instance, some hotels, which were normally in competition, organized staff-sharing arrangements during the Games.

The significance of changes caused by the Games was very often a product of locational characteristics. Thus, in addition to temporal and relationship factors, a spatial dimension was evident (see discussions of stratified geography in Chapters 3 and 4). In this case, the impact on a business was affected by whether it was located in:

- The host city

- The host state, outside Sydney

- Other states in Australia

Within the city, proximity to certain routes and sites that attracted the largest number of Olympic visitors determined the type of impacts that were experienced (Brown, 2001). Some of the impact spread beyond Sydney to other areas of the state of New South Wales (NSW) which were able to host Olympic visitors. However, some areas experienced a decline in tourism demand. The dominance of the Games served to capture the attention and resources of visitors to the detriment of attractions that were effectively competing with the event. This situation was compounded when tour operators were unable to offer their normal services in the absence of buses that had been committed to the Games.

A desire to present the 2000 Olympics as a national event, for the whole of Australia, was contingent upon a sense of engagement by people throughout the country. Thus, strategies to spread tourism benefits were developed. These included attempts to encourage visits by international teams for pre-Games training and to stage events, as celebrations, to coincide with the arrival of the Olympic torch (cf. discussions of London 2012 in Chapter 10). The need for coordinated planning to achieve these objectives was one of the reasons for the formation of the Tourism Olympic Forum and its activities will be discussed in the following section.

The Tourism Olympic Forum

The Tourism Olympic Forum was established in January 1994 by Tourism New South Wales, the government agency responsible for tourism in the host state. It had been recognized that the success of the Games would require coordinated planning across the host city; at locations beyond the event venues for which SOCOG was responsible. In addition to the coordinating role, the Forum sought to maximize the strategic opportunities presented by the Games by working with industry representatives and by making representations to the government on behalf of tourism interests.

The Forum operated until 2000 with the Chief Executive of Tourism New South Wales acting as the Chair throughout this period. Membership, at the invitation of the Chair, mainly comprised of senior representatives of industry associations. Local, state and national interests were represented by the mix of public and private sector organizations (Table 7.1). Meetings were held four times per year. Although membership numbers remained quite stable throughout the life of the Forum, the level of active participation by individual members varied according to the perceived importance of the issues under consideration at different times.

The activities of the Forum could be divided into three periods: 1994–1996, 1997–1999, and 2000. The initial period, between 1994 and 1996, was characterized by activities that reflected the uncertainty that existed at this time. This concerned the likely impact of the Games, the demands that might be placed on tourism facilities and services and the timing of any controls or regulations

Table 7.1
Members of the Tourism Olympic Forum

Government Agencies
  Australian Tourist Commission
  City of Sydney
  Office of National Tourism, Department of Industry, Science and Resources
  Tourism New South Wales

Industry Associations
  Australian Federation of Travel Agents
  Australian Hotels Association
  Australian Tourism Industry Association
  Board of Airline Representatives of Australia
  Bus and Coach Association
  Canberra Tourism and Events Corporation
  Caravan and Camping Industry Association
  Catering Institute of Australia
  Charter Vessel Operators Association
  Council of Tourist Associations
  Federal Airports Corporation
  Hotel, Motel & Accommodation Association
  Inbound Tourism Organization
  Meetings Industry Association
  Motor Inns & Motels Association
  Motor Traders Association
  National Roads and Motorists Association Ltd
  New South Wales Council of Tourist Associations
  New South Wales Special Events Agency
  Outdoor Tour Operators Association
  Pacific Asia Travel Association
  Regional Airlines Association
  Registered Clubs Association
  Restaurant & Catering Association
  Retail Traders Association
  Sydney Airport
  Special Events Ltd
  Sydney Convention & Visitor Bureau
  Taxi Council of NSW
  Tourism Council Australia
  Tourism Task Force
  Tourism Training Australia
  Tourism Attractions Association

Olympic Organizations
  Olympic Co-ordination Authority
  Olympic Media Centre
  Olympic Roads & Transport Authority
  Sydney Organizing Committee for the Olympic Games
  Sydney Paralympic Committee Organizing Committee

that might be introduced to accommodate event-specific planning. Thus, an emphasis was placed on information gathering. This involved a form of network extension by seeking to form relationships with informed decision-makers within government agencies and departments of SOCOG. The need for research was recognized. A specialist library, devoted to Olympic literature, was established and new studies were commissioned. An accommodation needs analysis that was conducted on behalf of the Forum found that 5600 extra hotel rooms would be required in the lead up to the Games. A desire to learn from the experience of other host cities resulted in visits to Barcelona, Nagano and Atlanta by members of the Forum. In each case, information from representatives of the cities' tourism and hospitality industries was sought. The 1996 Games provided the best opportunity to understand the implications of the Olympics for Sydney and three 'missions' to Atlanta were made; before, during and after the Centenary Games.

In the second period, between 1997 and 1999, the emphasis of the Forum shifted more towards planning with a series of issues addressed by sub-committees (Table 7.2). Each sub-committee had a Chair with membership reflecting the particular interests of the Forum's members and the expertise they were able to offer. A strategic framework was developed to plan activities for each of these issues. Examples for *Access* and *Packaging/Distribution* are given in Table 7.3.

The activities of the sub-committees were reviewed at Forum meetings, with work undertaken between the meetings. The inclusion of experts from outside the membership of the Forum who were able to make valuable contributions to the work of the sub-committees was encouraged.

During the final period, in 2000, the work of the sub-committees and the decisions taken at Forum meetings reflected

Table 7.2
Sub-committees of the Tourism Olympic Forum

Branding/Positioning
Media/Publicity
Access
Sponsors
Packaging/Distribution
Visitor Services/Information
Capacity
Service Quality
Regional Dispersion

Table 7.3
Tourism Olympic Forum Strategic Framework

Strategic Issue 3: Access

Rationale

- Easy movement into and around Sydney and New South Wales will leave visitors with a positive impression and promote repeat visitation and word-of-mouth promotion.

- Benefits, including yield, can be increased by assisting visitors to easily access a wide range of places and activities.

Strategic Directions

- Assist/influence transport operators to provide easier access to activities and places attractive to visitors.

- Present tourism needs in key Forums where decisions affecting routing and timing of transport services are determined.

- Work with key public/private transport groups to facilitate integrated tourism transport system for Sydney (with regional linkages).

- Incorporate transport access information into the main visitor information system.

Responsibility

- Bus and Coach Association, Chartered Vessels Association, Retail Traders Association, Sydney City Council, Department of Transport, Federal Airports Corporation, Tourism Task Force, Motor Traders Association.

Strategic Issue 5: Packaging/Distribution

Rationale

- The distribution network is different from source market to source market. Thus, each market requires a tailored approach to packaging and distribution of the Olympic related tourism experience.

- Appropriately structured packages associated with the Olympics are a key mechanism to convert interest in a destination into an actual visit.

Strategic Directions

- Work with the designated National Olympic Committee (NOC) appointed wholesalers to incorporate Sydney/New South Wales into their Olympic packages.

- Explore the wide range of electronic distribution options (e.g., Internet) for travel to Australia associated with the Olympics.

Responsibility

- Inbound Tourism Organization of Australia, Australian Tourist Commission, Pacific Asia Travel Association, Australian Federation of Travel Agents, Tourist Attractions Association.

---

a move away from planning to a greater concern with implementation strategies. Thus, activities under the headings of *Hosting/Welcome* and *Visitor Information* received greater prominence. An example of outcomes associated with the different stages of the work of the Forum is provided by the Media Centre that was built at Darling Point, in Sydney. This was a separate facility to the official Centre for accredited media that was located at Olympic Park. Participants in the Forum's 'missions' to Atlanta returned with a clear understanding of the problems that had been created in the absence of facilities and services that met the needs of the non-accredited media. Subsequent, planning for the Media Centre formed part of the work undertaken by the Forum's Media sub-committee which also sought the necessary funding to build the Centre from State and Federal agencies and from Olympic sponsors. During the Games, tourism information and tours were offered by members of the Forum to journalists using the Centre. This was designed to support the preparation of news items and stories that were consistent with tourism objectives (see discussions on leveraging Olympic media in Chapter 4).

In reviewing the role of the Forum, two features are particularly noteworthy; the importance of communication and the complexity of network development. The quarterly Forum meetings provided the main vehicle for members to share information and to develop comprehensive, integrated strategies for the tourism industry. Reports of specific projects undertaken by the sub-committees were given at the Forum meetings. Information was also presented by senior managers of SOCOG and by Forum members who were also members of other important planning committees. This provided a vital way of disseminating information about policies of critical importance to the tourism industry such as changes to airport procedures, the timing of road closures and security policies at hotels. As representatives of industry associations, Forum members reported relevant information, gained at the meetings, to their respective membership, making it possible for individual businesses to respond accordingly. In addition to these information flows, conferences were organized by the Forum, annually, from 1996 to 1999. The popularity of the conferences made it possible to communicate information about particular themes, reflecting the state of tourism preparations, to large numbers of people. Each of the conferences attracted approximately 600 delegates from around Australia. In 1996, information gathered during the 'missions' to Atlanta was presented under the conference title of *Lessons from Atlanta*. Subsequent titles, such as *Sharing the Knowledge* and *Getting Down to Business* illustrated the conference rationales.

The Forum is consistent with a partnership that was formed to address tourism issues associated with the 2000 Olympics however, its work can be analysed as a series of network relationships. These included participation in interdepartmental committees of the state government and a special Olympic planning committee of the Federal government that reported directly to the Prime Minister. Close links with SOCOG provided access to the 'Olympic Family' including members of the IOC, National Olympic Committees, Olympic sponsors and accredited Media organizations. Some of the relationships were formalized and a partnership was formed between Visa, an Olympic sponsor, and three Forum members (Tourism NSW, the ATC and the Sydney Visitor and Convention Bureau). Resources were invested by Visa to support a destination promotion campaign under the banner of 'Australia prefers Visa'.

The ATC was a key member of the Forum and was a central player in many of its most important activities (see discussions on policy legacies in Chapter 5). It also had distinctive responsibilities as the tourism agency responsible for marketing Australia as a tourist destination. Activities related to this role will now be discussed.

The Australian Tourist Commission

The marketing strategies of the ATC focused on:

- Identifying markets which have the greatest potential for delivering high yield arrivals to Australia.

- Generating tourism arrivals by raising international consumer awareness and interest in Australian destinations and tourism product.

- Dispersing tourism arrivals by providing information on diverse destinations within Australia. (ATC, 1998).

The Olympic Games were seen to offer extraordinary leverage opportunities with the level of international media interest making it possible to position Australia as a dynamic, sophisticated, technologically advanced country. The challenge was to create a strong association between the ATC's *Brand Australia*, that had been launched in 1995, and brands associated with the Olympics (Brown et al., 2004).

A specialist Olympic Business Unit was established at the ATC in 1995 and a four year Olympic strategy was launched in 1996 (Table 7.4). This was supported by A$12 million in additional funding from the Federal government. Work was conducted in

Table 7.4
Australian Tourist Commission Olympic Strategies

1. Maximize destination and product promotion for Australia by offering media relations services and resources to a greatly expanded media clientele.

2. Increase the ATC's capacity to handle media sponsored to Australia under the Visiting Journalist Program (VJP).

3. Protect the Australian tourism industry from the ill effect of a global media crisis by maintaining a highly effective media relations capacity.

4. Promote brand Australia in association with the XXVII Olympiad and related partners.

5. Service all Olympic related markets with destination information.

6. Encourage the establishment of a National Visitors Centre in Sydney and a National Telephone Enquiry Service.

7. Increase high-yield markets resulting from Olympic-related activities, such as MICE, promoting to a wider target audience of associations, exhibition organizers and corporations.

8. Create trade marketing programs for the industry to capitalize in the Olympic opportunities.

9. Identify and access Olympic opportunities through research which will enhance promotional support for consumer marketing programs.

10. Capitalize on tourism findings from previous host destinations of Olympic Games and hallmark events.

11. Build the ATC's profile with corporate Australia and government bodies through the Olympic and Paralympic Games.

12. Reinforce the ATC's position as the peak body responsible for Australia's international tourism marketing.

(ATC, 1998)

conjunction with traditional partners such as the state tourist commissions and industry associations but approaches were also received from Australian government departments and corporations which had demonstrated little interest in tourism prior to the Games.

Strategic alliances were formed with players that were new to the tourism industry in Australia such as the broadcast rights holders, Olympic sponsors and the sports marketing companies that managed the Sponsor's hospitality programs. These alliances greatly enhanced the ATC's ability to influence and participate in destination promotion activities. An internet site that was established by the ATC in 1996 made it possible for users to customize information about Australia as a holiday destination for the first time. It also provided links to web sites of the Commission's growing list of Olympic partners. Established distribution channels remained important with Olympic-specific information supplied by *Aussie Specialist* travel agencies and by the telephone *Helplines* that were operated by the ATC's main overseas offices. The vast majority of the ATC's projects were conducted in the period leading up to the Games but certain initiatives were necessary during the Games and a post-Games strategy sought to convert the heightened level of interest in Australia into visitor arrivals.

Marketing partnerships with Olympic sponsors such Visa International, Kodak and McDonalds resulted in an estimated additional A$300 million in advertising exposure (ATC, 2001). Examples of these partnerships included Visa billboards that showcased Australian images on Shanghai's Bund boulevard and a *Down Under Tour* roadshow in conjunction with US Olympic sponsor, Bank of America. This was a travelling exhibit of Australian attractions that visited 48 cities in the United States.

The ATC's Olympic media strategy generated A$3.8 billion in publicity between 1997 and 2000 (ATC, 2001). This included hosting more than 5000 international journalists through the Visiting Journalist Program, providing services for another 5000 non-accredited media at the Darling Point Media Centre and responding to more than 50,000 international media enquiries. The ATC provided story leads, production assistance and sound and vision resources at locations throughout Australia. This was designed to encourage media visits to dispersed locations, away from the host city. A particularly notable relationship was developed with the broadcast rights holder in the United States, when the ATC worked with NBC to develop a television advertisement in 1997. It was titled 'Colours of Australia' and was shown, without cost to the ATC, during coverage of major sport events that attracted large television audiences such as the Superbowl. The ATC also provided support for NBC's *Today Show* that was broadcast live from Australia for two weeks. The show gained some of the highest ratings in its 49-year history (ATC, 2001).

During 2000, there was concern that many visitors would avoid Australia due to uncertainties caused by the Games. Thus, the *Australia 2000 – fun and games* promotion was launched to communicate the message that it 'was business as usual' in Australia. Information about special packages was provided and a web site was developed for the international travel trade that gave information about flights and accommodation availability, the torch relay and some other, timely, issues such Y2K and taxation changes in Australia. The ATC invited 50 of its most important business partners, from eleven countries, to attend Olympic events. The hospitality was used to retain the good-will of people who had been negatively affected by the disruptive influence of the Games on their normal pattern of business activities.

The opportunity to take advantage of the positive publicity generated by the Games led to a post-Games strategy. This included tactical advertising, promoting special packages, in the six months following the Games. For example, a price-led, joint campaign with Qantas was aired on national television in the United States. It was supported by press advertising and generated more than 100,000 responses. Additional activities included a A$6 million direct marketing campaign and a number of initiatives focussed on further developing the lucrative MICE sector. The extensive list of initiatives by the ATC gave rise to the claim that:

> Since winning the Games bid, the ATC has worked tire-lessly to ensure that every possible opportunity from hosting the Games was maximised. Well over 1,000 individual projects were implemented to ensure that at the end of the 2000 Olympic Games, when Australia had a permanent seat on the world stage, the tourism industry would be the one to reap the benefits. (ATC, 2001:1)

The impact of the Sydney games

Accurate measures of the impact of the Sydney Olympic Games on tourism are not available as little research to specifically examine this issue has been conducted. As is the case with most major events, considerable effort was spent to gain support for and to justify the bid and to ensure that the event could be staged successfully. However, impact analysis received less attention as people with relevant knowledge move on to work on the next event. In contrast, considerable research informed the planning stages. In fact, there was evidence of duplication. For instance, studies to estimate visitor numbers and traffic flows were conducted independently by SOCOG, the Olympic Road and Transport Authority (ORTA), the Sydney Airport Authority, Ansett Australia and others. The objectives, in each case, varied slightly but the research agenda could have been more effectively coordinated. Timing issues, inter-agency rivalry and confidentiality seemed to work against achieving this objective. Some of the findings from these studies were reported at meetings of the Tourism Olympic Forum and without the Forum acting as a vehicle to communicate and disseminate information the situation would have been worse.

The complexity of the event meant that subtle differences in relationships had considerable implications for tourism. For instance, companies organizing hospitality programs for corporations that were not Olympic sponsors were more likely to include tourism components in their Games packages. This was because they did not have direct access to tickets for Olympic events nor to venues in the city controlled by SOCOG. This provided an opportunity for tourism organizations but it was also harder to identify these groups as they did not attend the hospitality workshops organized by SOCOG.

Research was conducted by the ATC to track awareness of the Olympics in overseas markets and to monitor community attitudes towards the Games in Australia. In 1999, the highest level of awareness about the Games was recorded in New Zealand (92%) followed by China (75%), Korea (71%), Germany (70%) and England (58%). Significant increases in awareness had occurred between 1998 and 1999 in Korea (from 47% to 71%), Malaysia (from 34% to 43%), Taiwan (from 28% to 38%) and England (from 38% to 58%). Nearly half of potential travellers in India (45%) were found to be more likely to consider going to Australia as a result of the Games. The likelihood in China and Malaysia had increased between 1998 and 1999; from 30 per cent to 37 per cent and from 33 per cent to 41 per cent, respectively. Between 1998 and 2000 there was a steady increase in the perception of the host population that the Olympics would boost the image of Australia (1998:25%, 1999:27%, and 2000:29%). However, there had also been a fall in the perception that the Games would bring economic benefits to the country (from 25% in 1998 to 19% in 2000) (ATC, 2000).

Data from the Australian Bureau of Statistics reveals that there was a 15 per cent increase in the number of international arrivals to Australia in September 2000, the month of the Games, compared to the previous year with changes from markets closely associated with the Olympics being particularly noticeable. The number of tourists from the USA nearly doubled. Within the city, locations that housed 'Live Sites', such as Darling Harbour, were crowded throughout the Games and retail sales for businesses in the Harbourside complex increased considerably. This contrasted with the situation in regional areas of Australia where a 10 per cent–15 per cent decrease in normal visitation levels was recorded (Brown, 2001).

Indications immediately after the Games suggested that Australia would gain the anticipated tourism benefits. There was 9.7 per cent increase in visitor arrivals in October 2000 compared to October 1999 and tour operators throughout Europe and North America were reporting unprecedented interest in and bookings to Australia (Brown, 2001). A record 565,700 international visitors arrived in December 2000, a 23 per cent increase on 1999; the highest number ever for a single month (ATC, 2001). These increases helped arrivals for the year 2000 to reach a record 4.9 million but everything changed in 2001. The combined impact on demand from the terrorist attacks in New York in September 2001, the outbreak of severe acute respiratory syndrome (SARS) in Asia and the collapse of Ansett Australia meant that visitor numbers to Australia declined for the next two years. This was the first time this had happened in Australia.

Even an event on the scale of the Olympics that is accompanied by a comprehensive tourism promotional strategy is clearly insufficient to counter the magnitude of change imposed by international crises. Visitor numbers to Australia have increased since 2003 but it is now impossible to determine the role played by any residual Olympic effect. This is disappointing but it does not minimize the lessons that are offered to other host countries by the strategies developed by the tourism industry in Australia that sought to maximize the benefits offered by the Sydney Olympic Games.

The Games of the XXVIII Olympiad in Athens (2004)

The story of the Summer Olympics in Athens in 2004 begins with the 1996 Summer Games in Atlanta and then goes back in time to over 100 years ago, and then to up to 3000 years ago, before returning to the current era for the Games of the XXVIII Olympiad in Athens. The Greeks, of course, have a special place in Olympic history and heritage, having been the hosts of the first 'modern' Olympic Games in 1896, and having given the name to the event which is traced back to the 'Ancient Games' held in Olympia.

Within this context, the city of Athens had bid for the 1996 Olympic Games, the celebration of the Centenary of the modern Olympic Movement. All of Greece and most of the world believed that the 1996 Centenary Games would return to Athens. On 18th September 1990, in Tokyo, the then President of the International Olympic Committee, Juan Antonio Samaranch announced the host for the Centenary Games: 'The International Olympic Committee has awarded the 1996 Olympic Games to Ath . . . '. Unfortunately, as a Spaniard, Samaranch speaks English with a slight lisp, and so while cheers made their way from hearts to mouths in Athens, Samaranch completed the sentence: 'Ath-lanta'.

As Athens got over the disappointment and prepared to launch its bid for the 2004 Olympic Games following the Atlanta Games in late 1996, Ian Thomsen of the *International Herald and Tribune* had noted that 'These days the International Olympic Committee is not only the protector of the Olympic ideal, it is also the world's greatest tour operator' and as such, the IOC's view of the Athens 1996 bid had been: 'Never mind the Acropolis. Tell us about the buses, the computers, how many hotels have you got and what is everybody going to do during their spare time'. The IOC felt that the 1996 bid had relied too much on history and had failed to pay attention to the detail of the bid. The mistake of the bid for Athens 1996 had been the belief that the IOC 'had to reward the founders of the Games; they had a moral obligation to Greece' (Poulios, 2006). The Greek president, Costis Stephanopoulos, still felt this was the case as the bid for Athens 2004 was being constructed, stating in November 1996 that:

> No other city awaits with such impatience the IOC's decision than Athens. However, I express my bitterness over losing the 'Golden 1996 Olympics'. I believe that in case our country does not win these Olympic Games, it should never again submit its candidacy.

This was, of course, not a particularly subtle or well advised statement, but many had sympathy with Greece and Athens as the Olympics are a key part of Greek culture going back up to 3000 years.

The Ancient Olympic Games

The Ancient Olympic Games are cited as the earliest documented example of sports-related travel by a number of authors across the last 35 years (Baker, 1982; Davies, 1997; Finley and Pleket, 1976; Standeven and De Knop, 1999; Van Dalen and Bennett, 1971; Weed and Bull, 2004). Traditionally, the date of the first Games is held to be 776 BC (Golden, 1998), but Crowther (2001) suggests that spectators were common at the Ancient Olympics at the turn of the eighth century BC when wells were first dug to cater for the drinking needs of increasing numbers of spectators. As has been widely documented, the Games at Olympia were not unique, but they were the largest of a number of festivals/sports events in Greek cities that included the Pythian Games, held in Delphi, the Nemean Games, held in Nemea, and the Isthmian Games held in Corinth, which have come to be known collectively as the Panhellenic Games. In addition, the Panatheniac Games were held every four years in Athens as a part of an annual religious festival, the *Panathenia*, which became the *Great Panathenia* every four years when the Games were also held. The Panatheniac Games included a torch race that is sometimes quoted as being the origin of the modern Olympic Torch Relay.

However, as the largest and most important of these ancient Greek festivals, it was the Games at Olympia that gave their name to the modern Games, and there are some analogies with the modern event in the 21st century. For example, infrastructure was built and updated to facilitate travel to the Games:

> the festival at Olympia with its influx of visitors only occurred once in four years. Hence it is conjectured that roads and bridges, for example, were repaired for the festival and buildings at the site, such as stables for horses, renewed or replaced. The hippodrome, including the famous *aphesis* or starting gate, would have to be reconstructed although part of it may have been stored away for future use. (Crowther, 2001:40)

As today, people were prepared to travel significant distances to attend the Games. Olympia is 320 km from Athens and Crowther (2001) suggests that the surviving sources that refer to these journeys (Xenophon *Memerobilia* 3.13.5) imply that the journey took five or six days by foot. Taken with the five or six days of the event, this would mean a total trip time of two to three weeks. Of course, for those travelling from outside mainland Greece, sea travel was necessary, and the journey consequently longer. As a result, the Ancient Olympic Games were the only Panhellenic Games to offer a pre-Games training period (another analogy for 21st century Olympic tourism) that was perceived as being important not only for athletes:

> Like athletes, horses would have needed to acclimatise if they were to perform well. The one-month pre-Games training period at Olympia would help athletes recover from a long journey and increase standards. (Crowther, 2001:41)

The physical dangers of travelling, by a range of methods, to the site at Olympia led to the instigation of the famous Olympic Truce, which lasted for at least three months, one and a half months either side of the Games (Finley and Pleket, 1976). Crowther (2001) claims that the truce appeared to have been largely effective, although it was not just during the journey to the Games that hardship and hazards presented themselves. Sources from ancient times refer to confined spaces, tents, huts, choking heat and poor bathing facilities. Furthermore, both spectators and athletes at the Games were controlled with whips by brutal officials (Harris, 1964). Why, then, did people travel to the Games? For some it appears to have been for the aesthetic ideal of 'manly perfection, physical beauty, wonderful condition, mighty skill, irresistible strength, daring, rivalry, indomitable resolution and an inexpressible ardour for victory' (Weiler, 1997), for others it was for the 'remarkable spectacle' (Crowther, 2001). In later Roman times, the Games were part of an educative touristic experience (Casson, 1974) and (another analogy for 21st century Games) some travelled for trading opportunities (Crowther, 2001). It was this Olympic heritage that led the Greeks to believe that the 1996 Centenary Games 'belonged' to Greece, as had the first modern Olympic Games in 1896.

The revival of the Ancient Olympics and the Greek contribution to the modern olympic movement

The revival of the Ancient Olympic Games for modern times was less to do with the values attached to Greek athleticism and spectacle, and more related to the admiration of a French aristocrat, Pierre De Coubertin, for the values that sport could instill in young people through what he considered to be a proper physical education as he had observed in British public schools in the late 19th century (Muller, 2000). When De Coubertin arranged the Sorbonne Congress to establish an International Olympic Committee in 1894, his intention was that the first modern Games should take place alongside the World Fair in Paris in 1900 – an early indication of the links between the modern Olympics and both tourism and trade/commerce. However, the congress felt that six years would be too long before the first Games. Initially, a number of delegates suggested London as a potential host before the congress settled on Athens for the Games of the I Olympiad in 1896, and this cemented the link between the ancient and modern Olympic events.

The 1896 Games took place over a 10 day period in the Panatheniac stadium, which had hosted the ancient Panatheniac Games, and included nine sports. However, the influence of the Greeks and Athens on the modern Olympics does not end there. Following the success of the 1896 Games, the Greeks suggested that the Games should be located permanently in Greece and arranged every four years. There was some support for this as the stadium and accommodation was already in place, as was the organizational knowledge (things that have been important considerations in the awarding of Olympic Games in recent times). However, De Coubertin was determined that the 1900 Games would be in Paris alongside the World Fair, and the IOC agreed that this should be the case. Following the 1900 Games, which many had felt had been overshadowed by the World Fair, the IOC suggested a compromise in which a second set of quadrennial Games, held in between the Olympic Games, could be permanently held in Greece. As this suggestion was made in 1901, the Greeks felt that it was too late to organize an event in 1902, but what have since come to be known as the Intercalated Games were held in Athens in 1906, two years after the St Louis Olympics of 1904. The Intercalated Games were important in providing the Olympic Movement with many of the features that characterize the Olympic Games today. Following the disappointment of the 1900 and 1904 Games, both of which had been held over a period of months alongside World Fairs, the 1906 Intercalated Games demonstrated the benefits of holding the Games over a shorter period (in this case, 11 days), and as a spectacle in their own right rather than under the shadow of a Trade Fair. Although it quickly became obvious that a Games every two years was unsustainable, and the 1906 Games were the only Intercalated event, without the Games in Athens in 1906 it is possible that the Olympics may not have survived. Rome, which was due to host the Games in 1908 until Mount Vesuvius erupted and drew funds away from the venture in 1906, was also planning a Trade Fair, and many Europeans had been unable to make the long trip to North America for the St Louis Games. As such, the 1906 Games were an important event for the Olympic Movement.

The 1906 Athens Games were successful as a spectacle and contained, for the first time, opening and closing ceremonies as separate events in their own right, flags being raised for victorious athletes, and athletes participating as part of national teams rather than as individuals. As such, the Athens Games of 1906 may have rescued the Olympic Movement and gone some way to establishing the Games as the spectacle that they had been in ancient times. By the time London had stepped in (following Rome's withdrawal) to host the official Summer Olympics in 1908, national teams, opening and closing ceremonies in which athletes paraded behind national flags, and victory ceremonies at which national flags were raised were established as a central part of the Olympic programme, and the Games as an event with which entire nations could engage were begun.

The Greeks contribution to the modern Olympics was finally recognized with the awarding of the 2004 Games to the city of Athens on 5th September 1997. For some in the IOC, awarding the Games to Athens was seen as a salvation following the 'overwhelming commercialisation, heavy traffic congestion, and the bombing of the Centennial Olympic Park' at the Atlanta Games in 1996 (Poulios, 2006:18), and as such some parallels could be drawn with the role the Intercalated Games had played almost a century earlier. The Athens bid for 2004 still rooted the Games in their historical context, but also told a more convincing story of the organizational abilities and infrastructure projects that would underpin the Games, as well as the contribution that the Games would make to the Greek economy and to tourism.

The Greek tourism product

In 1993, *The Economist* noted that tourism is one of the few activities through which Greece could achieve competitive advantages through the redistribution of labour within Europe. Tourism is a major contributor to the balance of payments in Greece, with the Greek National Tourism Organization suggesting that its contribution to GDP was around 7 per cent in 2000, the start of the XXVIIIth Olympiad. However, Buhalis (2001) claims that tourism is of greater economic significance than official figures suggest because such figures do not account for economic activity in the 'para-economy' (the parallel or black economy), of which a range of tourism activities, such as the transfer and re-export of currency which is not processed through the Greek economic system, are part.

The problems for Greek tourism are provided by its inefficient and, at peak times, inadequate infrastructure, with telecommunications, transportation, police and health services, water supply and sewage systems all struggling to cope with the peak demand of the summer months (Buhalis, 2001). This, in itself, is derived from another major issue for tourism in Greece, its highly seasonal nature, which is further derived from the beach based nature of the majority of the product. Buhalis (2001) presented a SWOT analysis of Greek tourism based on strategic management research undertaken for Small and Medium Tourism Enterprises in the Aegean Islands (Buhalis, 1991; Cooper and Buhalis, 1992), and this is shown in Table 8.1.

While the strengths of the Greek tourism product were linked to friendliness, loyalty and personalization, its weaknesses

Table 8.1
SWOT analysis of Greek tourism in 2001

STRENGTHS	WEAKNESSES
• Flexibility	• Management
• Tailor-made product delivery	• Marketing
• Entrepreneurial activity	• Information technologies illiteracy
• Family involvement	• Dependence upon tour operators
• Natural and cultural resources	• Supporting markets
• Strong local character	• Lack of economies of scale
• Personalized relationships	• Human resources management
• Labour loyalty and low turnover	• Education and training
	• Transport and accessibility
	• Financial management and resources
	• Seasonality
	• Lack of standardization
	• Lack of quality assurances
OPPORTUNITIES	**THREATS**
• European Union support	• Environmental degradation
• European redistribution of labour	• Concentration and globalization
• Increase in tourism demand size	• Oversupply
• Trends in tourism demand	• Lack of visibility in Computerized Reservations Systems
• Low cost of living in periphery	• Infrastructure
• Information technology	• Wars/terrorism
• Infrastructure development	• Political intervention
• Transportation	
• Olympic Games	

Source: Buhalis, 2001.

revolve around issues related to quality and infrastructure, and a dependence on European tour operators that make little contribution to the Greek economy. Opportunities, unsurprisingly, relate to addressing these weaknesses, whilst many of the threats relate to the failure to do so. Somewhat prophetically, terrorism was identified as a threat in 2001 before the attack on the World Trade Centre in September. And, of course, the Olympic Games was identified as one of the key opportunities.

Early hopes for the 2004 Athens Olympic Games and tourism

The Greek authorities had originally hoped to employ a private sector model for the Games, with Athens 2004 SA, the company established to manage the infrastructure needs of the Games, seeking to establish private partnership funding for construction projects (Business File, 2004). However, contractors were not forthcoming and it was accepted that the state would have to take on the major burden of funding the requirements for the Games. Poulios (2006) claims that this was inevitable, noting that a country such as Greece with minimal economic power, would inevitably have to base the funding of the Games on public sources. However, although the Games may not have been viewed as a financial success, Poulios (2006:19) notes that the Games were an unparalleled opportunity for Greece to significantly develop the infrastructure of the capital city which, it was hoped, would have long-term benefits for the economy and the tourism industry.

Five years before the Athens Games, Papanikos (1999) estimated three tourism scenarios for additional arrivals as a result of the Games. This comprises 'Games-related' arrivals (i.e., IOC delegations, officials, athletes, teams, etc.) and 'Induced' arrivals (i.e., additional tourists to Greece as a result of hosting the Games). While the basis for these estimations are not particularly clear, and the factors that would lead to one of them being more likely not explicitly stated, the scenarios are presented here in Table 8.2 (pp. 162–163).

The first scenario was presented as the most pessimistic and 'less likely to happen' (Papanikos, 1999). However, it was noted that global political or economic instability, or a failure to leverage the Games (see Chapter 4), could lead to this rather low estimate, where the average yearly impact of the Games between 1998 and 2011 would be 90,000 visitors. In this respect, the World Trade Tower bombings on 11th September 2001, and the somewhat *lassiez faire* approach to planning for Olympic tourism in Athens and Greece, might be taken as set of conditions that might have resulted in the fulfilment of this scenario.

Scenario's 2 and 3 both exceed considerably the estimations in scenario 1, and are much closer in their total predictions. However, they represent very different assumptions about the distribution of Olympic tourism during the 14 year period under consideration. Scenario 2 assumes a smooth growth in additional visitor numbers from 1 per cent of the 'without-the-games-case' estimate in 1998 to 5 per cent during the four years surrounding the Games (2002–2005), with a smooth reduction back to 1 per cent in 2011. Conversely, scenario 3 assumes a very small effect (up to 1% of 'without-case') in all years except the four years

2003–2006, when additional arrivals are assumed to jump to 10 per cent of the 'without-case'. The problem with these estimations is that Papanikos (1999) does not discuss the conditions which might result in the various scenarios, or the assumptions that underpin them, and as such it is all but impossible to judge which might be likely in which situations. It is stated that scenario 3 'matches Barcelona's historical evidence', but this scenario does not reflect Barcelona's experience of a lasting growth as a tourism destination that remains today, 15 years after the Games were hosted. In fact, none of the scenarios allow for a lasting growth as they all assume a reduction in additional arrivals to 1 per cent or less of the 'without-the-Games-case' by 2011. What these estimates do show, however, is a general assumption that the Athens Games would be positive for the Greek tourism industry.

It is not just in terms of visitor numbers that the Athens Games were expected to have an impact. Buhalis (2001:454), in providing a strategic analysis and assessment of challenges for tourism in Greece, noted that the 2004 Games provided opportunities to develop the Greek tourism product:

> The Olympic Games in 2004 provide a unique challenge and opportunity for the city and the country to rebrand and redevelop itself and demonstrate its unparalleled heritage and cultural resources. The Games also provide the resources and funding as well as a 'deadline' for several infrastructural projects that were already scheduled but perhaps delayed. In addition, several projects are anticipated to improve the superstructure of the industry through both renovation of existing properties and through the development of new hotels and other facilities. It is anticipated that the regeneration of the city and the country in general will provide major opportunities for the attractiveness and competitiveness of the tourism industry.

In fact, the 2004 Games were seen as an opportunity to upgrade the Greek tourism product, and to diversify beyond its traditional sun, sea and sand tourism. In 2003, the Greek Minister of Culture, Evangelos Venizelos noted that:

> Until now Greece has followed a tourism model very similar to Spain's. Our goal is to bring our model closer to the Italian one: not only a resort-based summer holiday tourism but also urban tourism with an important cultural impact.

161

Table 8.2
Scenarios of the impact of Athens 2004 on Greece international arrivals (1998–2011)

Year	Games-related arrivals (constant for each scenario)	SCENARIO 1		SCENARIO 2		SCENARIO 3	
		Induced arrivals: Number (percentage of "without-Games" estimate)	Total number of additional arrivals	Induced arrivals: Number (percentage of "without-Games" estimate)	Total number of additional arrivals	Induced arrivals: Number (percentage of "without-Games" estimate)	Total number of additional arrivals
1998	500	1,426 (0.1%)	1,926	114,619 (1%)	115,119	114,619 (1%)	115,119
1999	1,000	12,312 (0.1%)	13,312	246,238 (2%)	247,238	123,119 (1%)	124,119
2000	1,500	12,991 (0.1%)	14,491	389,736 (3%)	391,236	129,912 (1%)	131,412
2001	3,000	128,003 (1%)	131,003	512,012 (4%)	515,012	128,003 (1%)	131,003
2002	6,000	135,416 (1%)	141,416	677,078 (5%)	683,078	135,416 (1%)	141,416
2003	12,000	136,251 (1%)	148,251	681,256 (5%)	693,256	1,362,513 (10%)	1,374,513
2004	87,000	144,075 (1%)	231,075	720,375 (5%)	807,375	1,440,750 (10%)	1,527,750

2005	0	150,868 (1%)	150,868	754,339 (5%)	754,339	1,508,678 (10%)	1,508,678
2006	0	148,959 (1%)	148,959	595,835 (4%)	595,835	1,489,589 (10%)	1,489,589
2007	0	156,371 (1%)	156,371	469,114 (3%)	469,114	156,371 (1%)	156,371
2008	0	157,207 (1%)	157,207	314,414 (2%)	314,414	157,207 (1%)	157,207
2009	0	16,503 (0.1%)	16,503	330,061 (2%)	330,061	16,503 (0.1%)	16,503
2010	0	17,182 (0.1%)	17,182	171,823 (1%)	171,823	17,182 (0.1%)	17,182
2011	0	16,991 (0.1%)	16,991	169,914 (1%)	169,914	16,991 (0.1%)	16,991
TOTALS	111,000	1,244,592	1,355,592	6,146,818	6,257,818	6,796,854	6,907,854

Source: Papanikos, 1999.

163

A year later in the run up to the Games, the Alternate Minister of Culture, Fani Palli-Petralia expressed the country's desire to use the Games to present a contemporary image of a country with a modern infrastructure that 'is creating investment ideas and constantly progressing'. A key goal for Athens was to 'link ancient with modern' in promoting the country's heritage but also presenting an image of a modern city and country that is socially, politically, and economically capable of staging one of the world's largest events. The country's position as the birth-place of the Games, in both the ancient and modern era, provided Athens with an ideal opportunity to link history and heritage with modern capabilities, and this was a central aspiration for the 2004 Games.

Chapter 6 on the Winter Olympic Games noted that modern Winter Games host cities have shown a desire to learn from pre-vious hosts, and the organizers of the Athens Games expressed a desire to follow the Barcelona model which focussed on urban development (Poulios, 2006). However, Beriatos and Gospodini (2004) claim that the Athens approach was very different to that used in Barcelona, and that it lacked focus in terms of a coherent urban development strategy (see later discussions). In fact, there were a number of worries among local businesses and policy-makers not only about the escalating costs of the Games (not an unusual thing for Olympic host cities), but also about the lack of planning. In 2002, Sports Business carried an interview with the President of the Athens Hotel Owners Association, Sypros Divanis, who claimed that while local hotel owners had invested over 500 million Euros ($437 m) in modernizing and expanding hotels, they were being let down by the government which had failed to produce a plan for tourism linked to the Games. Divanis claimed that:

> The Olympics are the most positive event that could happen to the Greek tourism industry, but while there's over-activity on the part of the hotel community, the state ... seeks sloppy solutions which will not offer the infrastructure needed.

One such 'sloppy solution', proposed by the head of the organiz-ing committee, Gianna Angelopoulos, was to accommodate visi-tors on islands or other tourist hotspots and to watch events on day trips to Athens. The lack of tourism planning for the Games was further highlighted in 2003, when the formal co-operation agreement between ATHOC (the Athens 2004 organizing com-mittee), the government and private enterprises was launched. At the launch, in August 2003, it was claimed that the focus needed to be on the development of business and tourism after, rather than during or before, the Athens 2004 Games (Yannopoulos, 2003). However, this approached was severely criticized by George Drakopoulos, Managing Director of the Greek Association of Tourism Enterprises (SETE), who stated:

> Tourism is the principal sector where the economic bene-fits from hosting the Olympics are obvious, even to a child. And yet, neither the government nor EOT [the National Tourism Organisation] have done anything all these years to formulate a marketing strategy that would make the Olympic the pole of attraction for millions of foreign visitors to Greece. Let's face it, we have forsaken the chance to make the Olympic theme the linchpin of our tourist publicity drive prior to the Games. Let's at least hope that its not too late to plan our steps to reap the benefits after the Games.

However, despite the claims of those launching the co-operation agreement, and the hopes of the Managing Director of SETE, four years later in early 2007, Haris Coccossis, the Executive Secretary of Tourism in the Greek Ministry of Tourism Development (which was only established in 2004), admitted that there was a need 'to plan carefully the post-Olympics use of facilties and include such considerations in a strategy for the development of tourism, something we missed in the past in Athens' (Ecoclub, 2007). Somewhat frustratingly for Athens and Greece, it was clear some years before the 2004 Games that detailed planning would be required to realize potential benefits (see Chapters 4 and 5). In 2000, the Greek Chamber of Commerce noted that:

> How much benefit [the 2004 Games] will bring will depend on the degree of seriousness on the part of the organisers and on the professionalism shown in the administration of the event, in order to ensure that long-term benefits can be derived from the profit, structural development and acquired technical expertise resulting from the Games. (Trade with Greece, 2000)

What, then, led to the lack of planning to leverage Olympic tourism for Athens 2004. Some of those associated with the organization of the Games would point to the diversion that was created by the attack on the World Trade Centre in 2001, and the ever increasing security fears for the Athens Games. For Sydney in 2000, US$200 million was spent on security, whereas Athens was forced to cancel some of the finishing construction touches, like the roof on the swimming pool (!), to release funds for the US$1.2 billion security budget (Knowledge@Wharton, 2004) to 'protect against every eventuality from assassinations to bombings to chemical – and even radiological – attacks' (Business File, 2004). While the organizers might have resented the circumstances that led to the need for this budget, there were plaudits to be taken in the wake of the Games, with the IOC President Jacques Rogge, with a nod towards the criticisms of Athens in the run up to the Games, declaring at the Closing Ceremony: 'Dear Greek friends, you have won! The 2004 Games were the unforgettable Games, the dream Games'. However, as Ritchie (1999) noted in his advice to the organizers of the Salt Lake City Winter Games in 2002, 'a successful event and successfully marketing the host city are distinctly different concepts'. In the case of Athens 2004, while the Games themselves were a success, it appears that there were major planning failings.

Beriatos and Gospodini (2004) use the Athens Games as a case study in their examination of the transformation of urban landscapes in the era of globalization. Their analysis sees cities as 'commodities' to be consumed by tourists and business interests:

> In the metaphor of 'commodification' of cities, mobile capital and tourists are the highly flexible consumers, cities are the product, and local government, organisations and institutions are the manufacturers, the marketers and the retailers.

As such, cities compete to sell themselves to tourists, and seek to use 'branding' strategies to create a unique place identity for mobile capital, for tourists and also increasingly for residents who are increasingly becoming similar to tourists in the consumption of their city as a cultural product (Lefebvre, 1996). In developing cities as products, Beriatos and Gospodini (2004) note that there appear to be two converging forces: first, an emphasis on local tradition, history and heritage in which to root place identity and, second, an emphasis on globalized modernity that displays all the signs and symbols of a cutting-edge, contemporary city. This convergence, which was a key aim of the Athens Games is referred to by Beriatos and Gospodini (2004) as 'glocalization'.

While Athens is by far Greece's most important city, Petrakos and Economou (1999) note that within the wider European context, Athens represents a large peripheral city with low-level influence in the region. This is a result of a range of spatial disadvantages, including unplanned residential areas on the outskirts, obsolete infrastructure, degraded built fabric, traffic congestion and environmental pollution, caused by unregulated rapid economic and physical growth as a result of rural immigration between 1950 and 1980 (CEC, 1992). Consequently, the 2004 Olympic Games presented a major opportunity to re-develop and re-brand the city. However, despite the city's expressed aim to follow the 'Barcelona Model' (Poulios, 2006), the development of Athens bore little resemblance to Barcelona's approach, and this might be seen as a planning shortcoming that has failed to leave the city with an infrastructure legacy that best provides for future tourism and inward investment. Specifically, some of the planning failings were:

- *Lack of integrated planning* – partial spatial interventions were not integrated into a strategic plan for Athens as a whole, especially in relation to the post-Games period (Beriatos and Gospodini, 2004).

- *Failure to re-develop brownfield areas* – Barcelona focussed on the re-development of run-down areas whereas Athens largely developed green spaces on the outskirts or undeveloped sites in the city. Beriatos and Gospodini (2004:198) express surprise that Eleones, 'a large declined area with light industrial uses centrally located in Athens' was not considered for development.

- *Architects and urban designers not given a central role* – Barcelona incorporated architects and urban designers on the bidding and organizing committees for the 1992 Games, whereas Athens only consulted a few 'big name' artchitects, and did so much later in the process.

- *Lack of spatial concentration* – perhaps the key failing in creating a long-term legacy for urban tourism was the failure to concentrate spatial interventions and landscape transformations in a limited number of strategic sites. Unlike the approach taken in Barcelona, development and re-development projects in Athens were scattered 'all over the plan of the city without a focus' (Beriatos and Gospodini, 2004:192).

However, despite these planning failings, there was a clear intention to create an urban legacy as around 95 per cent of Olympic projects were not temporary, but permanent spatial structures. There were also projects that sought to enhance the city's historic sites, in particular those carried out by the Agency for the Unification of the Archeological Sites of Athens, which sought to link together a geographically disparate range of historical sites and to enhance the city's 'historic physiognomy' (Beriatos and Gospodini, 2004:199). The intention, therefore, to link the historic local with the modern global existed, but was poorly implemented in practice.

Business File reported at the end of 2004 that tourism to Athens and Greece was 'lacklustre' during the Games and in Olympic year, and that Olympic ticket sales were much lower than expected. However, there remained hope in the Athens tourism sector that the tourism benefit would occur in the post-Games period, with a Gallery owner in Athens oldest neighbourhood commenting that despite lower than expected tourism in 2004, 'Next year will be better. We don't know, we just hope. It happened in other places and we think it will happen here too' (Business File, 2004).

Evidence in the time since the Games suggests that, despite the *laissez faire* approach to planning for Olympic tourism, the Athens Games have had a positive effect. A study by Alpha Bank, published at the end of 2004 estimated that the Games added 9 billion Euros to Greece's Gross Domestic Product between 2000 and 2004 (total GDP = 163 billion Euros in 2003). However, the most optimistic estimates remained predictions: namely that foreign visitors to Greece 'may reach 19–20 million by the end of the decade', from circa 13 million in 2004 (Alpha Bank, 2004). It is perhaps worth noting, though, that Alpha Bank was a major sponsor of the Athens Games, and thus had a vested interest in demonstrating a positive outcome from the Games.

Two years after the Athens Games, Catherin Sykianaki of the Organization for Planning and Environmental Protection of Athens analysed the potential for post-Olympic sustainable development in Athens, noted that the image of Athens as a place in which to live and do business has improved substantially as a result of the Games. In 2006, she identified the priorities for urban development in Athens (Sykianaki, 2006):

- Sustaining the momentum of economic, social and environmental improvements generated by the Games, as well as promoting post-Olympic use of facilities

- Evolving and expanding the metropolitan strategy, which was developed in the process of preparing the city for the Olympic Games

- Advancing the framework needed for the co-ordination between ministries, different layers of government, as well as encouraging co-operation and partnership between different development players, such as the public, private, community and voluntary sectors.

The tone of these priorities is a little revealing, as they were set out at a time when Greece and Athens should be reaping the benefits of its Olympic planning. However, it is only in 2006 that a 'strategic programme for post-Olympic sustainable development' is being produced. Similarly, in 2007, the Executive Secretary for Tourism in the Greek Ministry of Tourism Development was still describing how '(e)xtending the tourist season is an important tool in achieving one of our basic goals: to broaden and enrich the tourism product'. Yet, addressing seasonality and broadening the tourist product were intended as key outcomes of the Athens Games. That these are still emergent issues for Greece and Athens in 2007 can only be ascribed to the lack of planning to leverage both tourism and broader business development around the 2004 Games.

Empirical assessments of the actual or potential effects on tourism and business of the Athens 2004 Games are few and far between, and this is perhaps an extension of the failure to recognize the need to plan for and leverage tourism and business benefits from the Olympic Games. Athens and Greece, it appears, relied on reports from previous Games for re-assurance that a positive tourism impact would result from their Games. As empirical evidence is sparse, the tourism impact of the 2004 Games for Greece and Athens is likely to remain a matter of conjecture.

The Games of the XXIX Olympiad in Beijing (2008)

As the first of the two Games 'in prospect' at the time of writing, perspectives on Beijing obviously focus on aims and aspirations for the Games rather than on their outcome. Like the previous Games in Athens in 2004, the context for the Games in Beijing is provided by China's historical relationship with the IOC and the Olympic movement. However, unlike Athens and Greece, which have a central place in the development of Olympism and the Olympic ideal, the relationship between the IOC and China has been problematic and was rooted in the changing nature of international and Chinese politics in the second half of the 20th century.

The earliest Chinese relationship with the Olympic movement commenced in 1924 when the China National Amateur Athletic Federation was initially recognized by the IOC (Chan, 1985), a relationship that was formalized when the re-named Chinese Society for Sport Promotion was designated as the National Olympic Committee for China in 1931 (Ren, 2002). At this time, the country was governed by the Republic of China (ROC). However, following the establishment of the communist People's Republic of China (PRC) in 1949, the members of the National Olympic Committee fled to Taiwan with the ROC government where they maintained contact with the IOC and claimed jurisdiction over Olympic affairs both in the mainland and in Taiwan (Kolatch, 1972). On the mainland the PRC established the All-China Athletic Federation which, similarly, claimed jurisdiction over sporting affairs in both mainland China and Taiwan. This was the start of a 'two-Chinas' diplomatic conflict that spanned 30 years, with both the ROC government in exile in Taiwan and the PRC government on mainland China claiming that they were the sole government, and by extension the National Sports Federation aligned to them was the sole sports body for all of China (see Chan, 1985; Hill, 1996; Ren, 2002 for more details on the 'two Chinas' issue). Initially the international community recognized the ROC government based in Taiwan as the rightful Chinese government and, as the Olympic Committee based in Taiwan was already recognized by the IOC, this was convenient for IOC officials. However, over time the All-China Athletic Federation based on the mainland made a number of overtures to the IOC to be recognized as the sole Olympic organization for China, stipulating also that the Taiwanese Olympic Committee could not use any variation of the name 'Republic of China'. As time passed, the international community moved towards recognizing the PRC as a legitimate government, and this resulted in the IOC's acceptance of the PRC-based All China Athletic Federation's as a legitimate National Olympic Committee in 1979. However, there was still the tricky question of the PRC's refusal to accept that Taiwan represented a separate sovereign government. The result was what has become to be known as the 'Olympic formula' (Chan, 1985). The Olympic formula designated the PRC-based All China Athletic Federation as the 'Chinese Olympic Committee' (using the flag and anthem of the PRC), and required that the Taiwan committee be named the 'Chinese Taipei Olympic Committee' and that it should use a flag and anthem other than that currently used (i.e., that the ROC anthem and flag could not be used). While this was a disappointment for the Taiwan authorities, it allowed both Taiwan and mainland China to compete in the Olympic Games (and subsequently in most other international sport). This solution allowed the PRC to claim that Taiwan was 'subsumed' under China, as indicated by the respective names of the National Olympic Committees (Chan, 1985). However, it also allowed the Taiwanese authorities to show to the world that there was a separate Chinese entity in Taiwan to that on the Chinese mainland. Following the establishment of this 'formula' in 1979, it was not until five years later, at the 1984 Los Angeles Summer Games, that 'China' and 'Chinese Taipai' competed in the same Olympic Games for the first time since the London Games of 1948. As such, the 1984 Los Angeles Games heralded the return of China to the Olympic fold.

It was only seven years after China's re-appearance at the Summer Games of 1984 that the Chinese Olympic Committee launched a bid for Beijing to host the 2000 Games. For many in the Olympic movement this was too soon after their re-admission to the Olympic fold. However, there was also concern in the international community more generally about China's record on Human Rights. In this respect, both the United States Congress and the European Parliament passed resolutions calling for such human rights issues to be addressed before Beijing be considered as host of the 2000 Olympic Games, with the latter stating that:

> The European Parliament .... [is] aware of the deplorable violation of human rights in Tibet and the huge number of political prisoners ... and [t]akes the view that the Olympic Games should not be held in Beijing in the year 2000, unless significant progress is made in ensuring respect for human rights by the Chinese regime.

In this climate, Beijing polled very well in the IOC vote to decide the host of the 2000 Games (held in September 1993), leading the bidding until the very last round when the majority of the votes that had supported the UK bid from Manchester in the previous round unsurprisingly switched to Sydney, who were duly awarded the Millenium Games. Beijing, however, against some fairly widespread international criticism, had finished a creditable second, only two votes behind Sydney, and as such was encouraged by the result. Furthermore, the 2000 bid had the effect of increasing both knowledge of, and enthusiasm for, the Olympic Games throughout China (Ren, 2002) and this led to the launch of the bid for the 2008 Games, which were awarded to Beijing in July 2001.

The promotion of Beijing as a global city

Wei and Yu (2006) list the hosting of the 2008 Olympic Games in Beijing as one of four themes in a deliberate and sustained strategy by both the central national government of China and the municipal government of Beijing to establish the city as a 'global city' following years of isolation as a result of the People's Republic of China's (PRC) 'self-reliance' policies. In the years following the establishment of the PRC, Beijing recorded the fastest industrial growth amongst its peers in China, but had virtually no interactions with the global economy. Even following the introduction of limited reforms in 1978, there was little outside economic contact with Beijing until the 1990s as much of the early reform had focussed on rural areas and provinces in Southern China (Yu and Wei, 2003). Reform accelerated in the 1990s, with the national government declaring their intention to create a 'socialist market economy', focussing initially on reform of state-owned and collective owned enterprises which, in 1990, together accounted for 80 per cent of industrial output. Two years later, 70 per cent of state-owned enterprises had been transformed into shareholding enterprises, improving both productivity and competitiveness (Wei and Yu, 2006). At this time the *Beijing Master Plan* (for the period 1991–2010) announced the intention to make Beijing a 'first-class, modern global city' (Beijing Institute of Urban Planning and Design [BIUPD], 1992). It is important to note, however, that whilst the reforms promote the marketization and opening up of Beijing, the state is still the key factor in driving the globalization and development of the city (Wei, 2000). And, consequently, state goals for the development of Beijing are key to the city's strategy for the development of the Olympic Games which, alongside the attraction of foreign investment, infrastructure investment and the development of a central business district (CBD), and the development of a 'silicon valley' at Beijing Zhongguancun Science Park, are the key themes identified by Wei and Yu (2006) in the state's strategy for the development of Beijing.

The attraction of foreign investment and trade has been a key goal of the 'open door' policy implemented as part of the Chinese government's reforms, with the municipal government seeking, in particular, to attract Trans-National Corporations (TNCs) to 'development zones'. In 2002, more than two-thirds of companies in such zones represented inward foreign investment, including some key TNCs such as Motorola and Sony (Beijing Statistical Bureau, 2003). Infrastructure developments in Beijing had tended to be ignored under state socialism as the almost singular emphasis was on industrialization. However, the opening up of Beijing stimulated urban population growth, and the state realized that the city's outdated infrastructure was a barrier to further development. Consequently, the municipal government invested heavily in transport, telecommunication and public services to 'create the best investment environment to attract business' (Assistant Mayor of Beijing, 2003, quoted in Wei and Yu, 2006). The creation of a CBD was also a key part of this strategy, and in 2001 the Beijing CBD Administrative Commission was established, with the explicit support of both municipal and central government. However, while the CBD now gives Beijing a focal point for investors, critics have argued that it serves international investment and real estate interests at the expense of local residents, many of whom were displaced with poor compensation (Wei and Yu, 2006). This 'state will' to stimulate development at, what appears to be, the expense of poorer elements of the community has echoes of the accusations of human rights violations from the international community at the time of the city's bid for the 2000 Games and this, as noted later, was not to be the last time this issue arose in the run up to 2008.

The third of Beijing's development themes has been the development of a 'Chinese Silicon Valley' at Beijing Zhongguancun Science Park (ZSP) as a result of the Beijing Master Plan strategy that 'industrial development will concentrate on high-tech, high value-added industries' (BIUPD, 1992). Preferential policies are in place to attract foreign investment as this helps to 'promote the image of technology in the media and create a better social atmosphere for innovation and the growth of high-tech firms' (ACZSP, 2003). As in the case of the development zones mentioned above, these policies have been successful as leading international companies such as IBM, Hewlett-Packard and Microsoft have established research and development facilities in the ZSP.

The fourth development theme is, of course, the hosting of the 2008 Olympic Games in Beijing, and the strategic themes for the Games reflect aspects of the economic themes outlined above. These themes, a 'green', a 'scientific and technological' and a 'human' Olympics, are a clear indicator of the role of the state in the development of the Beijing Games. Whilst a 'green' Olympics might not seem like an economic strategy, it reflects a desire to improve the physical and urban environment of Beijing which, it is hoped, will make the city a more attractive place for inward foreign investment. The second theme clearly resonates with the state's desire to promote 'high-tech' investment in the city; however, the 'humanistic' theme does not, on the surface, appear to be related to economic strategy and, as such, is worthy of further exploration.

Ren (2002:12) claims that Chinese culture has much to offer the Olympic movement, and invokes the concept of 'harmony' in describing two key aspects of Chinese culture:

- On the relationship between individuals and society: *An emphasis on the collective spirit rather than the individual*

- On the relationship between humanity and the environment: *An emphasis on 'the natural way' and the integration of humans into the natural world*

Furthermore, Ren (2002:12) believes that these characteristics could complement and extend the Western conception of Olympism in four areas:

- Emphasizing mental and moral aspects as being at least as important as physical strength, thus strengthening the Olympic ideal

- Emphasizing internal body training may counterbalance the external body training stressed in Western sport

- Emphasizing the process as well as the outcome of sport may result in a healthier attitude to winning and losing

- Emphasizing harmonious relationships with the natural world may encourage host cities to be more environmentally and ecologically aware

However, while there may be a focus on Chinese culture and what it may bring to the Olympic Games, there is also an economic imperative to the 'human' goals for the Beijing Games. The Beijing Organizing Committee for the Olympic Games (BOCOG) suggests that the Games offer opportunities to 'improve your health through sports and better your soul through culture' (BOCOG, 2003). However, they also emphasize the potential to 'invigorate the economy with the Olympics and enrich the capital with civilization' thus building Beijing into 'a modern global city with concentrated cultural talents, complete cultural facilities, developed cultural markets advanced cultural industries and rich cultural styles' (BOCOG, 2003). Thus, Wei and Yu (2006:392) describe the 'human' goals for the Games as to 'present to the world a new image of Beijing as an emerging global city, with prosperity, advanced civilization, and highly motivated citizens'. Such goals are clearly related to the economic development strategies described above. Enhancing the image of Beijing as a welcoming place to live, work and visit is a key aspect of the state strategy for the 2008 Games. However, to be successful in this respect, the city must explore ways in which the perceived 'cultural distance' (Hofstede, 1980) between Beijing and many other regions of the world can be overcome.

'Cultural Distance' and the development of Beijing

'Cultural Distance' is a concept that emerged in the business studies literature following a landmark study by Hofstede (1980) in which he identified four value dimensions that distinguish people from different nations: power distance, uncertainty avoidance, individualism/collectivism and masculinity/femininity. Hofstede (1980) claimed that such differences could influence the likelihood of business links developing between companies and corporations in different countries and/or could influence the success of such links. In later work, Hofstede (2001) added a fifth dimension: long-term/short-term orientation. More recently, studies have applied these concepts to tourism (e.g., Chen, 2000; Crotts and Litvin, 2003; Pizam and Jeong, 1996), with Crotts (2004) finding support for the proposition that travel and travel behaviour will be affected if tourists are travelling, or considering travelling, to countries that they perceive contrast greatly with their own cultural norms (i.e., where there is greater cultural distance). The concept of cultural distance clearly resonates with the discussions of Leiper's (1979) model of the tourism system in the second half of Chapter 3. Leiper's model examines 'travel propensities', a macro-concept relating to the propensity of the population of a 'tourist generating region' to travel to a 'tourist destination region' (Boniface and Cooper, 2001:13). The travel propensity of a tourist generating region is influenced by local contextual and personal factors and, significantly in this case, also by contextual, personal and supply factors local to the tourist destination region. In particular, populations in tourist generating regions will be influenced by perceptions, often generated by a global media, of tourist destination regions that may either positively or negatively affect their propensities to travel. The multiple influences on travel propensities appear similar to the four main elements of culture, identified by Ng, Lee and Soutar (2007) that were likely to contribute to perceptions of cultural distance and thus affect travel behaviour. These influences (Ng, Lee and Soutar, 2007:2) were:

1. The tourist's national culture

2. The tourist's individual (internalized) culture

3. The destination's culture

4. The 'distance' between a tourist's home culture and a destination's culture

As noted earlier, Beijing, both historically and contemporarily, has had its development shaped by a municipal and central government that has evolved from 'state socialism' to an emphasis on a 'socialist market economy'. Undoubtedly, despite reforms, Beijing remains a society strikingly at odds with Western liberalism (Wei and Yu, 2006). In this respect, Hill and Kim (2000:2188) point out that 'emerging global cities' such as Beijing are different from global cities such as New York and London because of the state function:

> The economic base, spatial organisation and social structure of the world's major cities are strongly influenced by the national development model and regional context in which each city is embedded.

Consequently, this engenders 'cultural distance' from the Western societies with which the state government wishes to promote trade, business and tourism links. In the latter respect, Wei and Yu (2006:383) note that the number of foreign tourists to Beijing tripled between 1990 and 2002. However, the 3 million foreign visitors to Beijing in 2002 still falls short of the 12 million visitors to London (ONS, 2003) or the 6 million to New York (NYCvisit, 2007) in the same year (particularly as Beijing is approximately twice the population size of both London and New York), and suggests that travel propensity may be affected by the perception of cultural distance.

ITIM International (see www.itim.org) have attempted to quantify Hofstede's (1980, 2001) five cultural dimensions (see Table 9.1 for a description of each of these dimensions) for individual countries, and this allows a comparison between countries and regions. For the purposes of this chapter, therefore, it is useful to examine the differences on each of these dimensions between China and the key markets for both trade and potential Olympic tourism. Consequently, Table 9.2 and Figure 9.1 compares the scores on each of the five cultural dimensions for China with the averages for Europe, North America and Australasia, as well as the world averages.

Table 9.2 and Figure 9.1 show that on all dimensions except masculinity/femininity there are significant differences between China and the key tourism generating regions of Europe, North America and Australasia, and the world average. As such, there is considerable evidence for the assumption that there is clear cultural distance between China (and by extension Beijing) and the key markets for trade and tourism that are the targets of the Chinese state and the Beijing municipal government. Crotts (2004) suggests that a key aspect of cultural distance is unfamiliarity, which leads to a feeling of uncomfortableness with that with which people do not know. Re-inforcing this is some evidence that populations in countries that score high on individualism (which includes most of the key Olympic tourism generating regions) tend to choose similar destinations (Jackson, 2001). As such, an important role for the Beijing Olympics of 2008

Table 9.1
Hofstede's (1980, 2001) cultural dimensions

Power Distance Index (PDI) that is the extent to which the less powerful members of organizations and institutions (like the family) accept and expect that power is distributed unequally. This represents inequality (more versus less), but defined from below, not from above. It suggests that a society's level of inequality is endorsed by the followers as much as by the leaders. Power and inequality, of course, are extremely fundamental facts of any society and anybody with some international experience will be aware that 'all societies are unequal, but some are more unequal than others'.

Individualism (IDV) on the one side versus its opposite, collectivism, that is the degree to which individuals are inter-grated into groups. On the individualist side we find societies in which the ties between individuals are loose: everyone is expected to look after him/herself and his/her immediate family. On the collectivist side, we find societies in which people from birth onwards are integrated into strong, cohesive in-groups, often extended families (with uncles, aunts and grandparents) which continue protecting them in exchange for unquestioning loyalty. The word 'collectivism' in this sense has no political meaning: it refers to the group, not to the state. Again, the issue addressed by this dimension is an extremely fundamental one, regarding all societies in the world.

Masculinity (MAS) versus its opposite, femininity, refers to the distribution of roles between the genders which is another fundamental issue for any society to which a range of solutions are found. The IBM studies revealed that (a) women's values differ less among societies than men's values; (b) men's values from one country to another contain a dimension from very assertive and competitive and maximally different from women's values on the one side, to modest and caring and similar to women's values on the other. The assertive pole has been called 'masculine' and the modest, caring pole 'feminine'. The women in feminine countries have the same modest, caring values as the men; in the masculine countries they are somewhat assertive and competitive, but not as much as the men, so that these countries show a gap between men's values and women's values.

Uncertainty Avoidance Index (UAI) deals with a society's tolerance for uncertainty and ambiguity; it ultimately refers to man's search for Truth. It indicates to what extent a culture programs its members to feel either uncomfortable or comfortable in unstructured situations. Unstructured situations are novel, unknown, surprising, different from usual. Uncertainty avoiding cultures try to minimize the possibility of such situations by strict laws and rules, safety and security measures, and on the philosophical and religious level by a belief in absolute Truth; 'there can only be one Truth and we have it'. People in uncertainty avoiding countries are also more emotional, and motivated by inner nervous energy. The opposite type, uncertainty accepting cultures, are more tolerant of opinions different from what they are used to; they try to have as few rules as possible, and on the philosophical and religious level they are relativist and allow many currents to flow side by side. People within these cultures are more phlegmatic and contemplative, and not expected by their environment to express emotions.

Long-Term Orientation (LTO) versus short-term orientation: this fifth dimension was found in a study among students in 23 countries around the world, using a questionnaire designed by Chinese scholars. It can be said to deal with Virtue regardless of Truth. Values associated with Long-Term Orientation are thrift and perseverance; values associated with Short Term Orientation are respect for tradition, fulfilling social obligations, and protecting one's 'face'. Both the positively and the negatively rated values of this dimension are found in the teachings of Confucius, the most influential Chinese philosopher who lived around 500 BC; however, the dimension also applies to countries without a Confucian heritage.

Table 9.2

Comparison of cultural dimension scores

	PDI	IDV	MAS	UAI	LTO
WORLD	55	43	50	64	45
Europe	44	60	57	74	N/A
North America	40	85	57	47	26
Australasia	36	90	61	51	31
CHINA	80	20	66	30	118

Sources: Hofstede, 1980, 2001.

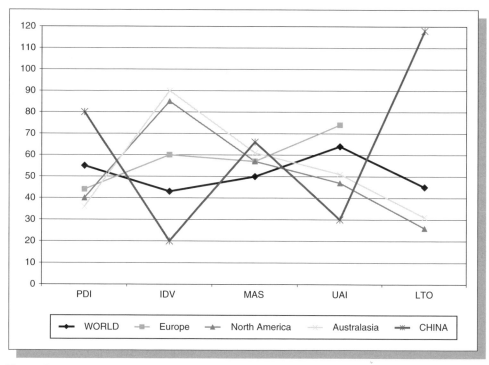

Figure 9.1

Illustration of cultural dimension scores.
Sources: Hofstede, 1980, 2001.

is to reduce the perception that cultural distance is a barrier to tourism (and, indeed, to trade) in key markets around the world by increasing the familiarity of these markets with the city, the country and its culture.

Olympic tourism to Beijing 2008 and the promotion of Chinese culture

A key goal of both the municipal government of Beijing and the national Chinese government is to harness aspects of traditional Chinese culture in presenting the city and the country to the world in the run up to and during the 2008 Olympics, and this will be a key part of the Olympic tourism offer (BOCOG, 2003). However, this may not be enough to entice Olympic tourists to the city and country. As the discussions, Figure 9.1 and Table 9.2 in the previous section have shown, there is considerable 'cultural distance' between China and key Olympic tourism generating regions in four of the five dimensions. Furthermore, more recent empirical research specifically addressing the tourism context found that, for Australians, China was perceived as the most culturally distant destination, whereas New Zealand, the USA, the UK and Germany were seen as the least distant (Ng, Lee and Soutar, 2007). The impact of cultural differences on travel propensies (see Chapter 3) has been the subject of debate in the tourism literature for some time, with Spradley and Philips (1972) suggesting that cultural differences, or perceptions of cultural differences, in food, language, cleanliness, pace of life, recreation, standard of living, transportation, humour, intimacy, privacy, etiquette and formality can affect travel propensies in tourism generating regions. However, it has also been suggested that absolute cultural distance may not be the issue, rather expectations of such (Ng, Lee and Soutar, 2007). Consequently, the problem is not the extent of cultural difference, but the tourist's expectation and awareness of it. If there is a consistency between the tourist's expectation of cultural difference and any actual cultural difference, then the impact of cultural distance on travel propensies can be ameliorated. This opens up two potential strategies to address the issue of cultural difference:

(1) To reduce the perception of cultural distance between a tourist destination region and a tourist generating region, thus increasing travel propensity.

(2) To increase the familiarity of the tourist generating region with the culture of the tourist destination region, thus ensuring that there is an expectation of cultural difference, but that this need not be a barrier.

The first strategy is one that has been employed by tourist destination regions such as the Spanish Costa's and the Greek Islands in promoting themselves to the UK as a tourist generating region.

These destinations have promoted themselves as places where the cultural differences are small, with the English language being widely spoken, English food being available and the existence of many English style bars showing English sport and television programmes. However, such a strategy is likely to be neither implementable nor desirable for Beijing and China.

The second part of Chapter 4 discussed the leveraging of Olympic media to promote destination image, and this should be a key element of Beijing's and China's approach to following the second strategy for addressing cultural distance. As such, the pre-Games period becomes particularly significant for Beijing and China in generating Olympic tourism as it is during this period that opportunities will be most widespread to increase familiarity, and by extension travel propensities, in key Olympic tourism generating regions. The Beijing Olympic Action Plan (2003) specifically states that a key aim for the Games is to make Beijing and China seem more open to the rest of the world, and recognizes that a 'new image' is required to do this:

> We aim to upgrade the opening-up of Beijing to a new level through the hosting of the Olympic Games and display to the world a new image of China which is developing rapidly and opening wider to the outside world. (Beijing Olympic Action Plan, 2003:3)

Elsewhere in the plan, the role of traditional Chinese culture in such an 'opening-up' strategy, as part of the humanistic 'people's Olympics' promotional theme, is clearly stated, for example:

> we will take the hosting of the Olympic Games as an opportunity to … promote the traditional Chinese culture, showcase the history and development of Beijing as well as the friendliness and hospitality of its citizens. We will also take the Games as a bridge for cultural exchanges in order to deepen the understanding and enhance the trust and friendship among the peoples of different countries. (Beijing Olympic Action Plan, 2003:2)

> Entertainment activities, which demonstrate the profoundness of the Chinese culture and its ever-lasting charm, will be organised to constitute a unique opportunity where the East meets the West. (Beijing Olympic Action Plan, 2003:4)

However, there are no discussions of the strategies by which this might be achieved, and there is certainly no stated plan to leverage Olympic media, which appears to be a key requirement for

Beijing's Olympic tourism and, indeed, trade strategy. Furthermore, the lack of such a strategy cannot be blamed on the need to concentrate on ensuring that the facilities and infrastructure are ready as, unlike Athens four years prior to the Games (see Chapter 7), Ritchard (2004:2) noted that:

> Beijing will be supported by world-class facilities and logistics planning. The city is well underway in developing its Olympic-related facilities, including a new airport, magnificent stadia, convention centre and a much-improved transport network. Construction is reported to be on time and, in some cases, ahead of schedule.

Such efficiency in construction might be expected in a country that has only relatively recently undergone a transition from a planned 'state socialist' political system to what is still characterized as a 'socialist market economy'. However, with construction and infrastructure projects appearing to be on, or even ahead of, schedule, the need to turn attention to media concerns might be seen as even more pressing. Ritchard (2004:3) claims that the efficiency of infrastructure development and construction has provided Beijing with a world-class tourism product to serve the 2008 Olympics and, as such:

> the greatest potential of the Beijing Games will be the marketing opportunity which will instantly create global consumer awareness of 'China – the brand'. ... Beijing – like no other previous Olympic city – has a fascinating extra dimension: the unveiling of what China really is and what it can achieve, showcased to a global audience which, generally, knows little about the country. (Ritchard, 2004:3)

Ritchard (2004) believes that the Olympic Games have come at such a point in the development of Beijing and China as to present 'an incredible co-incidence of timing' to showcase the opening up of the city and the country to the world. However, as the discussions earlier in this chapter have shown, there has been little co-incidental about the place of the 2008 Beijing Games in the city's and the country's strategy to present a new image to the world. Nevertheless, Ritchard (2004) is correct in noting that the Games provide an un-rivalled opportunity to place the city and the country in the spotlight of the global media to promote both trade and tourism and, in the latter case, to increase the travel propensities of a range of tourist generating regions around the world to Beijing and China as a tourist destination region. In this respect:

> Beijing 2008 will be the source of many 'first impressions'. The Games will be the most comprehensive [and nicely packaged] up-close look at China in half a century, and history will judge the event as the vehicle for demystifying the world's image of the country. (Ritchard, 2004:3)

The key question, though, is whether the 2008 Games, and the coverage of the city and country in the years before the Games, will be sufficient to 'convert public curiosity into travel bookings for conferences, leisure tours, city breaks, and business' (Ritchard, 2004:3). In this respect, China may not have such an easy ride, and it may not be the case that an Olympic media leveraging strategy is all that is required. One of the comments in the earlier section of this chapter introducing the concept of cultural distance was that, despite reforms, politically Beijing remains a society strikingly at odds with Western liberalism (Wei and Yu, 2006). Furthermore, one of the key aspects of this difference is the Chinese state's perceived attitude to, and record on, human rights (noted at previous points in this chapter), with organizations such as Amnesty International, Human Rights Watch and the Centre of Housing Rights and Evictions commenting both on the state's previous record and on alleged human right violations specifically linked to the preparations for the 2008 Games. The existence and coverage of such issues are likely to increase perceptions of cultural distance from China and Beijing as a tourist destination region and, consequently, are likely to reduce travel propensities in the key Olympic tourist generating regions, virtually all of which are liberal democracies with a distaste for human rights violations. Specifically, it has been alleged that, alongside censorship of the press, the 2008 Games has led to the exploitation of construction workers and the use of child labour and the enforced displacement of families and communities from their homes, which have been demolished to make way for Olympic infrastructure developments. Against this background, Ritchard's (2004) comments that 'China is absolutely committed to ensuring the success of the Olympic Games – whatever it takes.' (p. 2) and that the Games will be 'nicely packaged' (p. 3) become much more insidious. Of course, the displacement of residents to facilitate Olympic development is not a new phenomenon. Many of the criticisms of the 1992 Barcelona Games, which are often held up as the best example of the positive effects of the Olympics on long-term trade and tourism development (Sanahuja, 2002), highlighted the displacement of 624 families (approximately 2500 people) to facilitate the re-development of the waterfront area (COHRE, 2007). However, this is a mere drop in the ocean against COHRE's estimations that almost 1.25 million people have been displaced in Beijing to date, and that this figure is set to rise to 1.5 million by the time the Games commence in 2008 (COHRE, 2007). With the glare of the global Olympic media spotlight being concentrated on Beijing and China until 2008, these issues are likely to feature in Olympic (and other) media, and they cannot be addressed by a media strategy, only by addressing the human rights issues themselves. If such human rights issues become regular global stories, then this could significantly impact upon the way in which the 2008 Games affects 'China – the brand' with there being significant potential for perceived cultural distance in tourist generating regions to be increased, and thus for travel propensities to fall.

Conclusion

China's involvement with the Olympic movement and the Olympic Games has been controversial since the establishment of the People's Republic of China in 1949. The two-China's issue, and the attitude of the international community to this issue (shaped by the cold war and the PRC's 'state socialist' system) provides much of the context for the discussions of perceived cultural distance in the latter part of this chapter. Notwithstanding the reforms in China, and the efforts of the national and municipal government to develop and promote Beijing as a global city, residual perceptions, and continued concern over human rights remain key issues. The success of the Beijing Olympic Games as a tool to promote tourism and trade will depend on whether media messages familiarizing the world with the positive aspects of traditional Chinese culture can overcome more recent perceptions of a state socialist system with a poor record on human rights. Without a strategy for leveraging Olympic media, and with human rights issues unlikely to fade into the background, it would seem to remain a major task for China and Beijing to address the problem of perceived cultural distances, and consequently to increase travel propensities.

The Games of the XXX Olympiad in London (2012)

The Games of the XXX Olympiad in London in 2012 are the most recent Games to be awarded by the International Olympic Committee. Given the developing discourse of learning from previous Games, London 2012 has significant opportunities to draw on the experiences of previous Games in planning and developing its strategies. Consequently, the focus of this chapter will be on the structures and partnerships that have been put into place attempt to maximize the benefit for London and the UK of the 2012 Games.

With the hosting of the 2012 Games, London will become the first city in the modern era to host three Olympic Games. However, the 2012 Games will be the first time that London will have the opportunity to plan for the hosting of an Olympic Games. London has previously hosted the Games in 1908 and 1945, but on each of these occasions London 'stepped in' to host the Games at a relatively late stage. The 1908 Games were originally awarded to the Italian city of Rome, but in 1906 there was an eruption of Mount Vesuvius and the Italian government needed money to rebuild the area around the volcano. The Italians felt that in the face of such needs they could not allocate money to the hosting of an Olympic Games and asked the IOC to award the 1908 Olympics to another city. London put itself forward to host the Games, the IOC agreed, and with less than two years notice the 1908 Games were awarded to London.

As noted in Chapter 8 on Athens 2004, the 1908 Olympics in London introduced many of the innovations that first appeared in the Intercalated Games in Athens in 1906, and which are now a core part of the Olympic spectacle, such as opening and closing ceremonies, and the alignment of athletes with nations, national flags, and national anthems. In addition, it was at the 1908 Games that the current 'standard distance' for the marathon (26 miles and 385 yards) was set, for no other reason than this was the distance of a course that would allow the event to start at Windsor castle and finish in front of the Royal Box in the stadium.

In 1948, London again held the Games at short notice. The Games of 1944 were originally awarded to London shortly before the outbreak of the second world war in 1939. However, once it became obvious that the war was going to last for some time, these Games were cancelled. After the end of the war, the IOC invited London to host the 1948 Games. With less than three years to prepare, and with very limited resources following the expense of both the war and the re-building effort, London once again agreed to host. The Games of 1948 were very different to those of the current day, with post-war austerity meaning that athletes were put up in schools and military barracks rather than a purpose built Olympic village, and were even asked to bring their own meals with them!

Therefore, despite having twice hosted the Games before, the 2012 Games will be the first time that London will experience a full Olympiad (2008–2012) as host, and of course the first time that the city will have the opportunity to prepare for that Olympiad.

'A UK Games hosted in London'

In the UK, the Parliamentary Select Committee for Culture, Media and Sport, meeting in 2007 to consider the funding and legacy for the London 2012 Games, heard evidence from a number of sources that London 2012 should be considered 'a UK Games hosted in London'. In the two years since the Games were awarded to London in 2005, and in some cases before then, there has been a widespread interest in spreading the benefits of the Games throughout the UK. Part of the structure for the delivery of the Games comprises a 'Nations and Regions

Group' incorporating representatives from Scotland, Wales, and Northern Ireland and the nine English regions, with each of these areas having established their own steering groups and sub-groups to consider the potential opportunities that the Games may bring to them. As such, the primary focus of this chapter will be on the ways in which the UK is planning to spread Olympic benefits around the UK as a whole, and the ways in which tourism features in these plans.

The structure for the delivery of London 2012 is illustrated in Figure 10.1. As with all Olympics, the primary responsibility for the organization of the Games lies with the organizing committee, the London Organizing Committee for the Olympic Games (LOCOG), which is the body that reports to and liaises with the International Olympic Committee. However, LOCOG is only responsible for the organization of the Games, not for providing the sporting, transport and accommodation infrastructure that will serve the Games. As such, the accounts of LOCOG do not incorporate the building costs of stadia, facilities, transport systems and the Olympic Village accommodation, and it is for this reason that every Olympic Games Organizing Committee in the modern era has produced a surplus, as it is the organizing committee that receives the income from television rights and sponsorship. In the case of the London Games, an Olympic Delivery Authority (ODA) has been established to deliver the infrastructure requirements, and it is this body, funded by government, that will incur the majority of the costs associated with the 2012 Games. Providing the link between the work of LOCOG and the ODA, and ensuring that the requisite funding is in place for all aspects of London 2012, is an Olympic Board that comprises top-level representatives of the national government, the London Mayor's Office, LOCOG and the British Olympic Association (BOA). As of June 2007, these were Tessa Jowell (the government minister with designated responsibility for the Olympics), Ken Livingston (the Mayor of London), Lord Sebastian Coe (the Chair of LOCOG) and Lord Colin Moynihan (the Chair of the BOA).

Between them, LOCOG (and by extension the IOC), the ODA and the Olympic Board are responsible for delivering the London 2012 Olympic Games. However, as noted above, LOCOG has established a Nations and Regions Group (NRG), which as well as providing a forum for the nations and English regions of the United Kingdom to explore issues related to the 2012 Games, has primary responsibility for delivering 'a lasting legacy' from the 2012 Games. Consequently, the NRG also includes representatives of Visit Britain (the National Tourism Organization), Sport

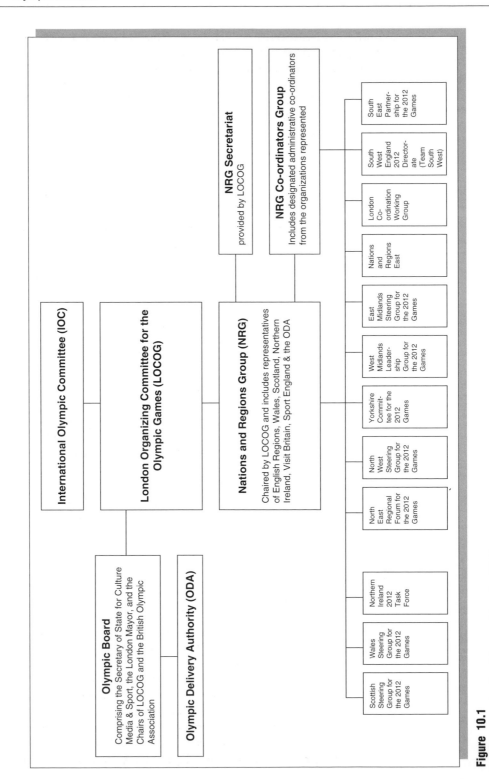

Figure 10.1

The structure for the delivery of London 2012.

England (the lead body for the distribution of government sport funding and for sport policy) and the ODA.

Figure 10.1 shows that the NRG is serviced by a secretariat provided by LOCOG and that, in addition to the meetings of organizational representatives, there is an NRG Co-ordinators group that comprises the designated administrative co-ordinators for 2012 from each of the organizations, nations, and regions. Each nation and region has established its own co-ordinating group/committee, with the lead organization varying, depending to a certain extent on the main objectives and aims that each nation and region has for the Games. To summarize this information, Table 10.1 lists, for each nation and region, the lead organization, the long-term aims for the Games as communicated to LOCOG, the identified priority areas, and the title of their Olympic strategy (if one exists).

The NRG identifies five core areas in which there are opportunities throughout the UK arising from London 2012: Business, Sport, Tourism, Culture and Volunteering. As Table 10.1 shows, each of the nations and regions identify most of these areas as priorities, although Scotland and Northern Ireland do not overtly highlight tourism or volunteering, whilst Yorkshire and the South West refer to 'community' rather than volunteering, and the South East refers to 'skills'. If the 'long-term aims' of the nations and regions are examined, there is generally a greater emphasis on sport and culture in the regions further away from London, whilst those grouped around London have a greater emphasis on economic development and tourism. Some areas, such as the West Midlands and the East Midlands, identify particular strengths, specific sports events and the facilities at Loughborough University, respectively, whilst others are much more generic in describing, for example, the enlargement of 'the region's sporting and cultural goals and programmes' (Yorkshire).

In relation to tourism, Visit Britain is a member of the NRG, whilst the Department for Culture, Media, and Sport of the UK government is represented via the Olympic Board and indirectly on the NRG. The Department for Culture, Media and Sport (in collaboration with Visit Britain and Visit London) has produced a consultation draft of 'Welcome Legacy: Tourism Strategy for the 2012 Games', published in July 2006 for which the consultation closed in November 2006. However, as of June 2007 a final strategy has yet to be produced and so the discussions and comparisons that follow are based on the consultation draft.

The Welcome Legacy tourism strategy consultation employs an Olympic tourism differentiation first suggested by Ken Robinson in his 2005 report to Visit Britain, 'Optimizing the Benefits of the

Table 10.1
Nations and regions – leadership, strategy and priorities

Nation/Region	Lead Organization	Long-term aim for London 2012	Priority areas/sub-groups	Title of Strategy	Representative on NRG
Scottish Steering Group for the 2012 Games	Sportscotland	• To inspire the nation to get active, to engage its schoolchildren and to bring communities together in celebration	• Sport • Culture & Education • Economic Development	No published strategy as of May 2007	Chair of sportscotland
Wales Steering Group for the 2012 Games	Welsh Assembly Government	• Following the hosting of the Ryder Cup (golf) in Wales in 2012, to use the 2012 Games as another opportunity to put Wales on the world map and to increase physical activity in a healthier Wales	• Procurement, Construction, Infrastructure, Employment & Skills, Business Promotion • Tourism • Sports Events • Wales' International Profile • Sport, Physical Activity and Health – elite, grass-roots, disability • Cultural Olympiad • Education Programme • Pre-Games Training Camps • Volunteering	No published strategy as of May 2007	Department Director in the Welsh Assembly Government

Organization	Lead body	Objective	Themes	Strategy	Lead
Northern Ireland 2012 Task Force	Department of Culture, Arts & Leisure, Northern Ireland Assembly	• To get more young people into sport at domestic and international levels and develop better facilities	• Sport • Culture • Olympic related events • Training and Holding Camps • Economic and business • Legacy	*Benefiting from London Olympics and Paralympics 2012: A Strategic Plan for Northern Ireland*	Permanent Secretary of the Department of Culture, Arts & Leisure
North East Regional Forum for the 2012 Games	One NE (the Regional Development Agency) & Sport England (North East)	• To develop and showcase the region's passion for sport and physical activity	• Business • Tourism/Image • Culture • Skills & Volunteering • Facilities • Performance Sport • Children & Young People • Health	No published strategy as of May 2007, but the North East "pledge" is titled *Passionate about Sport*	Chair of the Regional Sports Board

(Continued)

Table 10.1
(*Continued*)

Nation/ Region	Lead Organization	Long-term aim for London 2012	Priority areas/sub-groups	Title of Strategy	Representative on NRG
North West Steering Group for the 2012 Games	North West Development Agency	• To get more people active through sport and active recreation, with a 5 per cent increase in participation by 2012 • To capitalize upon the volunteering programme set up for the 2002 Commonwealth Games in Manchester • To build on links with Liverpool Capital of Culture (2008) and Manchester International Festival	• Sport & Physical Activity • Business • Cultural Olympiad • Tourism • Major Events • Skills & Volunteering	*Be Inspired*	Chair of North West Sports Board
Yorkshire Committee for the 2012 Games	Yorkshire Forward (the Regional Development Agency)	• To use the Games to help enlarge the region's sporting and cultural goals and programmes	• Profile & Tourism • Culture • Community • Sport & Physical Activity • Business	*Yorkshire Gold*	Executive Chair of the Yorkshire Committee for the 2012 Games

West Midlands Leadership Group for the 2012 Games	West Midlands Regional Assembly	• To promote the region as a world-class sporting region through events such as Birmingham's hosting of the European Indoor Athletics Championships (2006) and Coventry's hosting of the UK School Games (2007) • To build upon Much Wenlock's history as the inspiration for the modern Olympic Games	• Business Opportunities & Skills • Tourism • Culture & Cultural Olympiad • Performance Sport • Physical Activity & Health • Pre-Games Training • Volunteering	*Giving it our All*	Chair of the West Midlands Leadership Group for 2012 Games (a West Midlands Assembly member)
East Midlands Steering Group for the 2012 Games	East Midlands Development Agency	• To build on the success of Loughborough University to create the world's most successful sporting region • To use the Games to help encourage participation in sport and make the area flourish	• Sport • Pre-games Training Camps • Business • Tourism • Cultural Olympiad • Volunteering • Education • Health & Wellbeing	*Championing the East Midlands*	Chief Executive of East Midlands Development Agency

(Continued)

Table 10.1 (*Continued*)

Nation/ Region	Lead Organization	Long-term aim for London 2012	Priority areas/sub-groups	Title of Strategy	Representative on NRG
Nations and Regions East	East of England Development Agency	• To create a sustainable legacy, including economic development and regeneration, employment, skills, tourism, and culture	• Tourism • Business & Economic Development • Education, Skills, Training & Employment • Sport • Culture • Infrastructure & Transport • Volunteering	*Rising to the Challenge*	Chair of Nations and Regions East (a local government elected representative)
London Co-ordination Working Group	London Mayor's Office	• To use the opportunities created for jobs and training, increase skill levels through volunteering • To involve the diverse London communities in 2012 cultural activities • To provide new homes and leisure space in the Olympic Park			

		Objectives	Themes	Strategy	Role
South West England 2012 Directorate ('Team South West')	South West of England Regional Development Agency/Sport England South West	• To maximize the tourism benefits of the Games by increasing local skills and creating vibrant international sporting and cultural events using the sea, the natural environment and the World Heritage coastline	• Business Development • Tourism & Regional Image • Sporting Opportunity • Cultural Celebration • Community Engagement	*South West England Legacy Strategy for the 2012 Games*	Chair of South West of England Regional Development Agency
South East Partnership for the 2012 Games	South East England Development Agency	• To build on the region's creativity • To strengthen the region's involvement in the environmental and technology sectors	• Sport • Business & Foreign Direct Investment • Visitor Economy • Culture & Communities • Skills, Employment & Education • Transport & Infrastructure	*Compete, Create, Collaborate for a World Class Performance*	Chief Executive of South East England Development Agency

2012 Olympic and Paralympic Games'. Both the Robinson report and the DCMS consultation differentiate between:

> Games-related tourism (i.e., for the period of the Games themselves) [and] Games-motivated tourism (i.e., additional business events or tourist visits to Britain as a result of heightened awareness of the destination, and of its appeal, generated by the hosting of the Games). (DCMS/Visit Britain/Visit London, 2006)

However, whilst this definition has been embraced by many policy-makers in the UK, who have been attracted to its simplicity, it does not give a full indication of the range of Olympic tourism products discussed in this book. In particular, the range of sports-related Olympic tourism products that might be consumed outside of the Games period (see Chapter 1) are not adequately provided for within this definition, as only visits during the Games ('Games-related tourism') and generic tourism outside of the Games period leveraged by Olympic media, as discussed in the second part of Chapter 4, ('Games-motivated tourism') fall within its scope. As such, key Olympic tourism products, such as Sports Training tourism (e.g., pre-Games training and acclimatization camps) and Sports Events tourism (e.g., Olympic warm-up events) do not clearly fall within this differentiation. Furthermore, the simple binary nature of the Robinson differentiation fails to highlight the multi-faceted nature of Olympic tourism flows (see Chapter 3), specifically that Olympic tourism flows may be positive, negative or neutral, and that a consideration of such flows must recognize their stratified geography (i.e., that the effect of flows may change according to the geographic unit of measurement).

The remainder of this chapter seeks to link the activities in the nations and regions of the UK with the work of the DCMS, Visit Britain and Visit London in developing 'Welcome Legacy'. In particular, the discussion will focus on the potential of the approaches and issues outlined in Welcome Legacy to lead Olympic tourism development in the pre-, during, and post-Games periods in London, in nations and regions outside London, and in the UK as a whole. While this may seem a lot to ask of an Olympic tourism strategy at the consultation stage, the *raison detre* of such a strategy must be to cater for the full range of needs and aspirations for Olympic tourism, and it should be judged on its potential to do so.

The Welcome Legacy document is explicitly differentiated from other tourism strategies as having a specific purpose: 'the Government believes that it is important that the tourism sector's work towards 2012 should be identified and prioritized separately.' (DCMS/Visit Britain/Visit London, 2006:5). As such, its focus is on areas of priority and work that are seen as central in delivering a successful tourism product during 2012 and the impact that 2012 can have on the tourism industry. The document is structured around five key areas:

- Structures – getting the tourism structures for the games right

- Positioning – presenting the UK as a world-class tourism destination

- Quality – improving the quality of both accommodation and service

- Links – ensuring tourism links into the wider 2012 effort in other sectors

- Targets – setting ambitious and stretching targets for Olympic tourism

In relation to structures, there is a clear statement that the most appropriate structures to deliver Olympic tourism must be put in place:

> the operational structures adopted by VisitBritain and Visit London with LOCOG, regional and local delivery and support organisations, and the industry itself must be equally clear, must allow for full and effective collaboration, must encompass all relevant interests, and must be robust and flexible enough to cope with developments over the next six years. (DCMS/Visit Britain/Visit London, 2006:12)

However, much of the work on structures for Olympic tourism has focussed on liaison with bodies that have a limited life, such as LOCOG, the Nations and Regions Group and the Olympic Delivery Authority, and this may affect the extent to which London 2012 will be able to leave what was referred to in Chapter 5, and by Weed (2006c), as a 'policy development legacy'. Much discussion of the legacy of the Olympic Games, and indeed of mega-events more generally, focuses on the sporting, economic development, community/national pride and, of course, the tourism legacy. However, Weed (2006c) notes that there is also the potential for a policy development legacy in which organizations that have not always collaborated in the past 'learn' to work together, and learn of the benefits of working together, as a result of the Games. As such, the potential policy development benefits of London 2012 could be to establish long-term sustainable policy collaboration and liaison mechanisms and relationships between sport, tourism, and other sectors that can exist long after the Games has come and gone. Such collaborations, stimulated by mutual interests in relation to London 2012, can potentially continue and broaden in scope to become long-term 'legacy' collaborations dealing with the full range of issues on which it might be expected that sport, tourism, and other agencies might collaborate. However, such legacy policy development benefits will only be realized if operational and policy structures for London 2012 incorporate those agencies and interests that play key roles in the development of broader policy in these areas. As the Olympic-related structures and organizations established to serve London 2012 inevitably have a fixed life-span, it will be those agencies that will outlast such Olympic-structures that will be the key players in any legacy collaborations. Consequently, if the key players in London's Olympic tourism structures are agencies such as the Olympic Delivery Authority and the Nations and Regions Group, with agencies from sport, tourism, and other sectors playing a minor role, it is unlikely that any legacy liaison benefits will be realized as these agencies will not have had the opportunity to 'learn' how to work together. At present at national level, where no 'new' structure has been established for tourism, the lead agencies for Olympic tourism are the Department for Culture, Media and Sport, Visit Britain and Visit London, with no apparent involvement of Sport England or UK Sport. As such, it appears that the trend of agencies in the tourism sector demonstrating an involvement and interest in areas related to sports tourism, but without collaboration with sports bodies on such matters, as identified by Weed and Bull (1997a), is continuing at national level in the UK. In the regions, where the newly established NRG has some influence, there is much more evidence of collaborative working through newly established Olympic working groups. It will remain to be seen, however, whether such collaborations outlast the involvement of the NRG and the limited life of these groups.

In relation to positioning, the second of the priorities identified in Welcome Legacy, the strategy recognizes the importance of the Games in enhancing destination image, but the central focus is in relation to the Games period itself:

> During the weeks of the 2012 Games themselves, London will be the epicentre of the world's sporting and cultural interest … effective marketing and the management of international perceptions are vital to the full exploitation of the legacy. (DCMS/Visit Britain/Visit London, 2006:16)

What appears to be missing here is a recognition of the significant opportunities to leverage Olympic-media that exist in the pre-Games period, as discussed in the second part of Chapter 4. Other Games have recognized these opportunities with the 2006 Winter Games in Turin employing an 'Olympic Turin' promotion programme that focussed on generating positive stories about Turin in the non-sports media in the pre-Games period (see Chapter 6). Such opportunities are made all the more significant by the fact that the Olympic media spotlight will turn away from London and the UK before the spectators at the closing ceremony have left the stadium! There is very little opportunity to leverage Olympic media in the post-Games period.

Welcome Legacy also discusses a range of opportunities to harness the Olympics to develop business tourism, but states that while it may be possible for the regions to benefit, the majority of these opportunities will be for London:

> Visit Britain will work through the Nations and Regions Group to ensure that a significant proportion of business tourism generated by the Games opportunity accrues to parts of Britain other than London. But the capital is undeniably central to the sector. (DCMS/Visit Britain/Visit London, 2006:20)

This view contradicts the evidence somewhat. In Chapter 7, Graham Brown notes that the Sydney Convention Centre was unavailable for a considerable period before and during the Games of 2000, and that this resulted in some conference business switching to elsewhere in Australia. Furthermore, Brown (2007) has also noted that there was a general perception in the period up to a year and a half before the Games that Sydney would be too focussed on preparations for the Olympics to host conferences and exhibitions and that, in any case, businesses and conference organizers would prefer to avoid Sydney in Olympic and pre-Olympic year. While the Sydney Convention Centre did significantly increase its business in the years following the Games, undoubtedly the potential flow of business tourism from London to other locations in the UK (see discussions in Chapter 3) in the years before the Games represents a significant opportunity for the other nations and regions. In particular, the capital cities of Scotland and Wales, Edinburgh and Cardiff, could market themselves as alternative UK Capital Cities for business tourism and conferences in 2011 and 2012 which, of course, then offers the opportunity to generate further repeat business after 2012. And, of course, similar opportunities exist for other locations throughout the UK to 'pick up the slack' of 'Olympic aversion' markets in conference, business, and incentive tourism.

The concept of 'aversion' markets is not something that is recognized by Welcome Legacy, except in relation to the quality of the welcome and service, the third of the priority areas identified. The strategy notes that there is the potential for the Games to have a negative impact on the perception of the UK tourism product among those who visit for the Games and have a bad experience. In particular, the need to upgrade and improve disabled provision, accommodation, skills and service, transport and sustainability is discussed. However, as the discussion in Chapter 3 showed, there are a much wider range of aversion markets than those who have a bad experience during the Games, including those who decide not to visit because of the Games, those who switch to another UK destination because of the Games, and those London residents who wish to escape the Games. There is a limited recognition of this elsewhere in the document:

> a high proportion of tourism during the Games themselves is substitute in nature – many residents go away for the duration, and some inbound visitors will stay away. (DCMS/Visit Britain/Visit London, 2006:10)

However, this only recognizes that there will be aversion markets during the Games period whereas the analysis in Chapter 3 has shown that aversion markets exist in the pre-, during, and post-Games periods. Furthermore, there is no discussion of any need for strategies to address such aversion markets, only of increasing inward tourism. This is akin to owning a bucket with a hole in it and deciding to maximize the amount of water in the bucket by pouring in more water without attempting to plug the hole!

Of course, as Chapters 3 and 4 note, whilst Olympic aversion markets from London represent negative flows away from the capital, they offer opportunities for positive flows for other nations and regions in the UK, and present challenges to neutralize flows for the UK as a whole (i.e., to retain aversion markets within the UK rather than lose them to other countries). This is the *stratified geography* of Olympic tourism flows that is discussed in Chapters 3 and 4. Of course, stratified geography can work in London's favour, with inward flows from the nations and regions to London for a range of Olympic tourism products. However, there has been little recognition in either national or regional Olympic tourism strategies of the potential for this stratified geography of flows within the UK. This may be because there is a political imperative for London, the nations and regions, and the UK to all be seen to be working together towards a common goal. To a certain extent, the concept of a stratified geography of Olympic tourism flows may be politically unspeakable!

Whilst recognizing this stratified geography may be politically unspeakable, these discussions seem to highlight the clear need for strategies for Olympic tourism at three levels: (a) a strategy for London; (b) strategies for the other nations and regions; and, (c) a strategy for the UK as a whole. Furthermore, it should fall to the UK strategy to recognize that particular strategies for Olympic tourism to London may have negative impacts for the other nations and regions in the UK and vice-versa. As such, the role of a national strategy should be to balance the interests of London and the UK's other nations and regions and, most importantly, to ensure that the benefit for the UK as a whole is maximized. This could involve encouraging regions to provide tourism products for Olympic aversion markets (that will have a negative impact on London) to ensure that such aversion flows do not go outside of the UK. However, the consultation draft of Welcome Legacy gives the general impression of being an extension of a London Olympic tourism strategy, an impression that is reinforced by the fact that Visit London is one of the authors/publishers.

The fourth of the priorities identified in Welcome Legacy is the need for tourism to link in to the wider range of provision around 2012. In this respect, the strategy recognizes that:

> Tourism must make the most of the impressive range of cultural, sporting, artistic and other events planned for the run-up to, and during, the Games …. Plans to market these events at national, regional, and local levels to both the inbound and domestic markets should be in place at an early stage. (DCMS/Visit Britain/Visit London, 2006:28)

This section of Welcome Legacy is the strongest, and it highlights a range of Olympic tourism opportunities in both London and the nations and regions. In fact, some of the issues that have been highlighted as lacking in other sections of the strategy (such as the potential of the pre-Games period to generate tourism) are recognized, albeit not explicitly, in this section. In summary, the key areas highlighted (DCMS/Visit Britain/Visit London, 2006:28–31) are:

- The potential of the Torch relay (arriving around 2 months before the Games) to spread benefits around the UK.

- The Cultural Olympiad as a potential showcase for London and the rest of the UK in the pre-Games period. In the years before the Games, the cultural programme can showcase international and UK arts and culture, including a diverse range of festivals, events and artistic programmes. These begin with the handover ceremony at the Beijing Games in 2008, and dovetail with Liverpool's year as Capital of Culture in 2008.

- The potential for Games venues to attract visitors in the pre-Games period, and the tourism potential offered by training camps

- The expanded potential for sports event tourism. Additional major events in the run up to 2012, and the established UK draws such as Wimbledon, will take on greater significance as this country becomes the centre of the world's sporting attention over 2008–2012.

- Broadcasting and media opportunities for generating interest in the UK and its culture – not only during the Games themselves but over the four years of the Cultural Olympiad.

- Plans to harness film, live music and theatre, although largely focussed on 2012 itself

- The potential use of iconic heritage images and sites for Olympic-related activities

- Potential for big screens to be erected in Royal parks and open spaces in London

- Potential for special Olympic-themed exhibitions in London museums

- Potential to involve of the creative industries to ensure that the Games leave an appropriate cultural legacy.

These activities provide an impressive list of potential Olympic tourism opportunities and, notwithstanding the criticism of Welcome Legacy so far, indicate a much greater awareness of Olympic-related opportunities than that shown by many previous Games. However, while this section is less London-centric than other parts of the strategy, there is still a tendency towards focussing on the London-based opportunities. There is no reason, for example, why opportunities relating to big screens in open spaces and parks should be limited to London.

The theme of the relationship between opportunities for London and those for the other nations and regions is one that recurs in relation to the setting of ambitious and stretching targets, the final priority identified in Welcome Legacy, and this is a useful way to conclude the substantive discussions in this chapter. The need for targets to be relevant to 2012, to other

Government objectives, and to the existing tourism growth target is identified in the strategy, alongside the need for targets to 'be UK-wide in scope (and therefore to enjoy the support and commitment of the devolved administrations of Scotland, Wales, and Northern Ireland)' (DCMS/Visit Britain/Visit London, 2006:32). Much of the discussion of Welcome Legacy in this chapter has suggested that the strategy as it stands cannot adequately lead the UK-wide Olympic tourism effort because it assumes that strategies that benefit London will benefit the UK as a whole. As noted earlier, this fails to recognize the *stratified geography* of tourism flows discussed in Chapter 3, and the need for a national strategy that focuses on maximizing the benefits for the UK as whole and balancing the often competing interests of London and the other nations and regions. In particular, a UK national Olympic tourism strategy should not be co-authored and co-published by Visit London.

Conclusion

The discussions in this chapter have undoubtedly been more critical than those of the other 21st Century Olympic hosts in previous chapters. To a certain extent the fact that, five years prior to the London 2012 Games, an Olympic policy community (see discussions in Chapter 5) has developed to the point that national strategies (or consultations) have been issued in a number of policy areas (including tourism) in addition to a range of regional Olympic strategies, is testament to a significant change in attitude to Olympic planning. Certainly, in comparison with Athens 2004, London has a much more wide-ranging set of strategic planning arrangements. However, the criticisms in this chapter are derived, in part, from a recognition that London has benefited from a decade of research and knowledge transfer in relation to the opportunities that an Olympic Games can present. As such, in comparison to the Sydney Games of 2000, which are widely recognized as having set the benchmark for leveraging the benefits of the Olympic Games, there is, quite rightly, a higher expectation across a range of policy areas, including tourism, for London 2012.

Afterword

Many people picking up a text such as this might have expected a greater emphasis on the economic impacts of tourism to the Olympic Games. However, the decision not to focus on such economic impacts is a deliberate one, and was taken for two reasons. First, there are already a number of texts available examining the impacts of the Games, not least Holger Preuss' *The Economics of Staging the Games* (2004) which provides a detailed and extensive coverage of this topic. Second, in focussing on the ways in which Olympic tourism might be generated, the book is responding to the calls of a number of authors (e.g., Chalip, 2006; Downward, 2005; Gibson, 2004; Weed, 2007) to focus on the means rather than the end in relation to sports tourism and sports events. In other words, there is increasingly a need to move beyond asking 'what' questions (i.e., what impacts has the Olympic Games had) to ask 'why' questions (i.e., why and how were particular impacts generated) (cf. Gibson, 2004). Downward (2005:315) calls this 'ontic depth', noting that.

> explanations require 'ontic depth', that is moving beyond
> the level of events towards an understanding of the pro-
> cesses that produce them.

This book has sought to provide such ontic depth by progressing from an understanding of products (Chapter 1) and behaviours (Chapter 2) to an examination of the processes and flows induced in the consumption of such products (Chapter 3) which inform the development of strategy (Chapter 4) and policy (Chapter 5). In doing so, it is acknowledging:

> the fundamental nature of research on behaviours both in
> understanding impacts and, in turn, the policy and provi-
> sion requirements of such impacts, and in contributing to

the development of policy and management approaches. Undoubtedly, there is a clear link between behaviours, impacts and policy and management. (Weed, 2007)

This view assumes that if understandings of products, behaviours, consumption and processes have 'ontic depth', then the depth of this understanding can be capitalized upon in developing strategies to leverage benefits from an event such as the Olympic Games. Such a leveraging approach has been argued for by Chalip for some time (e.g., Chalip 2004; 2006; Chalip and Leyns, 2002), who summarizes the leveraging approach as follows:

> Unlike impact assessments, the study of leverage has a *strategic and tactical* focus. The objective is to identify strategies and tactics that can be implemented prior to and during an event in order to generate particular outcomes. Consequently, leveraging implies a much more *pro-active approach* to *capitalising on opportunities*, rather than impacts research which simply measures outcomes. (*emphasis added*) (Chalip, 2004)

This approach, within the context of a knowledge of products, behaviours, consumption and processes, was central to the first part of this text. The intention has been to suggest strategies and tactics to capitalize upon the opportunities for tourism that the Olympic Games provides to a host city/region and country, and to highlight the importance of being pro-active in capitalizing on such opportunities, rather than simply expecting positive impacts to materialize out of the ether. In this respect, as noted in its concluding sentences, Chapter 4 is perhaps the pivotal chapter in this book as it draws together the foundational knowledge from Chapters 1, 2 and 3 to inform a discussion of leveraging strategies.

As noted in the foreword, this book does not claim to present new empirical knowledge, rather it has sought to apply cutting edge and classic approaches from sports tourism, sport events and tourism research to the Olympic tourism context. In this respect, the key models, concepts and theories, which in most cases have been adapted or extended, have been: Weed and Bull's (2004) *Model of Sports Tourism Types* (Chapter 1) and *Sports Tourism Participation Model* (Chapter 2), Preuss' (2005) *Model of Event Affected People at Major Multi-Sport Events* and Leiper's (1979) *Model of the Tourism System* (Chapter 3), Chalip's (2004) *General Model for Sport Event Leverage* (Chapter 4), and Weed and

Bull's (1997a) *Policy Area Matrix for Sport and Tourism* and Weed's (2001b) *Model of Cross-Sectoral Policy Development* (Chapter 5).

While Part 1 of the book has sought to examine the application of a range of concepts, theories and models to the Olympic tourism context, part two of the book has sought to illustrate the application of these concepts, models and theories through an examination of previous and prospective Olympic Games in the 21st century. In doing so, these chapters have sought to highlight the very different contexts of the various 21st century Games. The differences between the potential tourism implications of, and the resultant strategies that might be employed in, the Winter and Summer Games were highlighted in Chapter 6. Here, the way in which the historical development of the Winter Olympics has affected the tourism strategies employed by and planned for the Winter Games of the 21st century are discussed. Furthermore, Chapter 6 highlights not only the specific context of the Winter Olympics, but the very different contexts of each individual host city/region. These varying contexts are highlighted in relation to the Summer Games in Chapters 7, 8, 9 and 10.

Graham Brown's guest contribution (Chapter 7) describes the first Games of the 21st century. He highlights how Sydney 2000 was the first Olympics at which any sustained planned attempts to leverage the Games were made in a context of little usable previous knowledge about how this should be done. The cultural context for the Athens Games was the country's and the city's historical place in the development of both the ancient and modern Olympics. In this respect, Athens wished to show itself as a county with a long-culture capable of staging a modern Games. However, while the Games themselves were successful, the leveraging opportunities were not capitalized upon as a result of a number of planning failures.

As the first Games in prospect at the time of writing (June 2007), the context for the Beijing Games of 2008 is China's history in terms of its relationship with the Olympic Movement (i.e., the 'two-China's problem') and its relationship with the international community (i.e., its emergence from being a 'closed' planned economy and its record on human rights). Each of these issues, and the way in which the Beijing organizers deal with them, and the rest of the world reacts to them, will be central to the extent to which China and Beijing can leverage the 2008 Games for tourism. The successful London bid for the 2012 Games emphasized the multi-cultural nature of the city and, therefore, its ability to engage with and inspire the world. However, the organizational context for London 2012 is one in which, unlike Sydney in 2000, a range of previous Olympic knowledge (and general knowledge on leveraging events) is available to draw upon in planning for the Games. Therefore, against this context London 2012 should perhaps be more critically evaluated than some of the previous Games in that it might be expected to be more effective in leveraging Olympic tourism.

Notwithstanding the comments regarding the greater availability of knowledge to inform planning for the London 2012 Games, specific empirical research on Olympic tourism remains sparse. This book has applied previous work in the related areas of sports tourism, sports events and general tourism to generate the perspectives on Olympic tourism that have been presented. Furthermore, it has established that opportunities to leverage Olympic tourism are both temporally and geographically broader than simply the period of the Olympic Games in the host city. Temporally, opportunities for Olympic tourism exist in both the pre- and post-Games periods, and geographically, opportunities exist for Olympic tourism throughout the host country. The challenge now for future empirical research is to build the evidence base relating to the scope, the nature and the extent of Olympic tourism.

References

Administrative Committee of Zhongguancun Science Park (ACZSP). (2003). *A brief introduction to the policies for the development of new and high tech industries in Zhongguancun.* Beijing: ACZSP.

Alpha Bank. (2004) *The Impact of the Olympic Games on the Greek Economy.* Athens: Alpha Bank.

Astrand, P-O (1978) *Health and Fitness.* New York: Skandia Insurance Company.

Astrand, P-O (1987) 'Setting the scene', in Coronary Prevention Group (eds) *Exercise Heart Health* (pp. 5–20). London: Coronary Prevention Group.

Australian Tourist Commission. (1996) *1996 Olympic Games Atlanta Report.* September.

Australian Tourist Commission. (1998) *Tourism and the XXVII Olympiad 1998–2000. Three Year Strategy.* January.

Australia Tourist Commission. (2000) *The Sydney Olympic Games.* ATC research Update. April.

Australian Tourist Commission. (2001) *Australia's Olympics.* Special Post Games Tourism Report.

Baker, W.J. (1982) *Sports in the Western World.* Totowa, NJ: Rowman and Littlefield.

Bale, J. (1989) *Sports Geography.* London: E. & F.N. Spon.

Bale, J. (2003) *Sports Geography*, 2nd edn. London: Spon.

Beijing Institute of Urban Planning and Design (BIUPD). (1992) *Urban Master Plan for Beijing.* Beijing: BIUPD.

Beijing Organising Committee for the Olympic Games (BOCOG). (2003) *Beijing Olympic Action Plan.* Beijing: BOCOG.

Beijing Statistical Bureau. (2003) *Beijing Statistical Yearbook, 2003.* Beijing: China Statistics Press.

Beriatos, E. and Gospodini, A. (2004) 'Glocalising' urban landscapes: Athens and the 2004 olympics. *Cities*, 21(3), 187–202.

Berridge, G. (2006) *Events Design and Experience*. Oxford: Elsevier.

Bondonio, P. and Campaniello, N. (2006) *Torino 2006: An Organisational and Economic Overview*. Working Paper 1/2006, Mega-Events Observatory, University of Turin.

Boniface, B.G. and Cooper, C. (2001) *Worldwide Destinations: The Geography of Travel and Tourism*. Oxford: Butterworth-Heinemann.

Boulton, R.E.S., Libert, B.D. and Samek, S.M. (2000) A business model for the new economy. *Journal of Business Strategy*, 21(4), 29–35.

Bramwell, B. (1997a) A sport mega-event as a sustainable tourism development strategy. *Tourism Recreation Research*, 22(2), 13–19.

British Tourist Authority. (1981) *Tourism, the UK – The Broad Perspective*. London: BTA.

Brown, G. (2000) 'Emerging issues in Olympic sponsorship' implications for host cities. *Sport Management Review*, 3, 71–92.

Brown, G. (2001) Sydney 2000: an invitation to the world. *Olympic Review*, 37, 15–20.

Brown, G. (2007) Olympic Sponsor Hospitality Programs: Maximising Benefits for Tourism. Paper to *Event Tourism: Enhancing Destinations and the Visitor Economy*, Bournemouth, UK, January.

Brown, G., Chalip, L., Jago, L. and Mules, T. (2002) 'Developing brand Australia: examining the role of events', in N. Morgan, A. Pritchard and R. Pride (eds) *Destination Branding. Creating the Unique Destination Proposition* (pp. 279–305). Oxford: Elsevier Butterworth-Heinemann.

Buhalis, D. (2001) Tourism in Greece: strategic analysis and challenges. *Current Issues in Tourism*, 4(5), 440–480.

Bull, C.J., Hoose, J. and Weed, M.E. (2003) *An Introduction to Leisure Studies*. Harlow: FT Prentice Hall.

Burbank, M., Andranovich, G. and Heying, C.H. (2001) *Olympic Dreams: The Impact of Mega Events on Local Politics*. Colorado: Lynne Rienner Publishers.

Burns, J. (2005) Written Statement to the US Senate Subcommittee on Trade, Tourism and Economic Development. *Field Hearing on The Economic Impact of the 2010 Vancouver, Canada, Winter Olympics on Oregon and the Pacific Northwest*. Washington: US Government Printing Office.

Business File. (2004) *Going for Gold? A Survey on the Economics of the 2004 Olympic Games*. Athens: Greek Special Survey Series.

Card Watch (1992). Olympic marketing on the cheap. *Credit Card Management*, June, 14.

Carpenter, G. and Priest, S. (1989) 'The adventure Experience Paradigm and non-outdoor Leisure Pursuits', *Leisure Studies*, 8, 65–75.

Carron, A.V. and Hausenblaus, H.L. (1998) *Group Dynamics in Sport*. Morgantown, Virginia: Fitness Information Technology.

Casson, L. (1974). *Travel in the Ancient World*. London: Allen and Unwin.

CEC. (1992) *Urbanisation and the Function of Cities in the European Community. Regional Development Studies*. Brussels: 4 Commission of the European Communities.

Chalip, L. (1990). The politics of Olympic theatre: New Zealand and Korean cross-national relations. In B-I. Koh (ed.) *Toward One World Beyond All Barriers* (Vol.1). Soeul, South Korea: Poong Nam.

Chalip, L. (2000). An interview with Maggie White, business manager Olympic Games for the Australian Tourism Commission. *International Journal of Sports Marketing and Sponsorship*, 2, 187–197

Chalip, L. (2004) 'Beyond impact: A general model for sport event leverage', in B.W. Ritchie and D. Adair (eds) *Sport Tourism: Interrelationships, Impacts and Issues* (pp. 226–252). Clevedon, UK: Channel View Publications.

Chalip, L. (2006) Towards social leverage of sport events. *Journal of Sport & Tourism*, 11(2), 109–128.

Chalip, L. and Leyns, A. (2002) Local business leveraging of a sport event: Managing an event for economic benefit. *Journal of Sport Management*, 16(2), 132–158.

Chan, G. (1985) The 'Two-Chinas' problem and the olympic formula. *Pacific Affairs*, 58(3), 473–490.

Chappelet, J-L. (2002) A Short Overview of the Winter Olympic Games. *University Lectures on the Olympics*, Centre for Olympic Studies, Barcelona, Spain.

Chen, J.S. (2000) Cross-cultural differences in travel information acquisition among tourists from three Pacific-Rim Countries. *Journal of Hospitality and Tourism Research*, 24(2), 239–251.

Centre on Housing Rights and Evictions (COHRE) (2007) *Fair Play for Housing Rights: Mega-Events, Olympic Games and Housing Rights*. Geneva: COHRE.

Collins, M.F. and Jackson, G.A.M. (1999) 'The Economic Impact of Sport and Tourism', in J. Standeven, and P. De Knop (eds) *Sport Tourism*. London: Human Kinetics.

Collins, M.F. and Jackson, G.A.M. (2001) Evidence for a Sports Tourism Continuum. Paper to *Journeys in Leisure*, Leisure Studies Association Conference, Luton, July.

Cohen, E. (1983) The social psychology of tourist behaviour. *Annals of Tourism Research*, 15(1), 29–46.

Cotton, B. (2005) Training and Holding Camps. Paper to Sport England One-day Seminar, *Going for Gold*, Bisham Abbey, UK, July.

Cooper, C. and Buhalis, D. (1992) 'Strategic management and marketing of small and mediumsized tourismenterprises in the Greek Aegean islands', in R. Teare, D. Adams and S. Messenger (eds) *Managing Projects in Hospitality Organisations* (pp. 101–25). London: Cassell.

Cooper, C.P., Fletcher, J., Wanhill, S., Gilbert, D. and Shepherd, R. (1998) *Tourism: Principles and Practice*, 2nd edn. Harlow: Pitman.

Council of Europe. (1992) *European Sport for All Charter*. Strasbourg: The Council.

Crompton, J.L. (1979) Motivations for pleasure vacation. *Journal of Leisure Research*, 6, 408–424.

Crotts, J. (2004) The effect of cultural distance on overseas travel behaviours. *Journal of Travel Research*, 43(4), 83–88.

Crotts, J. and Litvin, S. (2003) Cross-cultural research: are researchers better served by knowing respondents country of birth, residence, or citizenship? *Journal of Travel Research*, 42(2), 186–190.

Crowther, N. (2001) Visiting the olympic games in ancient Greece: travel and conditions for athletes and spectators. *International Journal of the History of Sport*, 18(4), 37–52.

Davies, N. (1997) *Europe: A History*. London: Pimlico.

De Knop, P. (1990) Sport for All and Active Tourism. Journal of the World Leisure and Recreation Association (italics), Fall, 30–36

Department for Culture, Media and Sport/Visit Britain/Visit London (2006) *Welcome Legacy: Tourism Strategy for the 2012 Games – Consultation*. London: DCMS/Visit Britain/Visit London.

Downward, P. (2005) Critical (Realist) reflection on policy and management research in sport, tourism and sports tourism. *European Sport Management Quarterly*, 5(3), 302–322.

Downward, P.M. and Mearman, A. (2004) On tourism and hospitality management research: A critical realist proposal. *Tourism and Hospitality Planning and Development*, 1(2), 107–122.

Duran, P. (2005) 'The impact of the Olympic Games on tourism. Barcelona: the legacy of the Games 1992–2002', in I. Urdangarin and D. Torres (eds) *New Views on Sport Tourism* (pp. 77–91). Mallorca: Calliope Publishing.

Ecoclub. (2007) The Ecoclub Interview: Haris Coccoccis (Executive Secretary of Tourism, Ministry of Tourism Development, Greece). *Ecoclub*, Issue 88, January.

Economist. (1993) Last Chance Sisyphus: A survey of Greece. *Economist*, 22nd May, 2–22.

Espy, R. (1979) *The Politics of the Olympic Games*. Berkeley: University of California Press.

Essex, S. and Chalkey, B. (2002) The changing infrastructural implications of the Winter Olympics, 1924–2002. *Bollettino della Società Geografica Italiana*, 7(4).

Ewart, A. and Hollenhorst, S. (1994) Individual and setting attributes of the adventure recreation experience. *Leisure Ssciences*, 16(3), 177–191.

Faulkner, B., Chalip, L., Jago, L., March, R. and Woodside, A. (2000). Monitoring the Tourism Impacts of the Sydney 2000 Olympics. *Event Management*, 6(4), 231–246

Fayos-Sola, E. (1998) The impact of mega events. *Annals of Tourism Research*, 25(1), 241–245.

Finley, M.I. and Pleket, H.W. (1976) *The Olympic Games*. Edinburgh: R and R Clark.

Fraser, K. (1998) 'The Hosts with the Most'. *Marketing and eBusiness*, December, pp. 29–35.

Gammon, S. (2002) 'Fantasy, Nostalgia and the Pursuit of What Never Was', in S. Gammon and J. Kurtzman (eds) *Sport Tourism: Principles and Practice*. Eastbourne: LSA.

Gammon, S. and Robinson, T. (1997/2003) Sport and Tourism: A Conceptual Framework. *Journal of Sport Tourism*, 8(1), 21–26.

Getz, D. (1997a) *Event Management and Event Tourism*. New York: Cognizant Communication Corporation.

Getz, D. (2003) 'Sport Event Tourism: Planning, Development and Marketing', in S. Hudson (ed.) *Sport and Adventure Tourism*. New York: Haworth Hospitality Press.

Gibson, H. (2004). Moving beyond the "what is and who" of sport tourism to understanding "why". *Journal of Sport Tourism*, 9(3), 247–265.

Gibson, H., McIntyre, S., Mackay, S. and Riddington, G. (2005) The Economic Impact of Sports Sporting Events and Sports Tourism in the UK: The DREAM Model. *European Sport Management Quarterly*, 5(3), 321–332.

Gibson, H.J. (1998) Sport Tourism: A Critical Analysis of Research. *Sport Management Review*, 1(1), 45–76.

Gibson, H.J. (2002) 'Sport Tourism at a Crossroad? Considerations for the Future', in S. Gammon and J. Kurtzman (eds) *Sport Tourism: Principles and Practice*. Eastbourne: LSA.

Gibson, H.J. (ed) (2006) *Sport Tourism: Concepts and Theories*. London: Routledge.

Girginov, V. and Parry, J. (2004) *The Olympic Games Explained*. London: Taylor & Francis.

Glyptis, S.A. (1982) *Sport and Tourism in Western Europe*. London: British Travel Education Trust.

Glyptis, S.A. (1991) 'Sport and Tourism', in C.P. Cooper (ed) *Progress in Tourism, Recreation and Hospitality Management* (vol. 3). London: Belhaven Press.

Golden, M. (1998) *Sport and Society in Ancient Greece*. Cambridge: Cambridge University Press.

Graburn, N.H.H. (1983) 'The Anthropology of Tourism'. *Annals of Tourism Research*, 10(1), 9–33.

Graburn, N.H.H. (1989) 'Tourism: The Sacred Journey', in V. Smith (ed) *Hosts and Guests: The Anthropology of Tourism*, 2nd edn. Philadephia: University of Pennsylvania.

Granson, E. (2005) The Big Event: Calgary 17 Years On. *Alberta Venture*, 9(3).

Gratton, C., Shibli, S. and Coleman, R. (2006) The Economic Impact of major Sports Events: A Review of Ten Events in the UK. *The Sociological Review*, 54(s2), 41–58.

Gratton, C. and Taylor, P. (1985) *Sport and Recreation: An Economic Analysis*, London: E and F N Spon.

Green, B.C. and Chalip, L. (1998) 'Sport Tourism as the Celebration of Subculture', *Annals of Tourism Research*, 25(2), 275–291.

Green, B.C., Costa, C. and Fitzgerald, M. (2002). Marketing the host city: Analysing exposure generated by a sport event. *International Journal of Sports Marketing and Sponsorship*, 4, 335–353.

Gunn, C.A. (1990) The New Recreation-Tourism Alliance. *Journal of Park and Recreation Administration*, 8(1), 1-8.

Gwinner, K.P., and Eaton, J. (1999). Building brand image through event sponsorship: the role of image transfer. *Journal of Advertising*, 28(4), 47–57

Hall, C.M. (1992) 'Adventure, Sport and Health', in C.M. Hall and B. Weiler (eds) *Special Interest Tourism*. London: Belhaven Press.

Hall, C.M. (2001) 'Imaging, Tourism and Sports Event Fever', in C. Gratton and I.P. Henry (eds) *Sport in the City: The Role of Sport in Economic and Social Regeneration*. London: Routledge.

Harris, H.A. (1964) *Greek Athletes and Athletics*. London: Hutchinson.

Hetherington, K (1996) 'Identity Formation, Space and Social Centrality', *Theory, Culture and Society*, 13(4), 33–52.

Higham, J. (ed) (2005) *Sport Tourism Destinations: Issues, Opportunities and Analysis*. Oxford: Elsevier.

Higham, J. and Hinch, T. (2002) Tourism, Sport and Seasons: The challenges and potential of overcoming seasonality in the sport and tourism sectors. *Tourism Management*, 23(2), 175–185.

Higham, J. and Hinch, T. (forthcoming) *Sport and Tourism: Globalisation, Mobility and Authenticity*. Oxford: Elsevier.

Hill, C. (1996) *Olympic Politics*. Manchester: Manchster University Press.

Hill, E., O'Sullivan, T. and O'Sullivan, C. (1995) *Creative Arts Marketing*. Oxford: Butterworth Heinemann.

Hill, R.C. and Kim, J. (2000) Global cities and development states: New York, Tokyo and Seoul. *Urban Studies*, 37(12), 2167–2195.

Hinch, T. and Higham, J. (2004) *Sport Tourism Development*. Clevedon: Channel View Publications.

Hinch, T. and Higham, J. (2005) Sport, Tourism and Authenticity. *European Sport Management Quarterly*, 5(3), 245–258.

Hofstede, G. (1980) *Culture's Consequences: International Differences in Work-Related Values*. Beverley Hills: Sage.

Hofstede, G. (2001) *Culture's Consequences*. Thousand Oaks: Sage.

Horne, J., Tomlinson, A. and Whannel, G. (1999) *Understanding Sport: An Introduction to the Sociological and Cultural Analysis of Sport*. London: Spon.

Houliham, B. (2003) 'Sport and Globalisation', in B. Houlihan (ed) *Sport and Society: A Student Introduction*. London: Sage.

Hudson, S. (2000) *Snow Business*. London: Cassell.

Hudson, S. (ed) (2003) *Sport and Adventure Tourism*. New York: Haworth Hospitality Press.

Hutchison, J. (2000) *Sydney Attracts Strong Post Olympic Business*. Sydney Convention and Visitors Bureau, News Release, June.

Industry, Science and Technology. (1995) Olympics 2000 - - - and the Winner Is? Report of the *Australian House of Representatives Standing Committee*.

International Olympic Committee (IOC) (2001) *Candidate Cities and Venues for the Winter Olympics*. Lausanne: IOC.

International Olympic Committee (IOC) (2004) *Marketing Revenue*. http://www.olympic.org/uk/organisation/facts/revenue/index_uk.asp (accessed 15/10/2004).

Inter Vistas Consulting (IVC) (2002) *The Economic Impact of the 2010 Winter Olympic and Paralympic Games: An Update*. Vancouver: State Government of British Columbia.

Iso-Ahola, S.E. (1980) *The Social Psychology of Leisure and Recreation*. Iwoa: William Brown.

Iso-Ahola, S.E. (1982) 'Toward a Social Psychological Theory of Tourism Motivation: a rejoinder', *Annals of Tourism Research*, 9(2), 256–262.

Iso-Ahola, S.E. (1984) 'Social Psychology Foundations of Leisure and Resultant Implications for Leisure Counselling', in E.T. Dowd (ed) Leisure Counselling: Concepts and Applications. Illinois: C.C. Thomas.

Iso-Ahola, S.E. (1989) 'Motivation for Leisure', in E.L. Jackson and T.L. Burton (eds) Understanding Leisure and Recreation: Shaping the Past, Charting the Future. State College, Pa: Venture Publishing.

Iso-Ahola, S.E. and Wissingberger, E. (1990) 'Perceptions of Boredom in Leisure: Conceptualisation, Reliability and Validity of the Leisure Boredom Scale', *Journal of Leisure Research*, 22(1), 1–17.

Jackson, G.A.M. and Glyptis, S.A. (1992) *Sport and Tourism: A Review of the Literature*. Report to the Sports Council,

Recreation Management Group, Loughborough University. Loughborough: Unpublished.

Jackson, G.A.M. and Reeves, M.R. (1998) 'Evidencing the Sport-Tourism Interrelationship: A Case Study of Elite British Athletes', in M.F. Collins and I. Cooper (eds) *Leisure Management: Issues and Applications*. London: CABI.

Jackson, G.A.M. and Reeves, M.R. (1996) Conceptualising the Sport-Tourism Interrelationship: A Case Study Approach. *Paper to the LSA/VVA Conference*, Wageningen, September.

Jackson, G.A.M. and Weed, M.E. (2003) 'The Sport-Tourism Interrelationship', in B. Houlihan (ed) *Sport and Society*. London: Sage.

Jackson, M. (2001) Cultural Influences on Tourist Destination Choices of 21 Pacific Rim Nations. *Paper to the CAUTHE National Research Conference*, Canberra, Australia, February.

Jennings, A. (2000) *The New Lords of the Rings: Olympic Corruption and How to Buy Gold Medals*. London: Simon & Schuster Ltd.

Jennings, G. (2003) 'Marine Tourism', in S. Hudson (ed) *Sport and Adventure Tourism*. New York: Haworth Hospitality Press.

Jordan, A.G. and Richardson, J.J. (1987) *British Politics and the Policy Process*. London: Allen and Unwin.

Judd, D.R. (ed) (2002) *The Infrastructure of Play: Building the Tourist City*. New York: M.E.Sharpe.

Knowledge@Wharton. (2004) Despite Lacklustre Ticket Sales, Can Greece Be a Big Winner in This Year's Olympics? *Knowledge@Wharton*, 25th August.

Kolatch, J. (1972) *Sports, Politics and Ideology in China*. New York: Jonathan David Publishers.

Kretchmarr, A.S. (1994) *Practical Philosophy of Sport*. Illinois: Human Kinetics.

Lambton, D. (2001) 'Changing Times on the Top Table', *Sports Business International*, 61, 54–56.

Lee, M. (2006) *The Race for the 2012 Olympics*. London: Virgin Books.

Lefebvre, H. (1996). *Writings on Cities* (translated and edited by E. Kofman and E. Lebas). London: Blackwell.

Leiper, N. (1979) 'The framework of tourism', *Annals of Tourism Research*, 6(4), 390–407.

Leiper, N. (1984) 'Tourism and Leisure: The Significance of Tourism in the Leisure Spectrum'. *Proceedings of the 12th New Zealand Geography Conference*. Christchurch: New Zealand Geography Society.

Lenskyj, H. (2002) *The Best Olympics Ever? Social Impacts of Sydney 2000*. New York: State University of New York Press.

Long, J. (1990) 'Leisure, health and wellbeing: Editor's Introduction', in J. Long (ed) *Leisure, Health and Wellbeing*. Conference papers, No. 44, Eastbourne: Leisure Studies Association.

Mannel, R.C. and Kleiber, D.A. (1997) *A Social Psychology of Leisure*. State College, PA: Venture Publishing.

Mannell, R. and Iso-Ahola, S.E. (1987) 'Psychological Nature of Leisure and Tourism Experience', *Annals of Tourism Research*, 14(3), 314–331.

Martin, P. and Priest, S. (1986) 'Understanding the Adventure Experience', *Journal of Adventure Education*, 3(1), 18–20.

Mathieson, A. and Wall, G. (1989) *Tourism: Economic, Physical and Social Impacts*. Harlow: Longman.

MacCannell, D. (1996) *Tourist or Traveller?* London: BBC Education.

MacCannell, D. (1999) *The Tourist: A New Theory of the Leisure Class*. London: Macmillan.

Maguire, J. (1999) *Global Sport: Identities, Societies, Civilisations*. Cambridge: Polity Press.

Masterman, G. (2004) *Strategic Event Management: An International Approach*. Oxfrod: Elsevier.

McIntosh, R.W. and Goeldner, C.R. (1986) *Tourism Principles, Practices, Philosophies*. 5th edn. Columbus, OH: Grid Publishing.

McLean, F. (1998) *Presentation to the IATA conference*, Berlin, September.

Mortlock, C. (1984) *The Adventure Alternative*. Cumbria, UK: Cicerone Press.

Moutinho, L. (1987) Consumer Behaviour in Tourism. *European Journal of Marketing*, 21(10), 5–44.

Muller, N. (2000) *Pierre De Coubertin 1863–1937. Olympism, Selected Writings*. Lausanne: International Olympic Committee.

Nauright, J. (1996) 'A Besieged tribe'?: Nostalgia, White Cultural Identity and the Role of Rugby in a changing South Africa. *International Review for the Sociology of Sport*, 31(1), 69–89.

Neulinger, J. (1991) *The Psychology of Leisure*, 2nd edn. Springfield Ill: Charles C Thomas Publishing.

Ng, S.I., Lee, J.A. and Soutar, G.N. (2007) Tourists' intention to visit a country: The impact of cultural distance. *Tourism Management*, in press.

NYCvisit (2007) *NYC Statistics*. New York: NYCvisit.

O'Brien, D. (2006) Event Business Leveraging: The Sydney 2000 Olympic Games. *Annals of Tourism Research*, 33(1), 240–261.

ONS (2003) *International Passenger Survey*. London: Office of National Statistics.

Parliamentary Select Committee on Culture Media and Sport (2007) *London 2012 Olympic Games and Paralympic Games: Funding and Legacy (First Report)*. London: HMSO.

Papanikos, G. (1999) *The 2004 Olympic Games and Their Impact Upon Greek Tourism*. Athens: Research Institute for Tourism (ITEP).

Payne, M. (2005) *Olympic Turnaround: How the Olympic Games Stepped Back from the Brink of Extinction to Become the World's Best Known Brand – and a Multi Billion Dollar Global Franchise.* London: London Business Press.

Pearce, D.G. (1993) 'Comparative Studies in Tourism Research', in D.G. Pearce and R.W. Butler (eds) *Tourism Research: Critiques and Challenges.* London: Routledge.

Petrakos, G. and Economou, D. (1999) 'Internationalisation and structural changes in the European urban system', in D. Economou and G. Petrakos (eds) *The Development of Greek Cities.* Athens: Gutenberg and University of Thessaly Publications.

Pigeassou, C. (2002) 'Contribution to the Analysis of Sport Tourism'. Oral presentation to the 10th *European Sport Management Congress*, Jyvaskyla, Finland, September.

Pizam, A. and Jeong, G. (1996) Cross-cultural Tourist Behaviour. *Tourism Management*, 17(4), 277–286.

Poulios, P.C. (2006) The 2004 Athens Olympics: A Cost-Benefit Analysis. *Entertainment and Sports Lawyer*, 24(1), 1 & 18–31.

Preuss, H. (2004) *The Economics of Staging the Olympics: A Comparison of the Games 1972–2008.* Cheltenham: Edward Elgar.

Preuss, H. (2005) The Economic Impact of Vistors at Major Multi-Sport Events. *European Sport Management Quarterly*, 5(3), 283–303.

PricewaterhouseCoopers. (2005) *Olympic Games Impact Study.* London: Department for Culture, Media and Sport.

Priest, S. (1992) 'Factor Exploration and Confirmation of the Dimensions of an Adventure Experience', *Journal of Leisure Research*, 24(2), 127–139.

Readman, M. (2003) 'Golf Tourism', in S. Hudson (ed) *Sport and Adventure Tourism.* New York: Haworth Hospitality Press.

Reeves, M.R. (2000) *Evidencing the Sport-Tourism Interrelationship.* Loughborough University: Unpublished PhD Thesis.

Ren, H. (2002) China and the Olympic Movement. *University Lectures on the Olympics*, Centre for Olympic Studies, Barcelona, Spain.

Rhodes, R.A.W. (1981) *Control and Power in Centre-Local Government Relations*, Gower/SSRC, Farnborough.

Rhodes, R.A.W. and Marsh, D. (1992) 'Policy Networks in British Politics: A Critique of Existing Approaches', in D. Marsh and R.A.W. Rhodes, (eds) *Policy Networks in British Government.* Oxford: Oxford University Press.

Riley, D. (2005) Written Statement to the US Senate Subcommittee on Trade, Tourism and Economic Development. *Field Hearing on The Economic Impact of the 2010 Vancouver, Canada, Winter Olympics on Oregon and the Pacific Northwest.* Washington: US Government Printing Office.

Ritchard, K. (2004) The Hotel Industry is Pinning its Hope on Gold at Beijing in 2008 – But is it a sure winner? *Hotel Asia Pacific*, December.

Ritchie, B. and Adair, D. (eds) (2004) *Sport Tourism: Interrelationships, Impacts and Issues*. Clevedon: Channel View.

Ritchie, J.R.B. (1984) Assessing the impact of hallmark events: Conceptual and research issues. *Journal of Travel Research*, 23(1), 2–11.

Ritchie, J.R.B. (1990) 'Promoting Calgary through the Olympics: The mega-event as a strategy for community development', in S.H. Fine (ed) *Social Marketing: Promoting the Causes of Public and Nonprofit Agencies*. Toronto: Allyn and Bacon.

Ritchie, J.R.B. (1999) *Turning 16 Days into 16 Years: A Calgary Perspective on Strategies for Enhancing the Success, the Long-term Impacts and the Legacies of the 2002 Olympic Winter Games on Salt Lake City*. Report to the Utah Division of Travel Development, Salt Lake City, Utah.

Ritchie, J.R.B. and Aitken, C.E. (1984) 'Assessing the impacts of the 1988 Olympic Winter Games: the research program and initial results', *Journal of Travel Research*, 22(3), 17–25.

Ritchie, J.R.B. and Aitken, C.E. (1985) Olympulse II – Evolving Resident attitudes Toward the 1988 Olympic Winter Games. *Journal of Travel Research*, 23(3), 28–33.

Ritchie, J.R.B. and Lyons, M.M. (1987) Olympulse III/IV: A Mid-term Report on Resident Attitudes Concerning the 1988 Olympic Winter Games. *Journal of Travel Research*, 26(1), 18–26.

Ritchie, J.R.B. and Lyons, M.M. (1990) Olympulse VI: A Post-Event Assessment of Resident Reaction to the XV Olympic Winter Games. *Journal of Travel Research*, 28(3), 14–23.

Ritchie, J.R.B. and Smith, B.H. (1991) The Impact of a Mega-Event on Host Region Awareness: A Longitudinal Study. *Journal of Travel Research*, 30(1), 3–10.

Robinson, H. (1976) *A Geography of Tourism*. Plymouth: Macdonald and Evans.

Robinson, T. and Gammon, S. (2004) A question of primary and secondary motives: revisiting and applying the sport tourism framework. *Journal of Sport Tourism*, 9(3), 221–233.

Rossi, B. and Cereatti, L. (1993) 'The Sensation Seeking in Mountain Athletes as Assessed by Zuckerman's Sensation Seeking Scale', *International Journal of Sport Psychology*, 24(4), 417–431.

Rotter, J.B. (1966) 'Generalised Expectancies for Internal versus External Control of Reinforcement', *Psychological Monographs: General and Applied*, 80(1), 1–28.

Ryan, C. (2002) *Recreational Tourism: A Social Science Perspective*, 2nd edn. London: Routledge.

Sanahuja, R. (2002) Olympic City – The City Strategy 10 Years after the Olympic Games in 1992. Paper to the *International*

Conference on Sports Events and Economic Impact, Copenhagen, Denmark, April.

Shaw, G. and Williams, A. (2002) *Critical Issues in Tourism: A Geographical Perspective*, 2nd edn. Oxford: Blackwell.

Simmon, B.L. and Ruth, J.A. (1998). Is a company known by the company it keeps? Assessing the spillover effects of brand alliances and brand attitudes. *Journal of Marketing Research*, 35(1), 30–42

Simson, V. and Jennings, A. (1992) *The Lords of the Rings: Powe, Money and Drugs in the Modern Olympics*. London: Simon & Schuster Ltd.

Slywotsky, A.J. and Shapiro, B.P. (1993) Leveraging to beat the odds: The new marketing mindset. *Harvard Business Review*, 71(5), 97–107.

Smith, V.L. (1977) (ed) *Hosts and Guests: An Anthropology of Tourism*. Philadelphia: University of Pennsylvania Press.

Snyder, E. (1991) 'Sociology of Nostalgia: Halls of Fame and Museums in America', *Sociology of Sport Journal*, 8, 228–238.

Sonstroem, R.J. (1982) 'Attitudes and Beliefs in the Prediction of Exercise Participation', in R.C. Cantu and W.J. Gillepsie (eds) *Sport, Medicine, Sport Science: Bridging the Gap*. Toronto: Callamore Press.

Sonstroem, R.J. and Morgan W.P. (1989) 'Exercise and Self Esteem: Rationale and Model. *Medicine and Science in Sports and Exercise*, 21, 329–337.

Stewart, P. (1993) 'Corporate Hospitality: Are running events missing out on a valuable component for sponsors?', *Road Race Management*, 137, 1–7.

Sofield, T.H.B. (2003) Sports Tourism: From Binary Division to Quadripartite Construct. *Journal of Sport Tourism*, 8(3), 144–166.

Sports Business. (2002) 2004 Olympics will not boost tourism. *Sports Business*, 7th March.

Sport England. (1999) *The National Lottery Sports Fund Strategy*. London: Sport England.

Spradley, J.P. and Philips, M. (1972) Culture and Stress: A Quantitative Analysis. *American Anthropologist*, 74, 518–529.

Standeven, J. and De Knop, P. (1999) *Sport Tourism*. Champaign: Human Kinetics.

Standeven, J. and Tomlinson, A. (1994) Sports and Tourism in South East England: A Preliminary Assessment. London: SECSR.

Sutton, J. (1993). Inside the credit card war. *Target Marketing*, December, 36–37

Swarbrooke, J., Beard, C., Leckie, S. and Pomfret, G. (2003) *Adventure Tourism: The New Frontier*. Oxford: Elsevier.

Sykianaki, C. (2006) *Strategic Program for Post-Olympic Athens Sustainable Development*. Athens: Organisation for Planning and Environmental Protection of Athens.

Toohey, K. and Veal, A.J. (1999) *The Olympic Games: A Social Science Perspective*. Wallingford: CAB International.

Trade with Greece. (2000) The Impact of the 2004 Olympic Games on Sectors of the Economy. *Trade with Greece*, November.

Travel Utah. (2002) *Beyond the Games: Assessing the Impact of the 2002 Olympic Winter Games and the Future of Utah Tourism*. Salt Lake City: Utah Division of Travel Development.

Turco, D.M., Riley, R.S. and Swart, K. (2002) *Sport Tourism*. Morgantown: Fitness Information Technology.

Turismo Torino. (2004) *Olympic Games and Tourism: Turin's Tourist Strategy for the 2006 Winter Olympics*. Torino: Turismo Torino.

Turismo Torino. (2007) *Torino 2006: One Year On*. Torino: Turismo Torino.

Turner, V. (1974) *Dramas, Fields and Metaphors*. New York: Cornell University Press.

Urry, J. (1990) *The Tourist Gaze*. London: Sage.

Urry, J. (2001) *The Tourist Gaze*, 2nd edn. London: Sage.

USA Today. (2006) Host city hopes Games recast its image; Torino officials think new look will boost business, tourism. *USA Today*, 17th February.

Van Dalen, D.B and Bennett, B. (1971) *A World History of Physical Education*. Englewood Cliffs, NJ: Prentice Hall.

Vester, H.-G. (1987) 'Adventure as a Form of Leisure', *Leisure Studies*, 6, 237–249.

Vrondou, O. (1999) *Sports Related Tourism and the Product Repositioning of Traditional Mass Tourism Destinations: A Case Study of Greece*. Loughborough University: Unpublished PhD Thesis.

Wahlers, R.G. and Etzel, J. (1985) 'Vacation Preference as a Manifestation of Optimal Stimulation and Lifestyle Experience', *Journal of Leisure Research*, 17(4), 287–295, S.E.

Weed, M.E. (1999) *Consensual Policies for Sport and Tourism in the UK: An Analysis of Organisational Behaviour and Problems* (PhD Thesis), Canterbury, University of Kent at Canterbury/Canterbury Christ Church College.

Weed, M.E. (2001a) Developing a Sports Tourism Product. Paper to the *First International Conference of the Pan Hellenic Association of Sports Economists and Managers, The Economic Impact of Sport*, February.

Weed, M.E. (2001b) 'Towards a Model of Cross-Sectoral Policy Development in Leisure: the Case of Sport and Tourism'. *Leisure Studies*, 20(2), 125–141.

Weed, M.E. (2002a) 'Football Hooligans as Undesirable Sports Tourists: Some Meta Analytical Speculations', in S. Gammon and J. Kurtzman (eds) *Sport Tourism: Principles and Practice*. Eastbourne: LSA.

Weed, M.E. (2002b) 'Organisational Culture and the Leisure Policy Process in Britain: How Structure affects Strategy in Sport-Tourism Policy Development'. *Tourism, Culture and Communication*, 3(3), 147–164.

Weed, M.E. (2003a) 'Why the Two Won't Tango: Explaining the Lack of Integrated Policies for Sport and Tourism in the UK'. *Journal of Sports Management*, 17(3), 258–283.

Weed, M.E. (2003b) 'Emotion, Identity and Sports Spectator Cultures'. Paper to the 11*th* *European Congress of Sports Psychology (FEPSAC)*, Copenhagen, July.

Weed, M.E. (2005a) Sports Tourism Theory and Method: Concepts, Issues & Epistemologies. *European Sport Management Quarterly*, 5(3), 229–242.

Weed, M.E. (2005b) A Grounded Theory of the Policy process for Sport and Tourism. *Sport in Society*, 8(2), 356–377.

Weed, M.E. (2005c) 'Sport Sponsorship and Tourism Flows', in J. Amis and B. Cornwell (eds) *Global Sport Sponsorship*. Chicago: Berg.

Weed, M. (2006a) Sports Tourism Research 2000–2004: A systematic review of knowledge and a meta-evaluation of method. *Journal of Sport & Tourism*, 11(1), 5–30.

Weed, M.E. (2006b) The Influence of Policy Makers' Perceptions on Sport-Tourism Policy Development. *Tourism Review International*, 10(4), 227–240.

Weed, M.E. (2006c) Olympic Tourism? The Tourism Potential of London 2012. *eReview of Tourism Research*, 4(2), 51–57.

Weed, M.E. and Bull, C.J. (1997a) Integrating Sport and Tourism: A Review of Regional Policies in England, *Progress in Tourism and Hospitality Research*, 3(2), 129–148.

Weed, M.E. and Bull, C.J. (1997b) 'Influences on Sport-Tourism Relations in Britain: The Effects of Government Policy', *Tourism Recreation Research*, 22(2), 5–12.

Weed, M.E. and Bull, C.J. (1998) 'The Search for a Sport-Tourism Policy Network', in M.F. Collins and I.S. Cooper (eds) *Leisure Management: Issues and Applications*. Wallingford: CAB International.

Weed, M.E. and Bull, C.J. (2004) *Sports Tourism: Participants, Policy & Providers*. Oxford: Elsevier.

Weed, M.E. (2007). Endpiece. In M.E. Weed (Ed.) *Sport & Tourism: A Reader*. London: Routledge.

Wei, Y.D.H. (2000) *Regional Development in China: States, Globalisation and Inequality*. London: Routledge.

Wei, Y.H.D. and Yu, D.L. (2006) State policy and the globalisation of Beijing: Emerging themes. *Habitat International*, 30, 377–395.

Weiler, I. (1997) Olympia. *Nikephoros*, X, 191–213.

Weinberg, R.S. and Gould, D. (1995) *Foundations of Sport and Exercise Psychology*. Champaign Ill: Human Kinetics.

Whitson, D. and MacIntosh, D. (1993) *The Hosting of International Games in Canada: Ecological and Ideological Ambitions*. Loughborough: Unpublished.

Whitson, D. and MacIntosh, D. (1996) The Global Circus: International Sport, Tourism and the Marketing of Cities. *Journal of Sport and Social Issues*, 20(3), 278–295.

Wilks, S. and Wright, M. (eds) (1987) *Comparative Government-Industry Relations*. Oxford: Clarendon Press.

Williams, C. (1994) 'Exercise and Well-Being'. *Unpublished Paper to the Sports Science Research Group*. Loughborough University.

Wilson, R.J. (2006) Review of 'Strategic Event Management: An International Approach' (Guy Masterman, 2004, Elsevier). *Journal of Sport & Tourism*, 12(1).

World Tourism Organisation (1991) *Tourism to the Year 2000: Qualitative Aspects Affecting Global Growth*. Madrid: WTO.

Wright, M., (1988) Policy Community, Policy Network and Comparative Industrial Policies, *Political Studies*, 36(4).

Yannopoulos, D. (2003) Entrepreneurs Set Eyes on Post-Olympic Windfall. *Athens News*, 26th August.

Yu, D.L. and Wei, Y.H.D. (2003) Analyzing regional inequality in post-Mao China in a GIS environment. *Eurasian Geography and Economics*, 44(7), 514–534.

Index